Transformative Challenges

Modern Civilization and Beyond

Transformative Challenges
Modern Civilization and Beyond

Contributions by Walter Reese-Schäfer, Hwa Yol Jung, Longxi Zhang, Jérôme Bindé, John M. Dunn, John A. Hall, Wolfgang Welsch, Nam-In Lee, Takashi Inoguchi, G. John Ikenberry, Bob Jessop, Rob Stones, Jae Chun Choe, Teckyoung Kwon, Inwon Choue

Edited by Inwon Choue and Yersu Kim

Published by Kyung Hee University Press
www.khupress.com

1 Hoegi-dong, Dongdaemun-gu, Seoul 130-701, Republic of Korea
82-2-961-0106/7 (tel), 82-2-962-8840 (fax)
press@khu.ac.kr (e-mail)

ISBN 978-89-8222-336-5 93300

Transformative Challenges
Modern Civilization and Beyond

Edited by **Inwon Choue and Yersu Kim**

Editorial Note

Human society is in the grips of a civilizational transformation. The civilization, based on the Enlightenment ideas of individualism, rationalism, scientism and teleology of progress, provided a sure point of reference as societies endeavored to deal with the tasks of survival and flourishing. Guided by this civilizational synthesis, some societies have achieved a degree of material affluence, political power and cultural achievement that set the measure of progress for the human society as a whole. The synthesis had such a preeminence in the minds and affairs of people that nations and societies were virtually unanimous in accepting the cultural model forged by a handful of European societies as the only means of ensuring a viable future.

Yet, there is a sense today that the old ideas and values that have served humanity so well over the past several centuries now seem to be increasingly irrelevant and even counterproductive. Science and technology are creating unheard of opportunities, even as they threaten the very foundation of human life. The globalizing economy is creating wealth for humanity, even as it widens the gulf between the haves and have-nots among individuals and nations. Increasing interdependence at the global level is giving prominence to the problems that can no longer be dealt with within the framework of nation-states.

It is this sense of historic crisis and the ensuing challenge for humanity that have informed the reflective efforts of Kyung Hee University to participate in and lead the global discourse on civilizational transformation through international conferences and publications. They are part of the long tradition of Kyung Hee University to search for a human society in which peace and prosperity reign supreme. One of the ways in which this tradition manifested itself has been to celebrate the United Nations International Day of Peace through various activities, including international academic conferences, held since 1981. Three meetings of particular significance were held during the last three years: "After Ideology: The 21st Century Talks" in 2005, "Reinventing Universality for the 21st Century: Beyond Freedom and Equality" in 2006, and "Transformative Challenges: In Search of New Humanity and Community" in 2007.

A number of presentations were made by international as well as Korean scholars. Although their topics range over rich and varied fields, they are united in their efforts to deepen understanding of the problems embedded in the present cultural model and to sketch the contours of the future to come. In this sense, these efforts represent continuation and expansion of the civilizational discourse on modernity and postmodernity. The present anthology combines fourteen essays into one volume under the title *Transformative Challenges: Modern Civilization and Beyond.* The papers are anthologized into four different chapters according to their thematic emphasis: "Humanity in Transition," "Reason, Ideology and Culture," "Global Civil Society and Governance," and "Community in Restoration."

The present volume opens with an introduction by **Inwon Choue**, which was delivered as the opening address in the 2006 International Conference to commemorate the United Nations International Day of Peace. Then Honorary Rector of the Global Academy for Neo-Renaissance* and the present President of Kyung Hee University, Choue sets out in a paradigmatic way the path toward a future society that serves humanity better than the ruptured modern society. This path is based on the idea of transcendental engagement, intended to bring an end to the closed circuit of absolute universality and open up a political world in which there is more dialogue, consensus, and a "compassionate" universality.

The four contributions comprising the first chapter are united in their efforts to discover ways to resolve what Hwa Yol Jung calls "the deadlock between Western modernity and postmodernity." **Walter Reese-Schäfer** explores the possibility of a world society. Rejecting the idea that radical individualism is the only normative conception appropriate for the development of a world society, he lays out its possibility from a communitarian perspective. **Hwa Yol Jung** gives prominence to the idea of transversality as a key concept that will enable us to navigate between the modernist obsession with universalism and the postmodern drive for pluralism. The future civilization of humanity depends on the interchange of thinking and doing at the crossroads of the East and the West, and the North and the South. **Longxi Zhang** attempts a reevaluation of the claim regarding the universality of Renaissance humanism as a force that have played a significant role in shaping the modern world, and finds it still gives us much to ponder and to learn. **Jérôme Bindé** criticizes modernity as marked by a dramatic divorce of sense and sensibility, and proposes aesthetics as the affective glue that can hold communities together. The future of values should be reconceived in this spirit.

The second chapter puts together four papers that deal with the questions of the meaning of ideology and the transformation of reason. **John M. Dunn** asks what it is to be free and how far equality can be a feasible and sustainable condition. He argues that we must not lightly turn away from preexisting habits and institutions and place

* The Global Academy for Neo-Renaissance was renamed the Global Academy for Future Civilizations as of June, 2008.

them in jeopardy of the demands of economic rationalization and subject to the short-term pursuit of wealth. **John A. Hall** points out that European modernity has not been singular. It has rather been multiple, and liberalism, socialism and fascism represent genuine moral visions. It is important to understand the reasons for their rise and acceptance at one time. Noting the present times as being increasingly transcultural, **Wolfgang Welsch** sees the need for people to carry out transitions between different social and individual cultural patterns. Transversal reason is the faculty that is needed in the current cultural change. Welsch notes that people are in fact making greater use of this potential of reason to enable them to move toward greater reciprocity between cultures. **Nam-In Lee** attempts to develop the concept of intuitive rationality, based on the tradition that considers reason to be intuitive. Intuitive rationality should be the core element of critical rationality in carrying out the critique of the crisis of modern society.

Three papers collected in the third chapter deal with the emergence of and possibility of the global civil society as an alternative to the Westphalian nation-state model of governance. **Takashi Inoguchi** examines four different versions of global governance: a realist interpretation represented by Michael Mandelbaum, a liberal version as expounded by G. John Ikenberry and Ann-Marie Slaughter, a social democratic view of governance by David Held, and, finally, a neoconservative meaning given to the concept by Robert Kagan. **G. John Ikenberry** examines the possible terms of international order that can be established around agreed upon universal norms and principles. He argues that the "great liberal ascendance" provides three such norms and principles: individual rights and protections, group rights and self-determination; procedural norms to settle disputes; and "modernity," consisting of a set of principles and norms about the progressive development of society and politics. **Bob Jessop** explores some decades into the 21st century, when the values and conduct of a reformed *homo reciprocus* might dominate the inclinations of *homo bellicus* and *homo economicus*.

In the first of three contributions in the fourth and last chapter of this volume, **Rob Stones** argues that the adequate realization of civic virtues in the 21st century requires "enlarged mentalities" based on the resources of moral philosophy, narrative storytelling and social theory. **Jae Chun Choe** makes a plea for reestablishing human beings as *homo symbious* in place of *homo sapiens*, arguing that mutualism or symbiosis can be more powerful than reckless competition. Echoing Edward Wilson, Choe gives expression to the hope that the 21st century will be the century when we achieve the consilience of all disciplines. He argues that such a union will be the beginning of a harmonized global community. **Teckyoung Kwon** puts forward the thesis of the "third space," that of the "sublime beauty," that would help restore the proper relationship between men and nature.

It is our hope that making these papers available for the larger public would contribute to the further stimulation of the global discourse on the transformative challenges for modern civilization and for what lies beyond it. We would like to thank the authors for their contributions. We are indebted to many friends at Kyung Hee University and the Global Academy for Future Civilizations who have helped to shape the international conferences out of which this volume grew. We owe deep gratitude to Dr. Inwon Choue, President of Kyung Hee University. We would like to acknowledge the invaluable efforts of Mr. Jong Ok Kim, Ms. Jeong-hyeon Yi and Dr. Neal D. Williams, Institute of International Education, who contributed significantly to the editing of this volume. Special thanks go to the staff members and assistants at the Global Academy, in particular to Kwang-yeop Lee and Huseyn Aliyev. Finally, we would like to thank the Kyung Hee University Press, particularly its director, Professor Young-Hak Yoo, for the loving care and expertise they put into the publication of this volume.*

* This was written by Yersu Kim, former Rector of the Global Academy for Future Civilizations of Kyung Hee University.

Contents

II Reason, Ideology and Culture

III Global Civil Society and Governance

IV Community in Restoration

Introduction
Modern Society of Rupture, Political World of Transcendental Engagement

Inwon Choue

On behalf of Kyung Hee University, I would like to extend a warm welcome to our guests today at the International Conference in Celebration of the 25th Anniversary of the UN International Day of Peace. I especially thank the distinguished scholars from abroad: Professors John M. Dunn, Scott Lash, G. John Ikenberry, Hwa Yol Jung, Walter Reese-Schäfer, Longxi Zhang, and Takashi Inoguchi. Also, I would like to express my deepest gratitude to Dr. Renate Bloem, President of the Conference of NGOs (CONGO) and Dr. Joan Kirby, Chair of the NGO/DPI Executive Committee.

Today we are celebrating the 25th anniversary of the UN Iternational Day of Peace. Over the past 25 years, we have held a series of conferences regarding such topics as "Human Society and Future Civilization" and "The UN and World Civil Society." These academic conferences have allowed us to maintain a long-standing tradition at Kyung Hee University. The 2005 conference, entitled "After Ideology: The 21st Century Talks," added a special meaning to this tradition.

For 2006, we proposed "Reinventing Universality for the 21st Century: Beyond Freedom and Equality" as the conference title. In hosting discussions and the sharing of ideas among domestic and foreign scholars, we wish to search for a "new universality" for the 21st century. I will now elaborate on the underlying philosophy that was developed during the planning process of this conference.

An understanding of human society lies in the knowledge that we live in an era of uncertainty. It is our mundane reality to live day-to-day while leaving behind the "problem of the origin." At the core of this *problematique* is our failure to look back over the chain of ultimate cause and effect. So we confront every day the limits of imagination and the consequences of relying on false realities. And these limits eventually and perplexingly lead us to run counter the unknown world known as the "fluctuation of nothingness."

Even today's modern society, replete with scientific rigor and reasoning, cannot be free of this mode of thinking. After conceptualizing myriad alternatives, we have settled on certain convictions and beliefs, rules and laws, and institutions and norms. Despite our efforts, however, they do not ultimately help us to understand the question of "origin." Civilization and history are formed and re-formed. They follow a certain rule of cause and effect. Nevertheless, their origin and essence remain unknowable. The reality of the modern mode of thinking is that constant changes in our consciousness are inevitable as we travel from the world of knowing to the realm of unknowing, and back.

Despite our inability to truly understand our realities, human societies have repeatedly created "civilizations of knowing" and "histories of rightness." Because we continually strive towards an understanding of the mechanism of cause and effect, and we hope to lead humane and modern lives, we have created a world in which certain principles are valued, such as:

Walking in the street is dangerous, but walking on the sidewalk is safe.

Working hard and earning money are pre-conditions of happiness.
The application of scientific construction methods yields productive and comfortable life spaces.
Only the development of science and technology can guarantee the wealth and well-being of humankind.

Applied principles such as these that are based in conviction and belief reflect a mode of reasoning unique to human beings who want to maximize existential well-being in an unknown world. They are also motivation for maintaining our modern lives.

The linear relationships of cause and effect on life and worldly phenomena provide some assurance about our ability to attain widespread societal well-being. They cannot, however, eliminate questions and doubts about our origins and purpose. This is because the relationship of cause and effect in human reasoning does not enable us to know the future and understand the reason for our existence. So, while we may think our hard and fast principles can guarantee a state of security and happiness, the sidewalk may not be safe, buildings might fall, and neither money nor hard work can guarantee happiness. Indeed, progress without the goal of science and technology may bring calamity upon the earth and mankind. For this reason, phenomenological bracketing of modern knowing and rightness, which excludes the possibility of unknowing and wrongness, allows for the possibility of infinite fallacy in cause and effect. Only when this fallacy is recognized and addressed can the true state of life and phenomena be accessed, possibly leading us to an ultimate reality and universality.

It is important to acknowledge the possibility of this fallacy as we enter a new era. If we do not concede that the fallacy could have negative consequences and must be rectified, opposition, conflict, exclusion and struggle may plague any complex modern society. Indeed, we must take into account that much will remain unknown to us even as we undergo the process of understanding and forming a political structure that encourages life, collective consciousness, and the living world of the future.

Such a political structure is controversial in its interpretation. Ultimately, though, it can be an expression of life formed in the process of pursuing our existential wellbeing and happiness. In this respect, politics should be an attempt to guarantee the creation of a universal world. The politics we encounter in the real world, however, does not appear to have this goal.

As an example, the "politics of the left," an axis of modern society, is based on the concept of politics as the superstructure of class relationships. It is both directly and indirectly influenced by the market. Politics as such represents an instrument of an economy in which class conflict as an unstable social relation of the capitalist mode of production is expressed. In order to realize an equal and just society, about which we all dream, the imbalanced politics of capital must be dismantled and a new politics to institutionally assure the rights of the alienated class must be established.

The "politics of the right," on the other hand, is based on an individual expression of life and self-realization, which are the result of a public struggle for recognition. From this perspective, politics is the process of identifying and mediating clashes in the public sphere, and of establishing agreement regarding the public good. The happiness of society and of the individual stems from a liberal democracy that maintains the proper political function of these clashing demands.

The different belief systems of the two sides have been dominant for many centuries, particularly the 20th century. They are still regarded as effective for understanding the real politics of our age. From the viewpoint of the left, the politics of the right exists only for capital and vested powers. From the viewpoint of the right, the resistant politics of the progressive is nothing but a struggle against a regime, causing much damage to the social stability.

The kind of logic that runs to both extremes—"from my point of view, you are wrong, and from your point of view, I must be wrong"—has engendered the divided universality pervasive in the modern era.

However, neither set of politics can decidedly determine what is right or wrong, or make the correct and incorrect tangible and therefore irrefutable.

Despite our inability to use politics to elucidate fundamental truths, there must be a single or infinite universality. Of course, what that universality is, we cannot know, because it is beyond our ability to grasp, which makes us "incomplete humans." This is even so when religious faith and conviction are excluded. If the meaning or origin of that single universality were revealed to an individual, then he would cease to be incomplete and human, and would take the position of a "god."

Logically, if someone has experienced the essence of universality, then it readily exists within the felt-necessity of humans. This universality becomes a reality because in essence it is a human artifact drawn from the horizons of the mind. Universal reality, or real universality, is the unknown realm of eternal, transcendental human consciousness. In this regard, when discussing the world of universality, what is possible logically or realistically is to seek a zone of interuniversal dialogue artificially constructed in an infinite and unknown realm.

A recent movement towards finding dialogue for universality is progressing widely in the real world beyond the academic realm. Tolerance and open society, diversity and global civil society, as we all know, were the aim of social discourse and practice at the end of the past century. As we enter a new era, academic reflections on "transversality" and "multiversality" are gradually percolating into society. This current trend evinces the emergence of a new understanding that places hope on the universality of the incomplete and the esthetic of difference until the ultimate reality of the universal world is revealed.

In this sense, we have gained a new interest in the "gray area." That there is a gray area does not imply "fence-sitting or opportunism." It refers to a middle zone between knowing and unknowing, or a zone of understanding both right and wrong. It also denotes an infinite space of creation. The space is not subordinate to the category of concepts aimed at capturing life and worldly phenomena. The realistic implication of the "fluctuations of nothingness," as the "origin of everything," is the growing importance of a new understanding of an open universality regarding this "gray area." This means that the gray area, or a limitless space of creation, can function as a "space of salvation," surpassing the linear chains of cause and effect prevalent in modern society.

Apart from this, our understanding of the "transcendental engagement" has also gained importance. The political idea based on transcendental engagement compels an alternative mode of thinking. It was designed to bring an end to the closed circuit of absolute universality, or absolute knowledge deeply rooted in modern era and real politics. Through reflective and inclusive creation that constantly overcomes and surpasses, we are trying to reach universality and inter-universal dialogue. Another aspect of "transcendental engagement" is the movement towards a new political possibility via a transformative episteme to incorporate human consciousness and practice.

In order to create and live in a future society that is better than the ruptured modern society, it is essential to reduce closed and exclusive authority, and remove the tyranny of the majority. We should instead engage the concept of transcendental engagement to reach out for dialogue, consensus and a compassionate universality for the time. There are more possibilities in a cultural world of transformation and creation and in a political world of transcendental engagement than in the existing political world of divisive struggle and oppression.

As the participants of this year's conference consist of civil society leaders and prominent scholars and experts, I believe that in-depth discussions on the exclusive universality of freedom and equality in today's society will proceed fruitfully. I am also confident that we will seek out an alternative plan and vision. I hope that this conference will serve as an opportunity for discussions and practice to open a new world of universality in the 21st century. *

* This speech was delivered as the opening address at the 2006 International Conference in Celebration of the 25th Anniversary of the United Nations International Day of Peace.

I

Humanity in Transition

Reinventing Humanity

Walter Reese-Schäfer

1. The Concept of Humanity: Intellectual History and Present Situation

The concept of humanity is a renaissance and enlightenment idea, which broke down and vanished after the invention of nationalism in the aftermath of the French Revolution of 1789. And, to avoid any misunderstanding, nationalism was not only a European movement of the 19th century, but a worldwide phenomenon from the start. European nationalism was copied in South and Central America, Venezuela, and Haiti since the end of the 17th century. It went on to Asia in the beginning of the 20th century, to the Arabian countries in the 1920s and 1930s and then further on as an anticolonial movement to Africa in the 1950s.

Nationalism had a double face from the beginning. It seemed to be unavoidable with the rise of democracy. When not only the parliamentary elites, but everybody was given the right to vote, it had to be made clear: Who is everybody? Who belongs to the electorate, who has the rights of a citizen and who is only a visitor, even if he, as a merchant, and asylum seeker or a foreign worker, lives in the country for a longer period of time? Citizenship became important with the establishment of democracy, and nationalism took profit from the positive image of sovereignty and self-determination. The answer to the question: who is this autonomous self, was one of the sources of most border conflicts from the 19th century on. Even democratic nationalism created a potential and the reasons for war, as could be seen in Germany in 1848, when the invasion of Denmark to regain the German language territories was planned, and in 1864, when this was pushed further by the Prussian army, followed by the wars against Austria in 1866 and against France in 1870-1871.

As a reaction against this process of militant nationalism, the Austrian poet Franz Grillparzer coined the famous line: from humanity through nationality to bestiality.[1] And he did not even know what was going to happen in the 20th century in the name of nationalism. But as a subject of a multicultural and multilingual empire, he had an inclination towards something like a cosmopolitan feeling. In Germany and in the German language countries, the year 1849 was the historical turning point from cosmopolitanism to nationalism, a process, which had started earlier in France. Until 1849 and, of course, in individual cases even later, the German merchants, the German liberal bourgeoisie considered themselves as citizens of the world. After the German unification in 1871, liberalism was in decline and put under pressure from the right and the left. The international, even cosmopolitan mind was under suspicion. The German Kulturkampf (which could be translated as cultural wars or cultural struggle) was led by the central government against Catholicism, because Catholicism was considered as a universal religion with loyalty to the pope and not to the national authorities. Nearly the same accusation was made against the German Social Democracy as "people without a fatherland," *vaterlandslose Gesellen*. The reason, of course, was the international orientation of the workers' movement in the time before the First World War.

One of the foremost German scholars of the history of ideas, Friedrich Meinecke, has described this development in his work *Weltbürgertum und Nationalstaat*,[2] in English language: *Cosmopoli-*

tanism and the National State. (Studies on the Genesis of the German National State.) The prevailing opinion in the 18th century was cosmopolitanism, which was replaced by nationalism. Meinecke considered nationalism as the newer and the more modern form of public opinion. From our point of view, nationalism looks much more like an aberration or a dead end. So it could be helpful to look back to the beginnings of this discussion. And, from my perspective, the beginning and one of the most exciting moments of this discourse is the work of Johann Gottfried Herder, sometimes called "The German Rousseau." Herder developed an idea of universal humanity, which left room for the development of cultural diversities. Human rights were universal, not national. In the eyes of Friedrich Meinecke this concealed the fact, that in reality only the nation state as the successor of the traditional Machiavellian Power State was able to guarantee human rights. The cosmopolitan and human motivation of the late 18th century was judged as a philosophical illusion by Meinecke and other hard boiled nationalists.

Through the influence of Herder and others, the new nationalisms won a rational and universal sense, which was important in the time of the Enlightenment, because public opinion longed for a motivation and foundation by reason. Many of the leading intellectuals would not have accepted the historicist irrationality that it just happened. They were looking for a deeper sense.

Herder's ideas grew out of the literary-philosophical field, but developed considerable political impact. They were very influential especially on the minds of the intellectuals of the newly developing nations in Eastern Europe. Even today the German scholarly institution, which concentrates and keeps contact with the small nations in Eastern Europe, is the Herder Institute, founded in 1950. The name Herder carried a message: no longer German or Austrian Paternalism and Imperialism against Eastern and Middle Europe, but, as Herder called it, *Billigkeit*, which is *fairness* against the other, even smaller nations. Herder outlined this idea in his 119th letter on humanity, where he wrote: "We need a sense of a community of nations." If someone crosses the border and tries to enforce his religion, art, ideas or ways of living on others, or if he destroys the welfare of others, he will be rightfully hated. But all other local and national customs have to be respected. If this common sense develops, there will be an alliance of all educated or cultured nations against the trespassers, or, as he wrote, against any single arrogant power.[3] Herder's letters on humanity were written in the first years of the French Revolution, when the German intellectuals like Herder, Kant, Fichte or Hegel had responded enthusiastically to this event. This opinions changed rapidly after they heard of the terror of the guillotine and even more after the imperial politics of Napoleon Bonaparte. Herder recommended a purified or chastened patriotism, because in the 18th century discourse patriotism was under critical scrutiny: It seemed too narrow, too local, too much preoccupied with the self-interest of small entities instead of with the great picture of general interest.

Herder's keyword and the central theme of his chef d'oeuvre *Ideas about the Philosophy of the History of Mankind*[4] and his *Letters for the Support of Humanity* was *Humanity*. In Herder's terminology, *humanity* does not mean a fixed ideal and refrains from a formal definition, but is used as a term to describe the general purpose of man, which is potentially present but has to be developed by education and enculturation, or, by *paideia*, to use the Greek word which Herder preferred. The self-education of mankind is at the core of this concept. At first sight, this sounds a bit pathetic, but, compared to the moral philosophy of Immanuel Kant, it is an easy, common-sense concept, which had wide ranging consequences in the fields of cultural anthropology, ethnology, and the social sciences. It is an anti-essentialist concept in the sense that it can be shaped and developed in present times, and, of course, in the future. It is open and not bound to an alleged essence or nature of man, which could be fixed in advance and from the beginning.

So Herder managed to escape from the formal rules of professional philosophy and to win the open space of the cultural and the social sciences. In an early and ingenious sketch of his *ideas*, he called them, knowing and communicating that it was something different, *Auch eine Philosophie der Geschichte der Menschheit*. In English Herder's political writings are translated under the title *Another Philosophy of the History of Mankind*. That means: this is philosophy, too, but of a different kind: narrative, evolutionary, taking irrationalism into account and keeping distance from the idea of progress. So he continued to use the word "philosophy," but he meant to replace traditional metaphysics by the cultural sciences. Rhetorically, it was a modest proposal, but the consequences lead to the dethronement of philosophy by the humanities—very similar to the work of the American philosopher Richard Rorty, who can be seen as a genuine successor of Herder.[5] In the last 15 years, the system of higher education has started to replace the traditional humanities with the more comprehensive and more theoretically demanding concept of the cultural sciences.

Herder's concept of humanity was developed parallel to the American and French declarations of human rights. The foundation of these rights is the same concept of humanity: only potentially present, but to be developed. The declarations are coined in pathetical and well-known words, seemingly like the early Roman laws fixed on stones, but actually they are only a temporary phrasing, a passing stage and, astonishingly for many observers, always open for new additions, for newly invented rights: already in 1791 there was Olympe de Gouges' *Declaration of the Rights of Women and Female Citizens*, then, in the course of the 19th century, there were social rights such as the right to work, to education, and in the 20th century there were cultural rights. The last two bundles of rights are continuously under dispute. The central argument for human rights is self-evidence. The American declaration starts with the famous words: "We hold these truths to be self-evident." Considered from the standards of justification in traditional philosophy, this sounds superficial and caused the reproach of shallowness against enlightenment philosophy. But it was a turning point: the social and cultural sciences became more and more the leading sciences and their standards of explanation were easier to handle than metaphysical foundationalism.

The development of human rights is the best example for the openness and fruitfulness of Herder's concept of humanity. No given definition, but an open-ended process. Of course, I did not refer to Herder to remain at the special historical situation of the end of the 18th century. But, like in our times, there was a sense of a new era coming. It was the coming up of a new wave of selfgovernment, the start of the establishment of mass democracies, of representative democracies. From then on we can observe four waves of democratization:[6] the first three waves were described by Samuel Huntington: the American and French Revolution, the processes of democratization after 1918, the wave in Southern Europe, Northern Asia and Latin America between 1974 and 1989, and a fourth wave has to be added: the democratization in Eastern Europe after 1989.

This worldwide process of democratization, which raised the number of democracies from 3 to about 120 shows, above all, that there may be many different models, but there are some fundamental criteria common to all: a constitutional government, which guarantees civil liberties, free elections with secret ballots, where everyone above a certain age is entitled to vote, peaceful changes of governments, the existence of a pluralist party system and a free press respective of free public discussion. These are requirements that are not met by certain "democracies with an adjective" like "people's democracies" with their one-party system, prefabricated lists of candidates and censured public opinion. The same is obvious in the case of the "Islamic democracy" in Iran, where the admission of the candidates to parliamentary elections is controlled by the non-elected council of guardians. However, at least, the Iranians have the opportunity to replace the president in elections. For Karl Popper, in his strictly reduced definition of democracy, that is sufficient grounds for calling a country a democracy. The majority opinion in political science today uses some more criteria and would, in cases like this, use the term "deficient democracy."

There has been a lot of talk about cultural differences, but my observation is that this kind of discourse has more the function of an apologetic argument against what is considered too much democracy by some ruling elites. But there is yet another argument, which is repeated very often and which has to be discussed thoroughly. It is the argument of Western universalism. The argument says: the process of economic and political modernization has its origins in the West and is therefore caused and contaminated by Western values. In particular, the basic human rights are considered individualist rights and, as such, not suitable for non-Western cultures, because a compliance with them would destroy traditional communitarian structures.

As a scholar who has published some books on communitarian political theory,[7] I dare to raise an objection against this picture: The complaint about the loss of family values and about the loss of social bonds is ubiquitous and could be heard in the West since modernization and industrialization started. In 19th century Germany Ferdinand Tönnies in his pioneering work *Community and Society* (*Gemeinschaft und Gesellschaft*) found impressive lamenting words. Peter Laslett, the British historian, described the lost life-worlds of preindustrial times.[8] This is similar to what I found, when I last visited Singapore: The Singaporean novels are full of complaints about anonymous modern housing with bathrooms and built-in kitchens, and full of nostalgia for the sixties, when many people lived in slums without hot and cold running water, but where the social communication was dense and intense. I don't want to mock about this attitude, because there are real things lost. But what I want to say is: The loss of family values, of familiar and local social cohesion is not the product of Western individualism, but the consequence of modernization. And this is going on everywhere. Societies where traditional cohesion is praised, normally are only one step behind and will catch up. The last and really impressive example was the development of labor relations in Japan: for some time this social model was recommended even to the U.S.: lifelong employment with the same company. But after the Asian crisis and a 10-year stagnation period it was abandoned, and now the Japanese economy is recuperating. The same seems to be imminent for the European social model, or the Rhinelandian model of capitalism respectively of social market economy.

And this is an interesting aspect, which harmonizes with the findings of empirical social research. I refer to Ronald Inglehart's *Modernization and Postmodernization. Cultural, Economic, and Political Change in 43 Societies.*[9] The prevailing social habits and opinions concerning community values and family values are remarkably similar in Japan and in Germany: in both political cultures you will find a majority of communitarians, whereas individualism is predominant in the United States, as could be expected, but also in Britain, Switzerland and France.[10]

So my consequence is: There are different cultures and they react differently to the process of modernization and, for that, postmodernization. But these habits and traditions are not "Asian," "European" or "American," and, even more, not very intensely correlated with religion (There is one exception: Islam, and up to now, the Islamic culture. This seems to be the hardest case, but possibly even this could be a phenomenon of transition). If you look deeper into the concrete value systems, you will find, that the Spenglerian or Huntingtonian theory of 7 or 8 cultural circles is too abstract.[11] It is a correlation of historical eras and geographical regions. It is based on the assumption that a culture will form in a certain territory and that the people living there will develop more or less a common value system or a common system of religious beliefs. This assumption was nothing more than a way to come to sometimes helpful, sometimes misleading generalizations of observations. If you change the research strategy and identify certain habits or values, you will find very similar attitudes in many societies, and you will find changes of habits correlating to political, social and economic changes. If you identify values instead of areas, then an intersocietal comparison is possible and dissociates value systems from what formerly was called blood and soil. I don't want to go so far as to criticize Spengler's research as a racist project, but I would like to make clear that a different approach in research enables unexpected insights and makes it possible to get rid of culturalist generalizations.

In the beginning of my paper I mentioned Herder as one of the founders of cultural theory. His approach, which is based on the concept of humanity, enabled him to overcome cultural and racial prejudices—not all, because there are some remarks on "Negroes," as he called them, which stand in absolute opposition to his struggle against the slave trade, slavery and colonization, and even though he respected the Asian high cultures very much, he remarked, that Asian societies tended toward immobility after having reached what they considered good social institutions. As we can observe in our times, this kind of lethargy has now taken over public opinion in Europe and caused continuous economic stagnation.[12] So even idleness is not necessarily connected to a specific culture.

2. World Society in a Communitarian Perspective

The concept of *world society* sounds interesting and "feels good," to put it like Niklas Luhmann. Nonetheless, the political sciences applied it only rather hesitatingly and reluctantly. Instead, there are varying terms like, *global order* or *international civil society* and many others. They share that they did not reach the breakthrough from a well-defined application to a genuine concept. The current notion of the term *world society* lacks some decisive elements of a convincing and generally acceptable conception.

I suggest the following working definition of the term *world society*: it is the attempt to signify the development of a globalised interaction instead of a variety of segmentary societies. At first sight the concept seems to be static, but at a closer look it becomes clear that it signifies a dynamic process. Our frequently used term globalisation accentuates this processual element even more, because it describes a direction of development, a trend, and thus emphasises the dynamic character even more precisely. This *world society* in the making can be seen as the actualization of the enlightenment idea of a *world citizen society (Weltbürgergesellschaft)*, which, for an example, Immanuel Kant outlined in his famous essay "An Answer to the Question: What Is Enlightment?"[13]

These old, but powerful universalist ideas were criticized because of their abstractness, not only by nationalists or traditionalists. They seemed to be far from reality and with very small prospect of realization. In contemporary political thought, especially communitarianism, has started the search for a model of a world society, which could be much closer to reality. Traditionally, communitarian political thought starts from small communties, as Emile Durkheim did or Ferdinand Tönnies did. They put the small communites of the family, neighbourhood, village, and small town against the large societies like the big cities and the nation-state. Tönnies' typology[14] displays an enormous persuasiveness and is just because of this, in some respect, a bit fallacious, for by its seductive concreteness it forecloses a priori to apply the idea of community to units larger than small towns.[15] The idea of a worldwide community seems to be an impossible phantasy. But that is just by definition and insofar not a really convincing argument. If we have a closer look, using even the terms and concepts of Emile Durkheim, we can observe worldwide waves of common emotions. They are fostered and accelerated by the globalization of mass media, but make no mistake: the spread of the ancient and medieval world religions, the spread of the reformation or the ideas of the French and American Revolution were possible in times before the invention of electronic mass media.

Durkheim coined the term collective *effervescence*, which means a sudden explosion of common emotions. One of Germany's foremost

Communitarians, Hans Joas[16] adopted this concept and described, in his study on the development of values, how new common values can suddenly flash up and become deeply implemented in collective feeling. He discussed the interesting possibility, that in a collective effervescence there will suddenly but sustainably emerge a universal *communitarian feeling*, rapidly exceeding the smaller communities and for a moment or longer opening up the emotions of people to embrace the whole world.

Collective effervescence describes a type of communitybuilding that is induced, stimulated or formed by a joint experience. The examples for this *emergence of a community* are usually looked for in the religious realm. For Durkheim the memory of the mass meetings of the French Revolution was exemplary.[17] I would add another famous example: the pleasant and peaceful experience of the Woodstock community in 1968, a famous Rock'n Roll concert in a small town in the U.S. was just as well a globally noticed generational experience that shaped many more than the estimated 500,000 people who were physically present: by the movies, by broadcast, by the album and by other means of communication. A myth was created. The phenomenon is familiar, can be put on stage, can be repeated and reproduced.[18] One only has to recall the reinvention of the Olympic Games in 1896 with the "Olympic Idea"—with exactly the same intention. This event at the end of the 19th century also referred to a rapid historical process of globalisation that at least in the West was incidentally experienced as optimistic and positive. It was a time of world expositions, international trade and, not to forget, an ephemeral second wave of colonial expansionism.

Hans Joas mainly focuses on the irrational, somehow Pentecostal notion of this worldwide emotionalised construction of a new community that, to put it a little more cautiously—accompanies the cooler process of world society building with its institutions like the WTO or the World Bank. A similar case of worldwide community building undoubtedly was the generational project of the 1960s student riots, which developed in the U.S., overleaped to Berlin in 1967 and until 1968, broadened to an enormous social movement from Prague over Paris to Italy, Yugoslavia and Mexico.[19] The similarity in the forms of protest and action seems to be significant. Some interpreters even called it—influenced by media theory—the first global revolution, mediated by television.[20] But, as I already mentioned, on a closer look there we can observe an analogue development in the Great French Revolution of 1789 that continued its effects until Haiti, in the July Revolution of 1830,[21] when the newspaper was the media of communication. How the arrival of the ship with the newspaper parcels at the tiny and far away island of Helgoland altered his life was portrayed in a very colorful way by the German writer Heinrich Heine in his *Letters from Helgoland*. The same effect happened in the European-wide revolutions of 1848.

It seems to be evident by now: It was only a too narrow version of Ferdinand Tönnies' typology, which led to the assumption that communitarians were not able to imagine a world community, but only small particularistic communities. The border transcending phenomena of community building—traditional as well as modern ones—, which are described by Hans Joas and others are so manifest, that one is amazed to see how the evident could have been so highly overlooked. The collective effervescence of the world religions gives additional evidence to this claim.

The political ethicists ask, if such morality producing mass events should not be looked at in a sceptical and critical way. In my own survey, "Political Thinking Today," I dealt intensely with this very aspect of Joas' theory.[22] For now it will be sufficient to state that Joas' specific communitarian view led him to analyze a phenomenon that so far has not been inquired about sufficiently. Of course, traditional political scientists classically will object that in a case of emergency, that is, in the case of a war, such crossborder normative community building will break down rapidly. They expect that cosmopolitan ideas would be replaced again by the traditional national and governmental forms of community. The best example for this hypothesis is the breakdown of the international labour movement in 1914. The realistic view is that, in a case like this, always those organisational units became crucial, which could provide firearms. I will not go further in discussing this point, because for my argument it is sufficient to state that the emergence of transnational community feelings is on the screen of the contemporary social sciences and that emotional communality is possible even outside of small groups of people.

In reference to Joas' idea of the emergence of values due to collective effervescence, the question, of whether or not communitarians can face a normative aspect of worldwide community building, can be answered affirmatively: Not only can they do it, but from their perspective, they have a kind of privileged access to forms of normative worldwide community building. Yet the—however profound and rational—description of an irrational phenomenon, remains a description and is not real *thinking* and, more importantly, it bears no normative consequences. So, the next step has to bring us to the question of political ethics. There are two communitarian political theorists, Michael Walzer and Amitai Etzioni, who address the question of the rationality and the universality of normative orientations.

3. Walzer's Conception of a Reiterative Universalism

Michael Walzer develops the idea of a specific communitarian universalism, which he calls *reiterative universalism*. Unlike the universalism of an all-embracing law, this type of normative universalism arises from individual experience and develops further by repeated political and societal acts of self-determination and of self-liberation. In game theory there is an analogous idea: repeated games can create trust and facilitate cooperation.[23]

Classical universalist philosophers like Ronald Dworkin, Thomas Pogge and other adherents of John Rawls would suggest the creation of a universal law. Walzer, however, pleads for learning by experience. Philosophically speaking, this is a contingent process, which unfolds in coincidental encounters. There is no logically necessary universal law. Instead, some pragmatic rules for situations of possible conflict have been developed, tried and tested and proven fairly reliable. That is Pragmatism, not Kantianism. Or in the words of the philosophy of science: It is the primacy of the *context of discovery* over the *context of justification*. This idea implies that the legitimation story of the generalised rules is not some kind of heroic narrative, that it is not told in a mentality of winners that condemns every particularity, but as a quasi-pragmatic measure to solve provisionally some complex problems of cooperation. So the approach of the *reiterative universalism* is more humble than the one of *covering law universalism*, which is Walzer's term for Kantian and Rawlsian approaches.

In this conception of reiterative universalism we can find what might be called a communitarian universalism. It rests on the reflexive interpretation of a real evolution and of practical everyday developments, instead of the constructivist establishment of international law. This is connected to Walzer's hermeneutic moral theory. The genesis of rules is identical with its location and proof in reality. Walzer rejects any other ideas of rule-emergence, for instance, as an invention of legislators like Solon and Lycurgus or as an act of a god or divine idea, whose out-comes Moses could pick up at Mount Sinai.

It would be an overhasty and therefore misleading conclusion to assume that an *a priori universalism* of a *covering law* and an *a posteriori universalism* by the communitarian model would have, as a result, the same set of rules. The *a posteriorism* abandons the idea of a world historic mission. It argues for a concept of nonintervention.[24] In his renowned study *Just and Unjust Wars*—written under the impression of the Vietnam War—Walzer is still a determined non-interventionist. Hence, he only accepts very few and narrow reasons for intervention.[25]

There is no doubt that the same results could be expressed in a universalistic way. That is always possible, if common moral standards are formulated. But nevertheless, these are *a posteriori*, not *a priori* formulations. Firstly and initially, it matters which moral standards are found. Then, in a second step, they can be tested by a procedure of generalization, and after that test they are proven as valid even for an international or an intercultural context.

Walzer assumes that a *covering law universalism* is inclined towards intervention much sooner than a communitarian universalism. *Communitarian universalism* would call the idea of liberation of foreign peoples a worthwhile general goal, whereas, nonetheless, any society should take its own steps in the direction of its emancipation without military intervention from the outside. Though he considers the liberation of other peoples and countries desirable, in his opinion there is no reason to advance it actively and by force. Anyway, Walzer's position is not without inconsistencies. So, on the one hand, he estimates sovereignty so highly that he regards it worth defending even in the case of dictatorships, yet on the other hand, he considers it appropriate to overrule the sovereignty of tyrannies in cases of civil war, of manifest cruelty or genocide.[26]

Unfortunately, the exceptions are not exactly defined, which is always dangerous in controversial matters. But then again, the communitarian will rely on experience. The relatively modest theoretical consistency of this type of political ethics enables openness for experience and evolution. Walzer's theory of the just war was developed in a reflexive interpretative examination of the Vietnam War, both World Wars and the American Civil War. Thus, it is possible and should be expected that the reflection of any new war, especially the Iraq War, might modify the theory further more. The hermeneutic idea in some measure substitutes the constraint of theoretic consistency by a pragmatic and technical conception of plausibility. It is, to say it in one term, a typical Aristotelian theory of politics as an applied science, not as theoretical science.[27]

4. Etzioni's Four Steps of Legitimacy

In his study on "The New Golden Rule," Amitai Etzioni provided a slightly different conception of communitarian universalism. The study asks the crucial question, "Who decides about the basic values of a community?" Etzioni outlines several theoretical steps. The crucial premise he makes is the obligation to give reasons for moral values, which strictly differentiates this discourse from expressions of taste or emotion:[28] The *first* step of reasoning is to verify, if certain ideals are approved by a community. Yet this alone cannot count as an adequate normative justification, but counts as an indication that such an ideal has taken the first hurdle. If others agree, it is more than a personal idiosyncrasy. It is important that the acceptance of certain moral values or ideals is not only ensured by the mere transfer from one generation to another—by tradition—but by democratic affirmation. We evaluate moral values based on democratic processes as superior, although it is clear that additional criteria are required. An additional qualification is a process of consensus building that exceeds a mere majority decision. This is yet not substantially more satisfying than majority decisions, but produces a higher legitimacy in comparison to ideals, which are imposed on a society by small elites or religious and ideological minorities. Nonetheless, the particularity of communities limits the first reasoning, because in the language of ethical theory, it only leads towards a community-bounded relativism.

Therefore, Etzioni considers it necessary to go to a *second* step of reasoning: Communitarians can contextualize the community by framing the values it affirms within a higher order of legitimacy. That is, a community's particular normative commitments will take precedence so long as they do not violate another set of normative criteria, to which the said commitments are additionally accountable. For instance, a community's values may be judged as legitimate if they are supported by majority voting or because they carry the imprint of consensus-building within the given community—but only as long as they do not violate the next order of normative criteria.[29]

The society and, accordingly, the constitution build this frame. Local laws and traditions do not always need to be substituted by universal values. Generally, they can be conceded a priority status. But in the case that they violate the framework, if they are not compatible with superior values, they have to conform. Going this *second* step, Etzioni is able to cover, theoretically, most of the cases that matter in reality, since "normative positions that pass the tests of both the community and the constitution will stand up under further normative scrutiny."[30]

Only where cultures, that differ a lot from one's own, are the subject of analysis, one has to go a *third* step. Thus Etzioni argues for a concept of normative economy: as few universalisms as possible. The method of generalization shall be used merely in cases that are otherwise insoluble. Hence, Etzioni discusses the idea of cross-border and cross-society moral dialogues, which he—unlike Habermas—does not want to construct in a proceduralistic technical way, but as concrete dialogues of persuasions.

In these dialogues, it is not necessary to separate values and facts artificially, as the Habermasian ideals of deliberation and reason demand. Etzioni gives, as an example, the dialogues about international environment regulations and the conferences on climate protection. So here as well: "Sharing of values that emerged out of moral dialogues has a higher moral standing than sharing that reflects values fostered by one group or another, or that results from the educational work of the state."[31]

But even if moral values have been shaped in dialogue, this cannot constitute an ultimately valid normative criterion, for even cross-cultural dialogues may produce erroneous and deficient outcomes. Here, Etzioni brings up the term of a *global community*, which, of course, is the one we are looking for. Normative communitarianism tries to suspend this step to universality as long as possible. That is not a peculiarity, because there are plausible reasons not to step onto this stage prematurely. To be sure, many moral philosophers would judge this to be the most elegant option to close the circle of legitimacy: if the values of a society do not offend against a worldwide valid canon of values, they can be taken for valid until further falsification, because if we have reached this level, only the dimension of the future has not been under scrutiny. But the problems of this solution should not be overlooked, and Etzioni addresses them in extenso: Worldwide values are only agreeable, if it is possible to disprove cultural relativism in a convincing way. That is hard to do. Empirical generalisations of existing rules are a weak and fragile criterion. They are weak, since only very few values like the condemnation of murder, rape or thievery may count as universal. The acceptance of human rights as laid down in the UN Charter is an insufficient criterion, too, because the interpretation and the order of precedence of those rights is controversial. Additionally, it has to be mentioned that human rights in some countries neither have been the result of genuine democratic processes nor the outcome of a worldwide moral dialogue, so that both their legitimacy and, yet more, the mere content have to count as an open question.

Still factually, there are cross-societal moral voices that are perceived. Indeed, only strong nation-states can enforce military and other instruments of power to implement these values. But the world listens even to smaller countries, like Switzerland, the Scandinavian nations or Israel. Individual rights, in Etzioni's mind, do not only represent specific Western values, even if they historically originated in Western countries. They are binding for every human being. The validity of moral standards for a global community can—unemotionally accounted—be ultimately assured only by the observation that certain values seem compellent by themselves, that they are *self-evident*. Etzioni acknowledges that this conception of virtually self-evident moral standards may be disputable or ambivalent. Notwithstanding the objections, he introduces it, because his functionalistic approach does not ask for origins or final reasons, but for "the constellations, processes, and structures that enable given societal traits or virtues to be sustained and recast."[32] Moreover, the consideration that there might be no other really convincing argument, suggests to him this answer. At its heart, Etzioni approaches an idea, which—in religious contexts—is called revelation. These ideas speak completely for themselves. The normative standing of moral order and autonomy for the communitarian paradigm is similar to the normative standing of life and health in medical sciences. Of course, theoretically, it would be possible to find moral virtue in death or illness—there are examples in literature for that—but that would be an eccentric perspective, and normally, order and autonomy would be preferred by most people.[33]

So the recourse to self-evidence might be seen as some kind of communitarian emergency brake against the final move towards a normative universalism. Yet, one has to admit that the argument of self-evidence is only needed in a few leftover cases that cannot be resolved by worldwide discourse. So, the argument of self-evidence does not constantly intervene in the moral everyday life of everyone, as, for instance, existentialism according to Sartre would claim, but should be taken as an encouraging and intuitional solution in cases that cannot be solved elsewise. So, here too, the principle of normative economy works: moral order and autonomy in balanced proportion are the ultimate values.

I am not convinced by the argument of self-evidence or, as I would call it, moral intuition, although it is highly respected in the relevant 20th century literature. So I, for my part, come to the conclusion that Etzioni indeed considered the global community as a benchmark and comprehensive moral criterion, but due to the, as yet, non-existence of this community he rejected this solution and replaced it by the idea of intuition. Etzioni did not choose the Kantian answer, to grasp this nonexistence as a not-yet-existence, that is, as a task of generalization, since for a sociological neofunctionalist—as Etzioni is—the active causation and establishment of a *world society* would be necessarily tied to such an idea. So what we can take from Etzioni is the typology of four steps of universalization and the insight that the recourse to the highest level of generalization should be used carefully and cautiously.

5. Provisional Result

I will sum up: Communitarian thought of the Etzionian type will maintain differences, specifics and particularities wherever possible. He sympathizes with particularities, but he considers the application of global standards the top priority in all cases of doubt or conflict, thus, in all the important cases. Simultaneously, Etzioni rejects resolutely the *tiersmondist* argument, which says that the generalization of Western standards should be considered as illegitimate. For Etzioni it is, "irrelevant, whence values originate. The underlying question is, if they are to justify or not. Values are not dependent on geographical factors."[34] Admittedly, a hermeneutic of suspicion may detect here nothing more than a perhaps modest variety of Western universalism. In my words, I would put it otherwise: Etzioni stands for a communitarianism with strong liberal elements. This, of course, entirely meets the communitarian self-conception to be an option within modern liberal thought and liberal societies.[35]

Thus the result: All of the three varieties of communitarian thought I introduced and discussed above, including the generalized waves of emotions Hans Joas speaks of, the reiterative universalism of Michael Walzer and Amitai Etzioni's typology of four steps of legitimation are compatible to a *world society* and, therefore, open the chance to accompany the factual process of globalisation with the respective steps of normative universalisation. In doing so, Hans Joas deals with an approach including emotions and moral sentiments like David Hume and Adam Smith in the age of enlightenment. Because of the irrationality included in emotions, he indeed provides the riskiest or most venturesome model.

Walzer chooses the reiterative evolutionary and stepwise way, comparable to Karl Popper's intellectual method of "piecemeal technology." Finally, Etzioni outlines a double-sided procedure: parallel with Walzer's method, the circle of generalisation has to be widened, if different communities and cultures come into the moral dialogue. The further the circle of legitimacy is widened, the higher the degree of legitimacy becomes.

But Etzioni rejects with sceptical reasons the final and supposedly most elegant step of generalisation, that is, the step to a global legitimacy. Instead, he suggests the argumentative emergency exit of self-evidence and moral intuition. This can be qualified as disappointing or as indication of intellectual probity.

None of the three possibilities is thought through in a perfect or absolutely convincing way. But in my opinion, they are sufficient to disapprove the idea that radical individualism should be judged as the only normative conception, which would be appropriate for the development of a world society. For it can be counted as evident that in a world society as well, subgroups and particularistic entities would play an important role, and simply therefore, a normative reflection has to pose the question as to how their particular norms could be restricted, reasoned or valuated.

An overarching consensus cannot be postulated from above. The communitarian idea is to find it in a bottom-up approach. Although communitarian universalism is not perfectly elaborated upon, it can be claimed that from a normativist perspective, world society is possible and imaginable, even if we do not take the isolated individual as a starting point. Or, in the language of another time, with the words of Jean-Paul Sartre: World society is imaginable, without paying the price of the seriality of atomised individuals.[36]

We have not to imprint the pale stamp of generalization on every individual in the world. Beside this argument of atomised individuality, there is another one in favour of the communitarian way: even if the liberal individualistic argumentation can be universalized in a somewhat cogent way, it is still not able to answer the crucial question: What can motivate people towards a normatively right behaviour?[37] Yet a theoretic design that is not able to solve the question of motivation, remains in the helplessness of the mere *ought*, as Hegel put it.[38]

So universalism can philosophically be judged as a weak idea. That should not necessarily be seen as a problem, because it avoids the perception that universalism is some kind of strong and frightening philosophic imperialism. It has not the power to enforce its ideas on people of different cultures, but only to give the encouragement and a possible direction for the development of a wider concept of societal and individual identity.

Notes

1 Franz Grillparzer, "Der Weg der neuern Bildung geht von Humanität durch Nationalität zur Bestialität," in Peter Frank and Karl Pörnbacher (eds.) *Sämtliche Werke. Ausgewählte Briefe, Gespräche, Berichte*, vol. 1 (München: Carl Hanser, 1960), 500.

2 Friedrich Meinecke, *Weltbürgertum und Nationalstaat. Studien zur Genesis des deutschen Nationalstaates*, 5th ed. (München and Berlin: R. Oldenbourg, 1919).

3 Johann Gottfried Herder, "Briefe zur Beförderung der Humanität," in Hans Dietrich Irmscher (ed.) *Werke in zehn Bänden*, vol. 7 (Frankfurt am Main: Deutscher Klassiker, 1991), 119, Brief 723.

4 Johann Gottfried Herder, *Ideen zur Philosophie der Geschichte der Menschheit* (Mit einem Vorwort von Gerhart Schmidt) (Wiesbaden, 1975).

5 Walter Reese-Schäfer, *Richard Rorty zur Einführung* (Hamburg: Junius, 2006).

6 Samuel Huntington, *The Third Wave: Democratization in the Late Twentieth Century* (Norman and London: University of Oklahoma Press, 1991). The waves are: 1) Die amerikanische und französische Revolution, 2) Die Demokratisierungen nach 1918, 3) Die Welle in Südeuropa und Lateinamerika zwischen 1974 und 1989, and 4) Die Demokratisierung in Osteuropa seit 1989.

7 Walter Reese-Schäfer, *Kommunitarismus* (Frankfurt and New York: Campus Fachbuch, 2001); Walter Reese-Schäfer, *Amitai Etzioni zur Einführung*, 3rd ed. (Hamburg: Junius, 2001); Walter Reese-Schäfer, *Grenzgötter der Moral. Der neuere europäischamerikanische Diskurs zur politischen Ethik* (Frankfurt am Main: Suhrkamp, 1997).

8 Peter Laslett, *Verlorene Lebenswelten. Geschichte der vorindustriellen Gesellschaft* (Frankfurt am Main: Fischer, 1991); originally published as *The World We Have Lost.*

9 Ronald Inglehart, *Modernization and Postmodernization: Cultural, Economic, and Political Change in 43 Societies* (Princeton: Princeton University Press, 1997).

10 *Ibid.*, Figure 3.5, 93.

11 *Oswald Spengler, Der Untergang des Abendlandes. Umrisse einer Morphologie der Weltgeschichte* (München: C. H. Beck, 1980); Samuel Huntington, *Der Kampf der Kulturen Die Neugestaltung der Weltpolitik im 21. Jahrhundert* (München and Wien: Europa,

1996); originally published as *The Clash of Civilizations.*

12 Cf. Herder, *op. cit.*, 399.

13 Immanuel Kant, *Political Writings* (Hans Reiss, ed.) (Cambridge: Cambridge University Press, 2006).

14 Ferdinand Tönnies, *Gemeinschaft und Gesellschaft. Grundbegriffe der reinen Soziologie* (Berlin, 1988) §6 and §§14-18.

15 Cf. critically Walter Reese-Schäfer, *op. cit.* (1997).

16 Joas is a member of the editorial board of the *Responsive Community* and addressor of the *Communitarian Platform*. Vide Joas 1997 passim and 94ff.

17 Hans Joas, *Die Entstehung der Werte* (Frankfurt am Main: Suhrkamp, 1997), 106.

18 This includes self-evidently the re-experience with sound or film.

19 Paul Berman, *A Tale of Two Utopias: The Political Journey of the Generation of 1968* (New York and London: W.W. Norton & Co., 1996).

20 Cf. W. Kraushaar, "Die erste globale Revolution," in *1968 als Mythos, Chiffre und Zäsur* (Hamburg: Hamburger Ed., 2000), 19-52.

21 On the 10th of August 1830, Heinrich Heine wrote with a revolutionary enthusiasm as well as longing for death (a combination that should become characteristic for the 20th century): "Lafayette, the tricoloured flag, la Marseillase. [...] Begone my longing for rest. Anew, I know, what I want, what I shall, what I have to. [...] I am son of revolution and again I grasp the weapons proofed that mother revolution spelled her blessing on. Flowers! Flowers! I will crown my head for death-struggle. And now the lyre, hand me the lyre therewith I sing a battlesong."(1977: 53ff.) I cite this to illustrate the ambivalences of this attitude. [This and any further quotations in my own translation].

22 Walter Reese-Schäfer, *Politisches Denken heute. Zivilgesellschaft, Globalisierung und Menschenrechte* (München and Wien: Oldenbourg, 2007), here 244ff.

23 Michael Walzer, *Lokale Kritik—globale Standards. Zwei Formen moralischer Auseinandersetzung* (Hamburg: Rotbuch, 1996), 146.

24 *Ibid.*, 146.

25 Michael Walzer, *Gibt es den gerechten Krieg?* (Stuttgart: Klett-Cotta, 1982), 141.

26 Walzer, *op. cit.* (1996), 151.

27 For this classification of Michael Walzer's and communitarian thought, see Thomas Gutschker, Aristotelische Diskurse. *Aristoteles in der politischen Philosophie des 20. Jahrhunderts* (Stuttgart, Weimar: Metzler, 2002).

28 Amitai Etzioni, *Die Verantwortungsgesellschaft. Individualismus und Moral in der heutigen Demokratie* (Frankfurt and New York: Campus, 1997), 278.

29 Amitai Etzioni, *The New Golden Rule: Community and Morality in a Democratic Society* (New York: Basic Books, 1996), 224.

30 *Ibid.*, 222.

31 *Ibid.*, 231.

32 *Ibid.*, 243.

33 *Ibid.*, 244.

34 Etzioni, *op. cit.* (1977), 299.

35 Cf. Walter Reese-Schäfer, *op. cit.* (2001), 134, Etzioni's self-characterisation as a communitarian liberal.

36 Jean-Paul Sartre, *Kritik der dialektischen Vernunft*, Bd. 1. *Theorie der gesellschaftlichen Praxis* (Reinbek: Rowohlt, 1967), 270ff.

37 Cf. Walter Reese-Schäfer, *op. cit.* (1997), 16-58 and passim. In this book, I argue that not only foundation, but also application, motivation and institutionalization are indispensable elements of ethical theory.

38 G.W.F. Hegel, *Wissenschaft der Logik. Theorie-Werkausgabe* (Eva Moldenhauer and Karl

Markus Michel, eds.), vol. 5 (Frankfurt am Main: Suhrkamp, 1970), 265.

On Humanity in Transition: The Past, Present, and Future

Hwa Yol Jung

In Memory of My Wife Petee

Where there is no vision, the people perish. The scholars are the priests of that thought which establishes the foundation of the earth. **Ralph Waldo Emerson**

If we keep on speaking the same language together, we're going to reproduce the same history. **Luce Irigaray**

What is your aim in philosophy?—To show the fly the way out of the fly-bottle. **Ludwig Wittgenstein**

Just as there is sleepwalking, there is also sleepthinking. **José Ortega y Gasset**

Prologue

We are living in interesting times because we are challenged today by multiculturalism and globalization where and when the exchange (ex-change) and interchange (inter-change) of diverse cultural ideas and values take place. The general theme of this conference is "After Ideology: The 21st Century Talks," which intends to advance the lofty and hopeful ideal of "world peace and human prosperity." I was specifically asked to speak on the subject of "On Humanity in Transition: The Past, Present, and Future." It is indeed an inexhaustible and demanding subject.

The nature of the subject on hand requires me to speak in generalities. At the same time, however, it asks for "a fitting response" to facilitate communication and the Arendtian notion of "judgment," that is to say, a concrete response to a concrete question and a critical assessment of a specific issue in its specificity. In other words, generalities without specifics are empty, while specifics without generalities are blind.

There are two keywords in the suggested subject of my talk: (1) humanity and (2) metamorphosis. The purpose of this conference, as I understand it, is to envision or forge a new humanism after the fashion of the Renaissance, which is the epoch sandwiched between the Middle Ages and modernity in the periodization of European history. It is distinguished by its attempt to bring back to Europe the cultural norms and values of ancient Greek civilization. In this sense, the term "neoRenaissance" as an analytical concept or without reference to the historical context of Europe would be redundant. Be that as it may, Emerson's and Irigaray's epigraphs, which I quoted in the beginning of this essay, which go hand in hand, are a perfect fit for my talk in this plenary session.

Emerson is regarded as the first American "public intellectual." He is an unrivaled essayist whose pithy words and passages are often quoted and misquoted in the American intellectual circle. For that matter, this conference shares the kindred spirit of Emerson in envisioning the revival of Renaissance humanism. I do have, however, one serious reservation concerning Emerson's epigraph. It is the designation of "scholars" as "priests." I take a cue from Leszek Kolakowski's[1] contention that throughout the ages there is an incurable antagonism between "a philosophy that perpetuates the absolute" and "a philosophy that questions accepted absolutes." There is, in other words, the antagonism between the "priestly" and the "jesterly," which are the two most general forms of intellectual disposition at any given period of time and in history. The "priestly" attempts to preserve the absolute and established ideas, while the "jesterly" distrusts the absolute and stabilized system and intends to deconstruct it.[2] There is a strong undercurrent of the "jesterly" in the humanism of the Renaissance, which is a carnivalesque culture. In this context, it is worth quoting in full a passage from Harvey Cox's work[3] *The Feast of Fools* that describes the anti-ideological "political vision" of carnivalesque culture as follows:

> The rebirth of fantasy as well as of festivity is essential to the survival of our civilization, including its political institutions. But fantasy can never be fully yoked to a particular political program. To subject the creative spirit to the fetters of ideology kills it. When art, religion, and imagination become ideological tools they shrivel into caged birds and toothless tigers. However, this does not mean that fantasy has no political significance. Its significance is enormous. This is just why ideologues always try to keep it in harness. When fantasy is neither tamed by ideological leashes nor rendered irrelevant by idiosyncrasy, it can inspire new civilizations and bring empires to their knees.[4]

By making the existing world upside down and inside out, the aim of the carnivalesque *dispositif* is to bring about a "reversible world." It symbolizes a culture of *dissensus* (*dis-sensus*). The spirit of carnivalesque culture in the Renaissance is embodied in Rabelais, Erasmus, and Bruegel.

The carnivalesque is the "jesterly" play of difference that aims at the creation of an alternative or "reversible world" order. As a ludic form of transgression and subversion, it intends to transform playfully a "real" world into a "possible" world: in short, it nonviolently deconstructs the world. Carnivalesque culture attempts to create a "reversible world" in which the "master" is placed at bottom and the "servant" on top. Humans as players (*homo ludens*) dethrone the stable and established hierarchy of all kinds. In the Bruegelian and Rabelaisian themes of Mikhail Bakhtin's dialogical body politics, which is opposed to Enlightenment rationalism and contains a hidden critique of Stalin's totalitarianism based, rightly or wrongly, on the Hegelian and Marxian dialectic, to carnivalize the world is to dialogize it: in them carnivalization and dialogization go hand in hand. As a protest against the monological "misrule" of (Soviet) officialdom, the carnivalesque model of life transgresses and transforms the canonical order of truth and the official order of reality. As Bakhtin writes forcefully:

> [It] is past millennia's way of sensing the world as one great communal performance. This sense of the world, liberating one from fear, bringing one person maximally close to another (everything is drawn into the zone of free familiar contact), with its joy at change and its joyful relativity, is opposed to that onesided and gloomy official seriousness which is dogmatic and hostile to evolution and change, which seeks to absolutize a given condition of existence or a given social order. From precisely that sort of seriousness did the carnival sense of the world liberate man. But there is not a grain of nihilism in it, nor a grain of empty frivolity or vulgar bohemian individualism.[5]

As it is exemplary of *dissensus*, the carnivalesque celebrates dialogue and community; it liberates people and brings them together and invites them to participate in communal living. In this light, the scholar is a (Kolakowski's) jester and (Camus's) rebel rather than a (Emerson's) priest and dialectical revolutionary. He changes the world by *first* changing the conception of it.

Parenthetically, the jesterly culture of the Renaissance deconstructs the priestly interpretation of Greek philosophy. It has nothing to do with the essentialist idea of discovering the truth as ready-made or eternally immutable. The eighteenth century anti-Cartesian and anti-Enlightenment Neapolitan philosopher Giambattista Vico is forthright in formulating the thesis that we understand history with certainty only because we "make"/"re-make" and "unmake" it (*i.e., verum ipsum factum*). On the other hand, the influential political philosopher Leo Strauss put forth an essentialist rendition of classical political philosophy which is exemplified in the philosophy of Plato and Aristotle in arguing against what he calls "historicism" or "relativism" that calls for the historical transformation of truth and the cultural variations of morals. Strauss left behind him a circle of such notable disciples as Allan Bloom, Francis Fukuyama, and Paul D. Wolfowitz. Bloom authored the bestseller *The Closing of the American Mind* (1987) which is anti-Nietzschean, anti-feminist, and anti-multiculturalist for obvious reasons; Fukuyama is the famed author of the "endofhistory" thesis; and Wolfowitz was a brain-trust and strategist of the American war in Iraq, whose ultimate task is to export and propagate "missionary democracy"[6] beyond the soil of the United States.[7]

As her epigraph makes it clear, the paradigmatic French feminist philosopher Irigaray, who calls herself *une philosophe*, means to *reverse* the mainstream (i.e., "malestream") tradition of Western philosophy. She offers a helping hand to a paradigm shift in philosophizing. Notably in the East with which she attempts to familiarize herself, the reputed Chinese *Book of Changes* (*Yijing*) is predicated upon the basic thesis that change is the order of things in the cosmos, that is, everything changes except change itself without a philosophical baggage of linear progress as in Western modernity. Standing by a river, Con-fucius, too, remarked that everything, like a river, flows ceaselessly, day and night. The *esprit de corps* of the Renaissance as carnivalesque culture, too, defies for its namesake the linear progression of time and cultural meanings as *être de longue durée.* For it, change is "cyclical" rather than "linear." Indeed, it rebirthed the Greek conception of time and history as the "myth of the eternal return."[8] Time does not travel in a unilinear direction. It travels multidirectionally: it travels forward and backward and even multilaterally. In this sense, the past is never prosaic and irrelevant. Even the prodigal son of the past is allowed to come back home again. Here again, the invocation of Bakhtin, who admires the personages of Dostoevsky as well as Rabelais, is helpful. For him, the recycling of past meanings for today and tomorrow is infinite. To use his own expression, it is "unfinalizable." According to the often-quoted epigram of the American novelist William Faulkner, "The past is never dead, it's not even past."[9] Meanings in the past can be recouped for the present and can conserve them for the future, as is the case with the rebirth of Greek culture in the Renaissance. Bakhtin is immeasurably profound when he writes:[10]

> There is neither a first nor a last word and there are no limits to the dialogic context (it extends into the boundless past and the boundless future). Even *past* meanings, that is, those born in the dialogue of past centuries, can never be stable (finalized, ended once and for all)—they will always change (be renewed) in the process of subsequent, future development of the dialogue. . . . *Nothing is absolutely dead: every meaning will have its homecoming festival* (italics added).

Indeed, Bakhtin's dialogism, which is totally open-ended, transcends the facile ideological dichotomy between "conservatism" (the preservation of the past tradition at all cost) and "radicalism" (change for the future by abandoning the past altogether) because radical changes can be made by the use of the past or past meanings. As the American philosopher George Santayana puts it wisely, those who forget the past or past mistakes are condemned to repeat them.

1. Transversality as a New Way of Transforming Thinking and Doing

The purpose of using the neologism *transversality*[11] in the context of this paper is to resolve or, better, dissolve the question of the One and the Many in the pluralistic world of multiculturalism in the postmodern age which is already on its way to globalization.[12] Recently I came to the realization that I had been speaking, albeit unself-consciously, the prose of transversality since the beginning of my academic career in writing about comparative philosophy, comparative culture, and intercultural hermeneutics. Be that as it may, transversality is a new way of thinking that is suitable for and accommodates the changing reality of today's world. It means to awaken us from the slumber of antiquated universality, which has been a Eurocentric idea because what is particular in the West is universalized or universalizable, whereas what is particular elsewhere remains particularized as "ethno-philosophy."[13] Transversality allows border-crossings of all kinds. It facilitates border-crossings both between academic disciplines and diverse cultures. It means to be thoroughly *intertextual*—to use the expression *au courant* of literary and philosophical minds today.

Enlightenment is the soul of mainstream Western modernity. Its legacy continues today. Some speak of modernity as an unfinished project, a second modernity, even the modernization of modernity, or the second coming of Enlightenment itself. They have an unswerving faith in it as the absolute "end of history." Enlightenment's unbridled optimism is alleged to promote and crown the Promethean progress of humanity based on the cultivation and universalization of pure and applied reason. Kant, who had a dim view of the non-Western world (especially Africa), spelled out the civilizing mission of Enlightenment in the clearest and simplest term: to sanctify the benefits of autonomous reason in rescuing and emancipating humanity—perhaps more accurately European humanity—from the dark grotto or slumber of self-incurred immaturity. In so doing, he institutionalized the major agenda of European modernity whose rationality was never seriously challenged until the auspicious advent of postmodernity in Friedrich Nietzsche, Martin Heidegger, Jean-François Lyotard, Michel Foucault, Gilles Deleuze, Emmanuel Levinas, Jacques Derrida, and others in the twentieth century. While privileging and valorizing the authority of reason for allegedly human progress and emancipation, European modernity unfortunately overlooks, marginalizes, and disempowers the (reason's) other whether it be (1) the Orient (or so-called non-West), (2) body, (3) woman, or (4) nature at the altar of Enlightenment's reason.[14] Orient, body, woman, and nature are not randomly isolated but are four interconnected issues: most interestingly, it is no accident that Orient, body, and nature are invariably genderized as feminine, while their counterparts—mind, culture, and Occident—are masculine or "malestream" categories.

The institution of Western thought called Eurocentrism[15] as well as the practice of imperialism is that habitus of mind which privileges Europe or the West as cultural, technological, political, economic, and moral *capital* of the entire globe. Modernization is nothing but the all-encompassing catchword given to the totalizing and hegemonizing process of this Eurocentric phenomenon. As the astute interpreter and critic of modernity Zygmunt Bauman relates:[16]

> From at least the seventeenth century and well into the twentieth, the writing elite of Western Europe and its footholds on other continents considered its own way of life as a radical break in universal history. Virtually unchallenged faith in the superiority of its own mode over all alternative forms of life—contemporaneous or past—allowed it to take itself as the reference point for the interpretation of the telos of history. This was a novelty in the experience of objective time; for most of the history of Christian Europe, time-reckoning was organized around a fixed point in the slowly receding past. Now, . . . Europe set the reference point of objective time in motion, attaching it firmly to its own

> thrust towards *colonizing the future in the same way as it had colonized the surrounding space* (italics added).

Indeed, this Eurocentric "chronopolitics" of colonizing the future born of "a little promontory in the continent of Asia" (Paul Valéry's expression) gives a new meaning to the conception of modernity as an unfinished project or the end of history.

A few words of caution are in order: understanding the other (the "foreign" other in particular), as anthropology and psychoanalysis have shown, is a difficult and demanding undertaking for no other reason than that the other as a moving target is always other than itself. Indeed, the other is the "black hole" of all understanding, all conceptualization, and all relationships. At a moment of frustration and despair, the existential phenomenologist Jean-Paul Sartre faces a real moment of this black hole: "Hell is other people." Furthermore, we should be aware of Akira Kurosawa's *Rashomon* that presents four equally plausible scenarios of one and the same murder scene. *Rashomon* is a telltale drama that raises a red flag for inter-cultural understandings.

There is also the intriguing question of John Hu or Hu Ruowang[17]—the first Chinese in record to travel to the West. He sailed to France from Canton (Guangdong) in 1722. Like the *Rashomon* tale, the question of Hu has an intriguing plot. Because of his "strange" (foreign) behavior, which astonished the Parisians, Hu was finally committed to the famous lunatic asylum of Charenton (Sha-lang-don) in 1723 and remained there until 1726 when he was ordered by the French government to return to China. Setting aside for a moment the Foucauldian question of insanity as a socio-cultural control mechanism in the age of reason, the relevance of the Hu question here is the question of whether he was committed to the asylum because he was "really mad" or perceived to be mad to the "foreign" Parisians because he was utterly "alien" to them. Either way, the question of Hu poses the "scandalous" difficulty of translating the dynamic chasms of intercultural perception, misperception, and even imperception.

Transversality is a keyword in the existential phenomenology of Calvin O. Schrag in pursuit of discovering a "diagonal" crossing (Xing) in resolving the deadlock between Western modernity and postmodernity.[18] Sitting in a philosophical cockpit, as it were, it is a balancing act of navigating through the stormy time and space between the dichotomous poles of the modernist obsession with identity and universalism, on the one hand, and the postmodernist exhaustive drive for difference and pluralism, on the other. Transversality actively seeks a transformation. It is, according to Schrag,[19] the recognition of difference that keeps open "the prospect for invention, intervention, transgression, recreation, etc." It looks for "convergence without coincidence"—to use his repeatedly emphasized expression. Thus, it broadens the "in-between" for the sake of the "beyond" by splitting the difference between modern identity and postmodern difference.

Transversality is primarily a derivative concept of geometry. It denotes the crossing (Xing) of two diagonal lines in any given parallelogram. Schrag exacts *l'esprit de finesse* by way of a geo-metric configuration: in addition to the two "diagonals" crossing or intersecting each other at the epicenter of any rectangle, there are also the hermeneutical "circle" and the rhetorical "triangle." By way of the "middle voice" of transversality, he means to subvert and transgress particularly the dichotomy between "the Scylla of a hegemonic unification"/"a vacuous universalism" on the one hand, and "the Charybdis of a chaotic pluralism"/"an anarchic historicism" on the other. Insofar as it is a negotiated or compromised "middle voice," transversality touches the soul and heart of Buddhism. The newly emerging face of transversality may be likened to the famous wooden statue of Buddha at a Zen temple in Kyoto whose face marks a new dawn of awakening (*satori*) or signals the beginning of a new regime of ontology, ethics, politics, and culture. From the crack in the *middle* of the old face of the Buddha's statue, there emerges an interstitial, liminal face that signifies a new transfiguration and transvaluation of the existing world. The icon of the emerging new face symbolizes the arrival of Maitreya (the "future Enlightened One") or *Middle Way*—the third enabling term of transversality, which is destined to navigate the difficult waters of intercultural border-crossings. We are warned not to take it as a middle point between two poles. Rather, it breaks through bipolarity (e.g., modernity and postmodernity, nature and society, mind and body, femininity and masculinity, and East and West). What is important here is the fact that transversality is the paradigmatic rendition of overcoming bipolarity itself. The bipolar solids melt into the air of transversality, as it were.

As disenchantment calls for transcendence, transversality is used here as a deconstructive concept. It deconstructs Eurocentrism the mission of which is to proselytize the universal and the "'catholicity' of the rational."[20] Transversality first dismantles or unpacks the status quo and then goes beyond what is given, received, or established by constructing a new formation of concepts. It, in short, attempts to challenge the assumed transparency of truth as universal and overcome the limits of universality as the Eurocentric canon of truth in Western modernity. It means to decenter Europe as the site of "universal truth" whose "identitarian" and "unitarian" motivation fails to take into account the world of multiculturalism. The pluralist Johann Gottfried Herder[21] challenges: "I find myself unable to comprehend how reason can be presented so universally as the single summit and purpose of all human culture, all happiness, all good. Is the whole body just one big eye?"

The French philosopher and sinologist François Jullien calls the effort of this decentering Eurocentrism or Western modernity—with Kant in mind—"a new 'Copernican reversal.'"[22] He contends that in "shaking up" Western modernity, China becomes a "philosophical tool." He uses Chinese thought to interrogate Western philosophy and to liberate it from its own "mental cage." Most radically, he wishes to replace the very concept of "truth" itself with that of "intelligibility" because the concept of truth is bound up with the history of Western philosophy. Jullien puts Foucault to the test in order to vindicate the Eurocentric "legislation" of truth for all global humanity. In his 1978 visit to Japan, the vintage Foucault remarked that as the warp of knowledge and the woof of political power are interwoven as one fabric, European imperialism and the era of Western philosophy together have come to an end. Foucault is not alone in conjecturing that philosophy of the future must be born "outside Europe" or in the "meetings and impacts" between Europe and non-Europe (see Jung, 2002b: 1).[23] The interlacing of the East and the West, in other words, will give birth to a new philosophy. For too long, the East has been living in the dark shadow of Western modernity. In this background there lurks an intriguing question that the Singaporean intellectual/statesman Kishore Mahbubani, who is now Dean of the Lee Kuan Yew School of Public Policy, asked a few years ago: "Can Asians think?" (1998).

Long before Foucault and Jullien, Maurice Merleau-Ponty spoke of the "lateral universal" and the lateral continuity of all humanity both "primitive" and "civilized" across history. He was unmistakably a consummate transversalist *avant la lettre*. The lateral universal is for him a new paradigm for world-making as well as philosophy. "Lateral" rather than "vertical" thinking is paradigmatic in that instead of digging the same hole deeper and deeper in which there is no exit in sight, it digs a new hole in another place. For Merleau-Ponty, all history is not only contemporaneous and written in the present tense but also an *open notebook* in which a new future can be inscribed. It is rather unfortunate, I think, that his deconstructive effort for comparative philosophy and his sensitivity to the global scope of philosophy have escaped the attention of comparativists as well as specialists alike. I would venture to surmise that this inattention is woven out of the same fabric in our Eurocentric propensity and orientation in philosophy.

Merleau-Ponty's deconstructive effort in philosophy, in comparative philosophy, is evidenced in his critique of Eurocentric Hegel who was a priest and missionary of the universal and the rational.[24] Merleau-Ponty[25] is critical of Hegel who arbitrarily draws "a geographical frontier between philosophy and non-philosophy," that is between the West and the East. Merleau-Ponty argues that philosophy is destined to examine its own idea of truth again and again because truth is "a treasure scattered about in human life prior to all philosophy and not divided among doctrines." If so, Western philosophy is compelled to reexamine not only its own idea of truth but also related matters and institutions such as science, economy, politics, and technology. Besides philosophy's own constant vigilance on what it is doing, Merleau-Ponty's phenomenological orientation demands its attention to the ethnography of the sociocultural life-worlds without which philosophy is a vacuous if not fatal abstraction.

The way of ethnography's thick description practiced by Marcel Mauss and Claude Lévi-Strauss, who also taught at the Collège de France, provides Merleau-Ponty with the idea of the lateral continuity of humanity between the "primitive" and the "civilized," that is, with the incessant ethnographic testing of the self by the other and the other by the self which has a "diacritical value" for humanity's coexistence and its planetary solidarity. Ethnography redeems Western narcissism precisely because it is the human science of understanding the "foreign other." Merleau-Ponty contends that, while for Hegel philosophical truth as absolute and universal knowledge is notarized and certified by the Occidental seal of approval alone, the Oriental past must also have an honored place in the famed hall of philosophies to celebrate its hitherto "secret, muted contributions to philosophy." He writes resolutely[26]: "Indian and Chinese philosophies have tried not so much to dominate existence as to be the echo or the sounding board of our relationship to being. Western philosophy can learn from them to rediscover the relationships to being and an initial option which gave it birth, and to estimate the possibilities we have shut ourselves off from in becoming 'Westerners' and perhaps reopen them." "If Western thought is that it claims to be," he challenges further, "it must prove it by understanding all '*life-worlds*'" (italics added) as multiple geographies of sociocultural realities.

Thus Merleau-Ponty suggests that in contrast to the "overarching universal" of objective sciences or, we might add, Western metaphysics, the "lateral universal" is acquired through ethnographical experience as the way of "learning to see what is ours as alien and what was alien as our own." His lateral universal is a passport, as it were, that allows us to cross borders between diverse cultures, enter the zone of intersections and discover cross-cultural connections and convergences. While the European geophilosophical politics of identity claims its validity as universal truth, the lateral universal takes into account "local knowledge" prior to planetary knowledge (*dubbed by some as "glocalization"*) and allows the hermeneutical autonomy of the other who may very well be right. Indeed, Merleau-Ponty's lateral universal is contextualized as an open-ended and promiscuous web of temporal and spatial (i.e., chronotopic) interlacings.

The (Eurocentric) universalist has failed to take into account seriously the question of diversity or multiplicity in the world of multiculturalism. He is still entangled in the cobweb of absolute universal truth and cultural relativism. As difference marks multiplicity and all relationships, Heidegger's *Differenz* as *Unterschied* edifies our discussion here because it plays and feeds on the coupled meaning of the words, which connect, preserve, and promote *both* difference and the relational in one breath. In *Differenz* as *Unterschied*, the other is neither assimilated/incorporated nor erased/segregated: the integrity of the other is well preserved. Here we would be remiss if, in light of Merleau-Ponty's above-mentioned "lateral universal" including a critique of Hegel's Eurocentrism, we fail to recognize the seminal contribution of the Caribbean francophone Édouard Glissant[27] to the making of the transversal world. Educated in philosophy and ethnography in France, he is a philosopher, a poet, and a novelist whose "poetics of relation" shaped Caribbean (*antillais*) discourse on "diversality" and "*créolité*" ("creoleness").

Glissant has an uncanny convergence in the name of transversality with Merleau-Ponty in his critique of Hegel the Euro-centric universalist and absolute rationalist when he articulates without equivocation that transversal relation means to replace "the old concept of the universal." "Thinking about One," Glissant puts it concisely, "is not thinking about All (La pensée de l'Un ne soit pas pensée du Tout)." Speaking of Hegel's conception of history, Glissant retorts:

> History is a highly functional fantasy of the West, originating at precisely the time when it alone "made" the history of the world. If Hegel relegated African peoples to the ahistorical, Amerindian peoples to the prehistorical, in order to reserve History for European people exclusively, it appears that it is not because these African or American peoples "have entered History" that we can conclude today that such a hierarchical conception of "the march of History" is no longer relevant.

Glissant unpacks Hegel's history by dissolving it as irrelevant or passé in the postcolonial world of diverse cultures that rejects "the linear, hierarchical vision of a single History."

Transversality is proposed and constructed by Glissant in opposition to and as a replacement of universality. For him, it is the "poetics" of cross-cultural encounters. It is the way of *crossing* and going beyond (i.e., creolized) ethnic, lingual, and cultural boundaries. It is indeed the site of hybridity. As Glissant himself puts it, transversality is "the site of converging paths" or the "convergence that frees us from uniformity." The British postcolonial theorist Robert J. C. Young,[28] who regards Eurocentrism as a "white mythology," makes an unusually interesting and astute observation that "[p]ostcolonialism is neither Western nor non-Western, but a dialectical product of interaction between the two, articulating new counterpoints of insurgency from the longrunning power struggles that predate and post-date colonialism." It may be said that the postcolonial mind works like a "double helix." More specifically, Paul Gilroy's[29] reputed thesis of "the black Atlantic" is in favor of hybridity or "double consciousness" that sums up the transcultural intermix of African and European things. Hybridity is a converging middle path of "multiple, interconnecting axes of affiliation and differentiation." In the final analysis, Gilroy's "black Atlantic" is constructed quintessentially as "a counterculture of modernity."

The so-called "recognition" or "acknowledgment" of difference, which is not one but many, is not the final but only the first step in the making of hybridity. In *In Praise of Creoleness/Éloge de la Créolité*—a Caribbean manifesto, which is purposely written bilingually (in French and English), "diversality" (*la diversalité*) in opposition to universality is defined as "the conscious harmonization of preserved diversities" (*l'harmonisation consciente des diversités preservées*). When harmonization is understood musically, it enriches the tonality and even coloration of "diversality" when two or more tones are put together (i.e., orchestrated), there emerges harmonization (or symphony) in which each individual tone is not lost but preserved, whereas when two colors are mixed together, there is no "harmony" but another color. In the name of "a polyphonic harmony," "diversality" frowns upon "the obsessional concern with the Universal." The above-mentioned Caribbean or "creolized" manifesto begins with the sentence: "Neither Europeans, nor Africans, nor Asians, we proclaim ourselves Creoles" ("*Ni Européens, ni Africains, ni Asiatiques, nous nous proclamons Créoles*"). The Creole (as hybrid) is neither unitarian nor separatist, but is likened to be a hybrid "butterfly" who frees himself/herself by breaking off from an "ethnocentrist cocoon." Glissant himself describes the principium of creoleness as the end of "diversality," which can hardly be paraphrased: [30]

> Diversity, which is neither chaos nor sterility, means the human spirit's striving for a cross-cultural relationship, without universalist transcendence. Diversity needs the presence of peoples, no longer as objects to be swallowed up, but with the intention of creating a new relationship. Sameness requires fixed Being, Diversity establishes Becoming. Just as

Sameness began with expansionist plunder in the West, Diversity came to light through the political and armed resistance of peoples. As Sameness rises *within* the fascination with the individual, Diversity is spread *through* the dynamism of communities. As the Other is a source of temptation of Sameness, Wholeness is the demand of Diversity. You cannot become Trinidadian or Quebecois, if you are not; but it is from now on true that if Trinidad and Quebec did not exist as accepted components of Diversity, something would be missing from the body of world culture—that today we would feel that loss. In other words, if it was necessary for Sameness to be revealed in the solitude of individual Being, it is now imperative that Diversity should "pass" through whole communities and peoples. Sameness is sublimated difference; Diversity is accepted difference.

2. Responsibility as First Ethics in the Twenty-first Century[31]

What is humanity? How do we make sense of it in the twenty-first century? The term *humanity* has "ten-thousand" faces—to use the Sinic expression. It is indeed a many-faced concept. If the devil can quote the Good Book, anti-humanists can call themselves humanists. If "secular humanism" is immoral, can we speak of religious inhumanism? Generally speaking, however, humanism—just like democracy—is a motherhood issue. Nobody disavows it: everybody claims to be a humanist.

In the main, humanity has a twofold meaning. In the first place, it is a collective term for humankind as a multitude. Thus it is not one but many. According to Michael Hardt and Antonio Negri,[32] humanity stands for neither "people" nor "masses" but a "multitude." They contend that the idea of "people" folds many into a unitary entity while "masses" is a term driven to indolent uniformity. Both "people" and "masses" fail to take into account difference or diversity. Hannah

Arendt, too, thought that without human plurality or diversity the word *humankind* or *humanity* is meaningless. To conserve diversity, "multitude" is preferred in describing the everyday sociocultural world (*Lebenswelt*), which is nothing but a web of multiple relationships. As it is a plurality of singular individuals, "multitude" for its namesake happens to be a fitting term for both the phenomenon of multiculturalism and the advent of globalization.

In the second place, more importantly, humanity stands for the ontological and moral quality of *being human* whose definition invites disagreements and controversies. Confucius is the standard-bearer of humanity as the moral quality of *being human* when he defines humaneness or benevolence (*ren*) as the highest and noblest virtue of humankind: as the wordplay has it, *ren* (the human) *is ren* (humaneness). The moral exercise of humanity is predicated upon the fundamental proposition that there is no "human nature" that is enframed theologically or philosophically. By human nature, I mean that quality of being human that is immutable or unchanging beyond the realm of history and culture. It is an invariable set of transhistorical and transcultural essences. The theory of human nature defies the idea that being human is constant becoming, that is, humans are capable of making/remaking and unmaking themselves, their history, and their culture. It is flawed, I submit, because it is deterministic: it allows neither change nor hope for the future. Moreover, the principle of making and unmaking for the future as the ontological and moral quality of being human calls for no prediction because it incorporates in them the phenomenon of self-fulfilling and self-denying prophecy. In most instances, socalled prediction in human events happens to be "postdiction" or what is known in American football language as "Monday-morning quarterbacking."

I would like to propose for the consideration of and experiment with this audience that responsibility be made "first ethics" and "first politics" as well as "first philosophy" for the twenty-first century.

Philosophy has made the "ethical turn" in the latter part of the twentieth century, which was previously unthinkable in the heyday of logical positivism when I was a graduate student in the late 1950s and early 1960s. Is this ethical turn a right turn, a left turn, a wrong turn, or a U-turn? None of the above. I would venture to call it a "Copernican turn" after the fashion of the nineteenth-century German philosopher Ludwig Feuerbach[33] who discovered (the importance and primacy of) "Thou" in speculating the future of philosophy. The reason for my proposal is twofold. First, it is an alternative to the American exceptionalism of "rights talk" whose (Daniel Bell's) "end of ideology" and (Francis Fukuyama's) "end of history" is tantamount to the triumphant declaration of Anglo-American liberalism turned into one universal ideology in disguise. The American exceptionalism of "rights talk," I would contend, is a misfit for the world of multiculturalism in the age of globalization, which demands the maximum of cooperation and harmony on its way to cosmopolitanism. Instead, it results in "clashes" the end of which is resolved by way of violence rather than dialogue toward the domination of one single ideology and one single nation. In other words, "rights talk" magnetizes, magnifies and even glorifies the self and one nation at the expense of others. Second, a new humanity for the future is in need of the ethics of responsibility for nature or the nonhuman world as well. Unlike the old tradition of humanity, this new humanity is no longer going to be anthropocentric. Anthropocentrism eventually brings the death of humanity as well as that of nature.

The ethics of responsibility has been overshadowed by and subservient to "rights talk." The hegemony of Anglo-American "rights talk" has obscured and misguided the importance of responsibility. "Rights talk" is directly founded in and funded by the liberal thought of John Locke which is judiciously characterized by the late Canadian political theorist C. B. Macpherson[34] as "possessive individualism." Possessive individualism places the individual at the center of the inviolable rights of possession which Locke called "property." Property is for him a composite of "life, liberty, and estate." "Estate" has been replaced with the "pursuit of happiness" in the American exceptionalism of "rights talk."[35]

The American political theorist Louis Hartz accurately measures the temperament of American ideology when he remarks that all Americans are born Lockeans. In *Rights Talk*, Mary Ann Glendon[36] characterizes the American "rights talk" as the dialect of the "*I's have it.*" She explains its pervasiveness and dominance when she writes concisely that "The American rights dialect is distinguished not only by what we say and how we say it, but also by what we leave unsaid." As America is the world, the so-called American "rights dialect" has become the universalized language of the world. To repeat: Fukuyama is the "last American liberal" whose "end of history" is a celebration of the global triumph of American liberalism. His "endism" is disguised in the garment of one ideology. Is the twenty-first century becoming American? Perhaps so. In his philosophy of history, Hegel envisioned America as "the land of the future."[37] However, it is far too early to tell with certainty.[38]

Lockean liberalism conceives of society as "a series of market relations" in which each and every individual enters voluntarily or contractually into a relationship with others with a view to maximize his own interest. As it heralds "economic man" (*homo oeconomicus*), economic rationality underwrites it. As the proprietor of his own person, the individual carries on his daily life as if he owes nothing to society. The theory of social contract stipulated in Lockean liberalism ensures and warrants its individualism. What must be recognized in Lockeanism is a sea change or paradigmatic shift from the primacy of the political to that of the economic when Locke makes unequivocally clear that the sole function of government is the protection of private property. With Locke political categories have become subservient to economic ones (i.e., economism). Economism is the distinct herald of Lockeanism, which has shaken and made Western modernity. Notwithstanding its fundamental opposition to Lockean liberalism as possessive individualism, Locke's economic rationality—especially its labor theory of value—is also the linchpin of Marxism in particular and socialism in general. To put it otherwise, economism is the ideological underpinning of Western modernity. The theory of "economics as a vocation" is yet to be written.

For Levinas, who is regarded by many as the most important moral philosopher of the twentieth century, ethics is "first philosophy" (*philosophie première* or *prima philosophia*).[39] As such it precedes both epistemology (Descartes) and ontology (Heidegger). "When I speak of first philosophy," he declares, "I am referring to a philosophy of dialogue that cannot not be an ethics." For him, heteronomy alone is the site of responsibility if not ethics itself.[40] By heteronomy, he means to favor the other in an asymmetrical relationship. The heteronomic ethics of responsibility is anchored in the *primacy* of the other over the self where the other ("Thou" or "you") rather than the self ("I") is placed at the altar ("higher place") of all relationships. Altruism for its namesake, therefore, is exemplary of responsibility. The ethics of responsibility, based on the othercenteredness ("heteronomy"), is a radical shift from "rights talk" which magnetizes the self in everything we do and think. The former is "otherwise" than the latter. What "rights talk" is to Ptolemaic geocentrism, the heteronomic ethics of responsibility is to Copernican heliocentrism. Responsibility thusly defined is a Copernican reversal of social and ethical thought, which began with Ludwig Feuerbach who discovered "Thou" at the center of human dialogue for the future of philosophy. In this connection, it is of utmost importance to note that Hannah Arendt's controversial reportage concerning Adolf Eichmann's "banality of evil" is correlated to "thoughtlessness." By "thoughtlessness," she meant Eichmann's *utter inability to think from the standpoint of an Other*, that is, the amnesia or erasure of the other's difference. Eichmann's "banality of evil" is indeed a sobering reminder that the politics of identity or the abolition of the other's difference results in the inhumane politics of cruelty, suffering, violence, and extermination.

The infliction of violence and terror by the invisible enemy was transparent in the faces of Americans on the fateful day of September 11(9/11), 2001. September eleventh and its ensuing events unmistakably prove that violence has its own vicious cycle. Shashi Tharoor, who was a high senior United Nations official, summed up the magnitude of the demolition of the World Trade Center twin towers as the birth of the twenty-first century. For him, then, the new millennium began with violence. It began with a big bang rather than a little whimper. The birth pangs are likely to last for some time.

The famous or infamous dictum of Karl Clausewitz's *Realpolitik* may be incontrovertibly true. It pertains to the inseparability of violence from politics since for him "war is the continuation of politics by other means." In his *Humanism and Terror* (1969/1947 in French), the French phenomenologist Maurice Merleau-Ponty declared that "humanism"—Machiavellianism notwithstanding—is not immune to violence. He asserted with firm conviction that one who abstains from violence toward the violent is an accomplice to violence itself. Not only is violence the common origin of all political regimes, but also violence is our lot as long as we humans are incarnate beings. However, we should not confuse "what is" with "what ought to be" on the one hand and hope on the other. The Southern Confederate General Robert E. Lee was pensive when he warned that we became too fond of war.

Violence is without doubt an utter failure of human dialogue, of communication.[41] It eschews responsibility: it is intrinsically an irresponsible act because it intends to efface, harm, or kill an Other. The abolition of difference courts violence, while the acceptance of difference is an act of civility.[42] Disagreement, too, governs our academic interdiscourses. To contradict or deny it is to authenticate it. As a freshman in college in 1954, I was introduced to Alfred North Whitehead's inspiring work *Adventures of Ideas*,[43] which left an indelible impression on me. It taught me the enduring idea that human civilization or human civility is the victory of persuasion over force.[44] Whitehead convinced me to date that violence has no place in civilization. As a measured failure of persuasion, violence takes a heavy toll on humans and nonhumans alike in abolishing differences. The breach of civility is predicated upon one's epistemological infallibility and moral inculpability, which is a deadly mix: I can never err and be morally wrong. J. Glenn Gray's *The Warriors*[45] is a classic and superb study of *homo furens* (warriors). Among the issues that Gray describes such as the appeals of battle, camaraderie, death, guilt, and even a delight of "fearful beauty" in destruction, there is the "abstract" image of *the* enemy that anestheticizes man the fighter. It is the monstrous—totally dehumanized—image of the enemy who is at best "subhuman." To repeat: violence is an irresponsible act because it intends to eradicate the other's difference.

I would be remiss if I fail to bring Václav Havel into my discussion here. He is a playwright who turned into a statesman of extraordinary courage, sagacity, and moral tenacity in coping with the political exigency of his time: he is truly a postmodern philosopher-statesman of our time. He has been the most prominent voice of post-Communist Eastern Europe. Havel was deeply influenced by Jan Patocka who was a student of phenomenology, an admirer of Masaryk's democratic humanism and Comenius's pansophic humanism, and an active political dissident who died in 1977 during a police interrogation. From the side of conservatives, Havel represents the death of communism as a totalitarian political system and the "end" of ideology and history as the transparent triumph of American liberalism. From the side of political radicalism, he is a champion of the powerless.

Havel is above all a Levinasian. He closely read Levinas during his prison years in Czechoslovakia. Following Levinas, he considered responsibility as the innermost secret of moral humanity. Havel's is an ethics of responsibility as humanity's "destiny" and "first politics." For Havel, freedom and responsibility are interlocked. Freedom is a requisite element of responsibility. The former, however, is not independent from responsibility. Responsibility is more inclusive than freedom because humans can be free without being responsible but they cannot be responsible without being free.

Havel's signature idea of "living in truth"[46] marks the heart of his conception of morality. He may also be likened to Bakhtin's dialogist who transgresses and subverts the canonical or "priestly" order of truth and the monological "misrule" of hierarchized officialdom. Havel's "dissident" is first and foremost Camus's "rebel" (*l'homme révolté*) (1958), who is a critic of Marxism as the dialectical metaphysics and eschatological politics of revolutionary violence. For the rebel is one who justifies the existentialist thesis that the human is the only creature who refuses to be what he/she is. He/she protests against death as well as tyranny, brutality, terror, and servitude. Havel's dissident is a true rebel who senses and cultivates his allegiance to human solidarity with no intention of obliterating the other. He is able to say that *I* rebel, therefore we exist. In an interview published as "The Politics of Hope," Havel[47] also talked about the role of an intellectual as a perpetually "irritant" rebel (or gadfly) who is self-consciously capable of detaching himself/ herself from the established order of any kind and who is vigilant to and suspicious of belonging to the "winning side." Havel shows that—to borrow the eloquent language of Roger Scruton[48] in writing about Masaryk and Patocka—"the individual soul is the foundation of social order and . . . the care of the soul, and the care of the *polis*, are two aspects of a single concern."

For Havel, in conclusion, morals are the basic stuff of all politics. Thus, politics is never a tetragrammaton (or four-letter word) precisely because it is deeply rooted in and inseparable from the moral makeup of humanity. He often speaks of politics as "morality in practice" "practical morality," "antipolitical politics," and even "the art of the impossible"[49] with Machiavelli's politics as the "art of the possible" in mind, which for Havel promotes "living in untruth," that is, manipulation, image-making, deception, and, above all, violence. In the end, the heteronomic ethics of responsibility is for Havel the postmodern alternative to *Realpolitik* as the modern "art of the possible."

3. Responsibility for Nature with Human(e) Face

For a very compelling reason, it is often said that we are living in the age of ecology. We have been playing dangerously and recklessly for centuries with the Promethean fire of modernization, which is driven by our interminable desire and appetite for more and more things for consumption (*pleonexia*) in the name of human progress and prosperity. Unfortunately, nature does not issue an insurance policy for humanity.

Ecology has rightly become our ultimate concern. It has a religious overtone. It has turned into the question of "*to be or not to be.*" The ecological crisis persists: there is no waning sign to it. It is a permanent fixture of the human condition everywhere. Alarmingly, this earth, our dwelling place, has progressively become an inhospitable, precarious, ruinous, and even deadly place for all earthlings both human and nonhuman. The ancient Hindu scriptural saying of *Bhagavad Gita* captures the dire predicament of the earthly condition today: I have become death. Indeed, we stand at the edge of history since the end of the earth or nature is also the end of history. Is there then a saving measure on earth to overcome our human-induced ecological crisis?

The ecological crisis signals human disembodiment and alienation from the earth as a "household" (*oikos*) whose "deed" is being taken away by nature's mutiny or silent rebellion. In sinography, "crisis" is spelled with two ideograms: "danger" and "opportunity." It means to seize an "opportunity" to save a situation from "danger." To overcome the ecological crisis, we are in need of inaugurating a geophilosophy grounded in fundamentals which, according to Deleuze and Guattari, "brings together all the elements within a single embrace"—only in fundamentals since, in following the advice of Einstein, not everything that counts can be counted. Merleau-Ponty's ontology or "there-being" ("*il y a*") of intercorporeality establishes and secures the firm foothold in such fundamentals for erecting the edifice of geophilosophy *as if the earth really matters.* Only by way of his intercorporeal ontology are humanity and the earth said to be bonded or intertwined. Without doubt the intercorporeal "generosity" of the whole earth will be a promising and defining moment of humanity in this millennium.

Western modernity demystifies, denaturalizes, and even deontologizes nature into an inert pile of use-objects. Francis Bacon[50] is the most eloquent voice of Western modernity as the age of science, technology, and quantitative economy. He is often called the "poet of science." Bacon advocated the convergence of theory and practice, of knowledge and utility, and of knowing and making for the sake of advancing what he called *philanthropia*, that is, for the sole benefit of humanity by cultivating the new experimental "inquisition of nature" in order to conquer it. The rationale of modern technology or technology's instrumental rationality is spelled out clearly by Bacon when he insisted that knowledge and power are one and discovered "in the womb of nature many secrets of excellent use." Speaking against the "degenerate learning" of medieval scholastics, Bacon felt that they had plenty of leisure in the cells of monasteries and colleges, but they knew no history of nature or "no great quantity of matter." In short, their "cobwebs of learning" produced "no substance or profit." He produced the perfect "instrumental rationality" for the modern-day justification of the earth as one gigantic power plant or energy station. By so doing, Bacon—like Descartes and Locke—cultivated no responsible and humane ethics for nature.

Synchronicity is the inviolable law of ecology (or geophilosophy). It refers to the ontological condition that in the cosmos everything is connected to everything else. M. C. Escher's lithograph *Verbum* (1942) depicts synchronicity or the (ecological) continuum of Interbeing (both interhuman and interspeciesistic). In the beginning was the Word (*verbum*). The Word was the Relation or Interbeing. Therefore, a new vision of humanity must interweave history and nature. The French philosopher Michel Serres[51] puts the matter poignantly: "At stake is the Earth in its totality, and humanity, collectively. Global history enters nature, global nature enters history: *this is something utterly new in philosophy*" (italics added). As such, geophilosophy *is* an entirely new philosophy. Since no earthly element— including humans—exists in isolation, what transpires in one element affects all the others on earth.

It is rather moving, I think, to recapture Havel's defining moment of conscience that includes our responsibility for the order of natural things. As he watched dense brown smoke scattered across the sky from a huge smokestack of a hurriedly built factory, Havel[52] writes with a poetic flair: "Each time I saw it, I had an intense sense of something profoundly wrong, of humans soiling the heavens. If a medieval man were to see something like that suddenly on the horizon—say, while hunting—he would probably think it the work of the Devil and would fall on his knees and pray that he and his skin be saved." Of course, his concern for the natural order is hitched to his ontological assumption that everything is "inter-being" with everything else in the world. Havel refers to the synchronistic effect of lepidoptery or— to put it simply—the "butterfly effect" (of chaos theory): "a belief that everything in the world is so mysteriously and completely interconnected that a slight, seemingly insignificant wave of a butterfly's wings in a single spot on this planet can unleash a typhoon thousands of miles away." Since humankind and nature are inextricably intertwined, there is no good reason why the responsible sense of humanity and that of nature cannot be synchronized. Furthermore, the death of nature signals the death of humanity with absolute certainty and not the other way around. Even if humanity perishes, nature remains. If the future of humanity depends on the generosity of nature, it stands to reason to emphasize that the responsible sense of nature must come before that of humanity. The "Earth First" movement in ecology tells us that to save humanity, we save nature or the earth *FIRST*.

Today "rights talk" has even invaded and colonized the nonhuman world of nature when speaking, albeit with good intentions, of the "rights of nature" and "animal rights" in addition to "civil rights" and "human rights." The "rights talk" of nature is nothing short of anthropocentrism—the shaping of nonhuman nature in human forms. Theriomorphism—the shaping of humans in nonhuman forms—is equally misguided because there are radical differences between humans and nonhuman nature. For example, all morals have their origin in humans but they are not necessarily anthropocentric. Long ago Confucius believed that it is impossible to understand humans without knowing the power of language. And he warned that human affairs can be carried out successfully only when their "names" are first rectified (i.e., *zhengming*, the "rectification of names"). Confucius issued his warning in the *Analects* long before George Orwell in *1984*.

There are more substantive reasons why ecology and "rights talk" are incompatible. In the first place, "rights talk" knows of no synchronicity. Lockean liberalism as possessive individualism begins with a *contractual* arrangement. In it, therefore, the individual is autonomous and sovereign, and he controls his own destiny. In the second place, more importantly, the concept of "possessiveness" of "rights talk" (i.e., "economism") goes against the deep grain of ecology. For Locke's possessive individualism, the utility of labor and industry is the source of material possession in exploiting the land. Labor alone produces the "value" of the land and the fruits of the earth. For him, wild things of nature have no "values," which is to say, they are useless, unless they are cultivated by labor and industry. He called the uncultivated land "*waste*" (his own term).

Locke, in sum, was ignorant of the wisdom of the deep ecologist Aldo Leopold[53] who advances the idea of the earth as "a biotic community," including not only humans but also—in his own words—"soils, waters, plants, and animals." Instead of the utilitarian and calculative *appropriation* of nature, Leopold argued for the aesthetic and meditative *appreciation* [i.e., what Heidegger calls "*Gelasssenheit*" (serenity) rather than "*Gestell*" (enframing)]. Leopold spoke of "conservation aesthetic." For him, the aesthetic delight of things wild is as indispensable as free speech. In his deep reverence for the land, he scorned the insatiable appetite for the "cash value" of land and wildlife or "the tedium of the merely economic attitude toward land." He had an utter distaste and disdain for reducing the land to a property or a set of commodities, for "skinning" the land for profit, for killing egrets for hats, for making farming only a business rather than an art.[54]

There is no need for us to emphasize that modern civilization is unmistakably technomorphic. Technology as *instrumentum* permeates every aspect of modern humanity. It is as absolutely necessary a part of modern humanity as *homo eoconomicus*. It has been a driving force of economic growth from the "take-off" to the "mass consumption" stage. It is a god, as it were, who dwells in the temple of what I call "economism." In such conditions, therefore, there must be a critique of the technological in addition to three (Kantian) critiques of the knowable, the practical, and the judgeable.

We—not all but many of us—have indeed become disenchanted with the world whose dominant prose is written in the language of technology and with the modern condition of humanity, which is enframed by the hegemony of technology including the cybernation of knowledge and the computerization and digitalization of society (i.e., what Heidegger aptly calls *Gestell*). We are all wired to, and become hostages of, the network of technology from which there is no easy and quick exit in sight. We are living, in other words, in the epoch when technology is totalizing, one-dimensional, planetary, and terribly banal and normalizing when microtechnology claims to have invented our "second self" whose "soul" may be imprisoned forever behind the invisible walls of gigantic technological Panopticon. History has become a nightmare from which there is no awakening—to emulate the language of James Joyce. Long ago the Chinese Daoist sage Zhuangzi warned that those who are too fond of technology would grow their hearts like machines.

The destructive power of technology, both visible and invisible, was unleashed in twentieth-century warfares: it destroyed not only humans but also nonhumans alike—for example, the chemical weapons we used during the Vietnam War deforested and made the Vietnamese countryside landscape look like beehives. Moreover, the pervasive and careless use of technology makes us banal or "sleep thinking": for instance, we ask why animals cross the roads we built to get killed instead of asking why we build roads where animals roam. It is instructive to note that in South Asia the Chipko movement tries to "hug" trees to protect them and prevent deforestation, whereas in the American Northwest environmental radicalism resorts to "spiking" to protect its woodland.

In today's world, more seriously, technology is no longer simply a means of human activity. It is not instrumental: it is not merely the application of science to *praxis*, but is itself autonomous in transforming *praxis*. It has become, in other words, an end in itself. As technology has a life of its own in reversing the end-means continuum, autonomous technology is technology-out-of-control. The rationale of technology as *instrumentum* or instrumental facilitation that serves the *telos* of human life became anachronistic. This, in fact, is the "categorical imperative" of technology as autonomous. It is not unreasonable, therefore, to argue, albeit against European and Anglo-American jurisprudence, that technology ought to be declared guilty before proven innocent.

Epilogue

Transversality replaces universality: it is spelled and comprehended as "trans(uni)versality." It is, as I have above proposed and intimated, the touchstone of correlating and negotiating differences in the postmodern world of multiculturalism. It makes connections—as Carol Gilligan[55] puts it—"in the face of difference." Instead of coming to hasty judgments and conclusions, therefore, we are obliged to study an anthropology of globalization thoroughly rather than selectively by taking stock of its losses as well as its gains. The transversalist is a "fox" rather than a "hedgehog." I am alluding here to Isaiah Berlin's line[56] from the fragments of the Greek poet Archilochus, which reads: "The fox knows many things, but the hedgehog knows one big thing." For the transversalist is one who has both deftness and agility to weave many ideas, whereas the universalist has one big thought.

I am hesitant to use unconditionally the term *humanism* both new and old because it is more or less anthropocentric. Therefore, I prefer to use the expression "a new philosophy of life" which is intrinsically organic rather than artificial. The *hope* of constructing a new philosophy of life for the future, more specifically for the twenty-first century, is hitched onto the very existential thesis that humans are capable of *making/remaking* and *unmaking* themselves and their world. *Hope* is nothing but the passionate and never-ending pursuit of the "impossible."

Interbeing (or "Midworld") has been the pivotal concern of Eastern thought, while Western philosophy has been preoccupied with and consumed by the question of Being. The way of transversality demands drawing insights from both East and West. What is deficient in one is augmented and supplemented by the other. Sinism, which is embodied in Confucianism, Daoism, and Chan (Zen) Buddhism, provides us with two indispensable ideas for a new philosophy of life in which the fabric of nature and humanity is inseparably interwoven—one is woof and the other warp: (1) Interbeing and (2) *homo ecologicus*. They are the two sides of the same coin, as it were, because they share the common ontological assumption that everything or every event is connected to every other in the cosmos and nothing exists in isolation. *To be in isolation is no longer to be.* It follows, therefore, that there cannot be just one center, the center is everywhere or multitudinous. Consequently, Euro-centrism or Sinocentrism must be decentered and unpacked.

A new philosophy of life is intrinsically organic rather than artificial. Life encompasses all life forms. As such, according to the principle of Interbeing, there is no reason why the helping hand of heteronomic responsibility cannot be extended to the *life-world* of nonhuman beings and things. What *homo ecologicus* is to the heteronomic ethics of responsibility, *homo oeconomicus* is to "rights talk." There is no need to emphasize here that human prosperity can never be measured solely by material things. To put it philosophically, "Being" cannot be identified with "Having": the former cannot simply be reduced to the latter. The economic, however important it may be, is only a means to the end (*telos*) of life. The heteronomic ethics of responsibility is based on an asymmetrical relationship that favors the other, while "rights talk" favors the self. Ethics in general and responsibility in particular, according to the long and cherished tradition of Sinism, is grounded in "fidelity" (*hsin*— literally, "the human standing by his/her words") and "sincerity' (*ch'eng*—literally, "word-performed" or "word-accomplished"). Sincerity is quintessentially *performative*: it means "we perform in action what we promise in words." To be sincere, speaking cannot be rendering just a "lip service." In sincerity, therefore, knowledge and action are correlative: knowledge without action is empty, while action without knowledge is blind. Sincerity is a prescription for what and how to do things with word and deed. It embodies the moral foundation of humanity.

Ultimately, the future cultivation of humanity in the world of multiculturalism depends on the interchange (inter-change) of thinking and doing at the "crossroads" (X-roads) of the East and West on the one hand and the North and South on the other. This transversal interchange may be called an "intercritique"[57] in search of cultural confluence/convergence, hybridity, or creolization. Globalization is nothing but the way of crosspollinating and cross-fertilizing cultural meanings, ideas, and values in multiplicity.[58] The new phoenix of postmodern cosmopolitanism, whose language is governed by the important prefix *inter*, *con*, or *trans*, has risen from the ashes of sovereign nation-states, which the modernist Hegel deified as the ultimate *telos* of his dialectic. With the newly rising phoenix, the "rights" of sovereign individuals, including their moral self-righteousness, give way to the heteronomic ethics of responsibility, which is accompanied by a *declaration of interdependence.* In the postmodern age of cosmopolitanism,[59] the virtue of civility promotes our communication and interaction with "foreign" others without holding their "foreignness" against them (i.e., xenophilism).[60] In the end, the good fortune (*fortuna, moira*) of globalization will be determined and sustained by the generosity or hospitality of the earth, which provides all earthlings both human and nonhuman a natural habitat.[61] In concluding my thought on "humanity in transition"or the cultivation of humanity, let me recite the celebrated devotional meditation of the English poet John Donne in its old original English: "No man is an Iland, intire of it selfe; every man is a peece of the *Continent*, a part of the *maine*; . . . Any Mans *death* diminishes *me*, because I am involved in *Mankinde*; And therefore never send to know for whom the *bell* tolls; it tolls for thee."[62]

Notes

1 Leszek Kolakowski, *Toward a Marxist Humanism* (Jane Zielonko Peel, trans.) (New York: Grove Press, 1968), 9-37.

2 There is a contrast between the masculine "priest" and the feminine "jester." Arendt notes that "The greatest enemy of authority . . . is contempt, and the surest way to undermine it is laughter." See Hannah Arendt, *Crises of the Republic* (New York: Harcourt Brace Jovanovich, 1972), 144. Woolf says: Laughter is "an antidote to dominance." Cf. Virginia Woolf, *Three Guineas* (New York: Harcourt Brace, 1938), 182.

3 Harvey Cox, *The Feast of Fools* (Cambridge, MA: Harvard University Press, 1969), 82.

4 *Ibid.*, 162. Cox writes elsewhere: "The world symbolized by the *Feast of Fools* is neither [B. F. Skinner's] *Walden Two* nor [George Orwell's] *1984*. It is much more heterogeneous, messier, more sensuous, more variegated, more venturesome, and more playful. It is a world for which a fiesta or even a love-in is a better symbol than a computer or a rocket. Technology need not be the enemy of the spirit in the modern world. But it should be a means to man's human fulfillment, not the symbol or goal of that fulfillment itself."

5 It is most interesting to note that "He [Bakhtin] felt that Rabelais drew his inspiration primarily from the comic grotesque of the Carnival, of life turned upside down and of the parody of everyday life: 'This was Rabelais's language.' Bakhtin condemned the mistaken interpretations of Rabelais as the poet of the flesh and of gluttony (Victor Hugo) and those who saw in him the expression of the bourgeois interest in the economic individual; Rabelais's style could only be understood as the translation of a popular, comic effect lay a whole cosmogony in Rabelais, and *his focus on orifices, protuberances, and outgrowths corresponded to corporeal parts that put the individual into*

contact with the external world" (Italics added). See François Dosse, *History of Structuralism*, vol. 2 (Deborah Glassman, trans.) (Minneapolis: University of Minnesota Press, 1997), 55.

6 Robert W. Merry, *Sands of Empire* (New York: Simon and Schuster, 2005), 193.

7 The episodic accounts of Leo Strauss's influence on American politics are found in Anne Norton, *Leo Strauss and the Politics of American Empire* (New Haven, CT: Yale University Press, 2004).

8 See Mircea Eliade, *The Myth of the Eternal Return* (Willard R. Trask, trans.) (New York: Pantheon Books, 1954).

9 Raymond Aron is quoted as saying that "we must accord to the past the uncertainty of the future." See François Dosse, *Empire of Meaning* (Hassan Melehy, trans.) (Minneapolis: University of Minnesota Press, 1999), 308.

10 Mikhail M. Bakhtin, *Speech Genres and Other Late Essays* (Vern W. McGee, trans. and Caryl Emerson and Michael Holquist, ed.) (Austin: University of Texas Press, 1986), 170.

11 For a decade, I have been on a transversality binge, so to speak. (See Jung, 1995, 2002b, 2002d, 2006a, 2006b, 2007a, and 2007b).

12 For Schrag, the idea of transversality initially played the role of midwifery between modernity and postmodernity. Most recently, however, he suggests that "The transversal logos replace the universal logos as the linchpin for the philosophy of the new millennium." (Calvin O. Schrag, *Convergence Amidst Difference* [Albany, NY: State University of New York Press, 2004], 76). The postmodern world is a transversal world. The anthropologist Michel-Rolph Trouillot makes the following point: "It [the postmodern world] is a world where black American Michael Jackson starts an international tour from Japan and imprints cassettes that mark the rhythm of Haitian peasant families in the Cuban Sierra Maestra; a world where Florida speaks Spanish (once more); where a Socialist prime minister in Greece comes by way of New England and an imam of fundamentalist Iran by way of Paris. It is a world where a political leader in reggae-prone Jamaica traces his roots to Arabia, where United States credit cards are processed in Barbados, and Italian designer shoes made in Hong Kong. It is a world where the Pope is Polish [now German], where the most orthodox Marxists live on the western side of a fallen iron curtain. It is a world where the most enlightened are only part-time citizens of part-time communities of imagination" (quoted in Hwa Yol Jung, "Postmodernity, Eurocentrism, and the Future of Political Philosophy," in Fred Dallmayr (ed.) *Border Crossings* [Lanham, MD: Lexington Books, 1999], 295).

13 In developing his new politics of cultural difference, West tries to avoid the Scylla of "ethnic chauvinism" and the Charybdis of "faceless universalism." See Cornel West, "The New Cultural Politics of Difference," in Russell Ferguson, Martha Gever, Trinh T. Minh-ha, and Cornel West (ed.) *Out There* (New York: The New Museum of Contemporary Art, 1990), 36.

14 See Hwa Yol Jung, "Enlightenment and the Question of the Other: A Postmodern Audition," *Human Studies* 25 (2002): 297-306.

15 See Edward E. Said, *Orientalism* (New York: Random House, 1978); Salah Hassan and Iftikhav Dadi, eds., *Unpacking Europe* (Rotterdam: Museum Boijmans Van Beuningen and NAi Publishers, 2001).

16 Zygmunt Bauman, *Legislators and Interpreters* (Cambridge, UK: Polity Press, 1987), 110.

17 See Jonathan D. Spence, *The Question of Hu* (New York: Alfred A. Knopf, 1988).

18 It is interesting to note that David Farrell Krell sketches *das Geviert* envisioned by Heidegger in the diagram of a rectangle which connects sky, earth, gods, and mortals with two diagonal lines having Being at its epicenter: the cross of Being is not a crossing *out* (*Durchstreichung*) but a crossing *through* (*Durchkreuzen*). See Hwa Yol Jung, "Heidegger's Way with Sinitic Thinking," in Graham Parkes (ed.) *Heidegger and Asian Thought* (Honolulu: University of Hawaii Press, 1987), n. 27.

19 Ramsey Eric Ramsey and David James Miller, eds., *Experiences Between Philosophy and Communication* (Albany: State University of New York Press, 2003), 26.

20 See Jean-Paul Sartre, *Anti-Semite and Jew* (George J. Becker, trans.) (New York: Schocken Books, 1965), 113.

21 Johann Gottfried Herder, *J. G. Herder on Social and Political Culture* (F. M. Barnard, trans. and ed.) (Cambridge, UK: Cambridge University Press, 1969).

22 François Jullien, "Did Philosophers Have to Become Fixated on Truth?" (Janet Lloyd, trans.), *Critical Inquiry* 28 (2002): 803-824; François Jullien, "China as Philosophical Tool," *Diogenes* 50 (2003): 15-21.

23 See Hwa Yol Jung, "Introduction," in *Comparative Culture in the Age of Globalization* (Lanham, MD: Lexington Books, 2002), 1-22. Before he became interested in Japanese aesthetic culture and the Iranian revolution, Foucault (Janet Afary, and B. Anderson Kevin, *Foucault and the Iranian Revolution* [Chicago: University of Chicago Press, 2005], 18) wrote with the inerasable sense of a great divide between the East and the West: "In the universality of the Western ratio, there is this divide that is the East; the East thought of as the origin, dreamt of as the dizzy point that is the place of birth, of nostalgia and promises of return, the East which offers itself to the *colonizing reason of the West* but is indefinitely inaccessible, for it remains always as a boundary, the night of beginning in which the West was formed but where it drew a dividing line, *the East is for the West everything which the West is not*, yet it is here that it has to seek whatever might be its originating truth. It is necessary to do a history of this great divide." It is worth noting that Heidegger expressed his bewilderment that the Japanese tend to forget the beginnings of their own thinking in their pursuit of the newest and latest in European thought. See Jung, *op. cit.* (1987), 217-218.

24 Hegel's lectures on the history of philosophy in three volumes were concerned with "Oriental Philosophy" (Chinese and Indian) in thirty-one meager pages in English translation. However, he was willing to make rather rash judgments about it. Hegel asserted with no substantiation whatsoever: "We have conversations between Confucius and his followers in which there is nothing definite further than a commonplace moral put in the form of good, sound doctrine, which may be found as well expressed and better, in every place and amongst every people. Cicero gives us *De Officiis, a book of moral teaching more comprehensive and better than all the books of Confucius. He is hence only a man who has a certain amount of practical and worldly wisdom—one with whom there is no speculative philosophy*" (italics added). See G. W. F. Hegel, *Hegel's Lectures on the History of Philosophy*, vol. 1 (E. S. Haldane, trans.) (London: Kegan Paul, Trench, Trüber, 1892), 121.

25 Maurice Merleau-Ponty, 'Everywhere and Nowhere,' in Signs (Richard C. McCleary, trans.) (Evanston, IL: Northwestern University Press, 1964), 121-158.

26 *Ibid.*, 139.

27 Édouard Glissant, *Caribbean Discourse: Selected Essays* (J. Michael Dash, trans.) (Charlottesville: University Press of Virginia, 1989); Édouard Glissant, *Poetics of Relation* (Betsy Wing, trans.) (Ann Arbor: University of Michigan Press, 1997).

28 Robert J. C. Young, *Postcolonialism* (Oxford, UK: Blackwell, 2001), 68.

29 Paul Gilroy, *The Black Atlantic* (Cambridge, MA: Harvard University Press, 1993).

30 Glissant, *op. cit.* (1989), 98.

31 In developing the heteronomic ethics of responsibility, I am deeply indebted to four philosophers: the Scottish philosopher John Macmurray, the Jewish-French philosopher Emmanuel Levinas, the Russian literary theorist Mikhail Bakhtin and the émigré American philosopher Hans Jonas. (See Jung, 1999a, 2000, 2001, 2002c, and Jonas, 1984).

32 Michael Hardt and Antonio Negri, *Multitude* (New York: Penguin Press, 2004), xiv-xv.

33 Ludwig Feuerbach, *Principles of the Philosophy of the Future* (Manfred H. Vogel, trans.) (Indianapolis: Bobbs-Merrill, 1966).

34 C. B. Macpherson, *The Political Theory of Possessive Individualism* (Oxford, UK: Clarendon Press, 1962).

35 Cf. Michaer Ignatieff, ed., *American Exceptionalism and Human Rights* (Princeton, NJ: Princeton University Press, 2005).

36 Mary Ann Glendon, *Rights Talk* (New York: Free Press, 1995).

37 See Lawrence W. Chisolm, *Fenollosa: The Far East and American Culture* (New Haven, CT: Yale University Press, 1963), 25.

38 Cf. Alfredo G. A. Valladão, *The Twenty-First Century Will Be American* (John Howe, trans.) (London: Verso, 1996).

39 Eaglestone (2004: 182) suggests that "postmodernism is first an ethical position before anything else." Perhaps he has Levinas in mind. See Robert Eaglestone, "Postmodernism and Ethics Against the Metaphysics of Comprehension," in Steven Connor, ed., *The Cambridge Companion to Postmodernism* (New York: Cambridge University Press, 2004), 182.

40 Gould attempts to "universalize" and "globalize" democracy on the basis of interculturalism and "human rights." (See Carol C. Gould, *Globalizing Democracy and Human Rights* [New York: Cambridge University Press, 2004]) Although she focuses on "rights," Benhabib comes close to the heteronomic ethics of care and responsibility when she speaks of the "rights of others." For an attempt to "internationalize" or "globalize" the feminist theory of care, see Fiona Robinson, *Globalizing Care* (Boulder, CO: Westview Press, 1999).

41 Glover is concerned with the moral history of humanity in the twentieth century. It is so littered with violence that the twentieth century may be characterized as the century of humanity's inhumanity to humanity. See Jonathan Glover, *Humanity* (New Haven, CT: Yale University Press, 1999).

42 See Mona Ozouf, *Festivals and the French Revolution* (Alan Sheridan, trans.) (Cambridge, MA: Harvard University Press, 1988), 12.

43 Alfred North Whitehead, *Adventures of Ideas* (New York: Macmillan, 1954).

44 *Ibid.*, 105.

45 J. Glenn Gray, *The Warriors* (New York: Harper and Row, 1967).

46 Václav Havel, *Living in Truth* (Jan Vladislav, ed.) (London: Faber and Faber, 1987).

47 Václav Havel, *Disturbing the Peace* (Paul Wilson, trans.) (New York: Vintage Books, 1991), 165-206.

48 Roger Scruton, "Masaryk, Patocka and the Care of the Soul," *in Philosopher on Dover Beach* (New York: St. Martin's Press, 1990), 88.

49 Václav Havel, *The Art of the Impossible* (Paul Wilson and others, trans.) (New York: Alfred A. Knopf, 1997).

50 Francis Bacon, *Selected Writings of Francis Bacon* (Hugh G. Dick, ed.) (New York: Modern Library, 1955).

51 Michel Serres, *The Natural Contract* (Elizabeth MacArthur and William Paulson, trans.) (Ann Arbor: University of Michigan Press, 1995), 4.

52 Havel, *op. cit.* (1987), 136.

53 Aldo Leopold, *A Sand County Almanac* (spec. commemorative ed.) (New York: Oxford University Press, 1987).

54 Carson's aesthetic appreciation of the earth or what Heidegger calls *Gelassenheit* is unsurpassable: "Those who dwell, as scientists or laymen, among the beauties and mysteries of the earth are never alone or weary of life. Whatever the vexations or concerns of their personal lives, their thoughts can find paths that lead to inner contentment and to renewed excitement in living. Those who contemplate the beauty of the earth find reserves of strength that will endure as long as life lasts. There is symbolic as well as actual beauty in the migration of the birds, the ebb and flow of the tides, the folded bud ready for the spring. There is something infinitely healing in the repeated refrains of nature—the assurance that dawn comes after night, and spring after the winter." See Rachel L. Carson, *The Sense of Wonder* (New York: Harper and Row, 1965), 88-89.

55 Carol Gilligan, *In a Different Voice* (Cambridge, MA: Harvard University Press, 1982).

56 Isaiah Berlin, *The Hedgehog and the Fox* (New York: Simon and Schuster, 1986), 1.

57 François Dosse, *Empire of Meaning* (Hassan Melehy, trans.) (Minneapolis: University of Minnesota Press, 1999), 345.

58 Multiplicity is typically a postmodern concept. According to Calvino, it refers to our "inability to find an ending." For him, there are five other memos or categories in addition to multiplicity: they are "lightness," "quickness," "exactitude," and "visibility." See Italo Calvino, *Six Memos for the Next Millennium* (Cambridge, MA: Harvard University Press, 1988), 110.

59 Woolf defines cosmopolitanism succinctly when she writes: "as a woman, I have no country. As a woman I want no country. As a woman my country is the whole world." See Woolf, *op. cit.,* 109.

60 Zygmunt Bauman, *Liquid Modernity* (Cambridge, UK: Polity Press, 2000), 104.

61 See Jacques Derrida, *On Cosmopolitanism and Forgiveness* (Mark Dooley and Michael Hughes, trans.) (New York: Routledge, 2001); Stephen Toulmin, *Cosmopolis* (New York: Free Press, 1990). Arendt (1958: 2) affirms humanity's dependence on the earth or nonhuman world: "The earth is the very quintessence of the human condition and earthly nature, for all we know, may be unique in the universe in providing human beings with a habitat in which they can move and breathe without effort and without artifice. The human artifice of the world separates human existence from all mere animal environments, but life itself is outside this artificial world, and through life man remains related to all other living organisms." (See Hannah Arendt, *The Human Condition* [Chicago: University of Chicago Press, 1958], 2.) In dealing with the issue of humanity's dependency on the earth or the natural world, a large number of us, unfortunately and sadly, belong to what Woolf calls the "ignorantsia" as opposed to the "intelligentsia." See Woolf, op. cit., 87.

62 Quoted in Jung, *op. cit.* (2002b), 10.

Renaissance Humanism Revisited

Longxi Zhang

One of the important lessons we learn from modern hermeneutics is that we understand the past from the perspective of the present, that our knowledge of history is itself historically constituted. "At the beginning of all historical hermeneutics," says Hans-Georg Gadamer in a crucial passage of *Truth and Method*, *"the abstract antithesis between tradition and historical research, between history and the knowledge of it, must be discarded."*[1] We become aware of the historicity of our knowledge when we realize that we are reflecting on Renaissance humanism and its claim to universality not out of some purely antiquarian interest, but because we believe that the Renaissance and its legacy are historical forces that have played a significant role in shaping the modern world, or at least the Western world today. In our investigation into past history, the questions we start with belong to the present, which in a way set both the agenda and the framework for our understanding.

It was Heidegger who brought time or temporality into the question of being and defined being as *Dasein*, that is, being inextricably connected with its particular moment and locale.

The particular historical givens—the language, culture, society, and time we are born into—form the perspective from which we see things, and constitute what Heidegger called the forestructure of understanding, or what Gadamer deliberately and provocatively called prejudice (*Vorurteil*). And yet, our "first, last, and constant task," Heidegger insists, "is never to allow our fore-having, fore-sight, and fore-conception to be presented to us by fancies and popular conceptions, but rather to make the scientific theme secure by working out these forestructures in terms of the things themselves."[2] Therefore, to discard the abstract antithesis between history and our knowledge of it does not mean that we only understand what we already know or have anticipated. The famous concept of the hermeneutic circle—that we understand the whole in terms of its parts, and we understand the parts in the context of the whole—does not imply that understanding is a circular movement that only confirms our prejudices or preconceived notions. Although we necessarily start with such notions, the point of the hermeneutic circle is not to prove the circularity of understanding, let alone to validate it, but to assume the internal coherence of the language we try to understand and the interactions between the interpreter and the interpreted. "All correct interpretation," says Gadamer in elucidating Heidegger's notion of the hermeneutic circle, "must be on guard against arbitrary fancies and the limitations imposed by imperceptible habits of thought, and it must direct its gaze 'on the things themselves.'"[3]

In understanding Renaissance humanism, then, what are the "imperceptible habits of thought" that we must pay special attention to in order not to be misled by "arbitrary fancies"? What are the "things themselves" to which we must direct our gaze so that we can understand properly? In thinking about Renaissance humanism at a time when a deep sense of *Weltschmerz* has set in after the devastation of two World Wars in the last century, with tension and conflicts running high in our own time, and a host of social and environmental problems facing humanity in today's world, it becomes almost a "habit of thought" to trace many of the current problems to past history, to the idea of modernity and to humanism as its basic intellectual foundation without carefully considering the historical context within which humanism has evolved since the Renaissance. In other words, because we are unhappy with the world we see at the present, our unhappiness and present anxieties may color the picture of the Renaissance we see from our own perspective as we trace the present problems to their roots in past history, without sufficient consideration of the historical context in which the Renaissance humanists found themselves and to which they responded in various ways. This can be seen, for example, in John Carroll's dramatic and highly rhetorical description of the present condition as the "wreck of Western culture":

> We live amidst the ruins of the great, five-hundred-year epoch of Humanism. Around us is that 'colossal wreck.' Our culture is a flat expanse of rubble. It hardly offers shelter from a mild cosmic breeze, never mind one of those icy gales that regularly return to rip men out of the cosy intimacy of their daily lives and confront them with oblivion. Is it surprising that we are run down? We are desperate, yet we don't care much any more. We are timid, yet we cannot be shocked. We are inert underneath our busyness. We are destitute in our plenty. We are homeless in our own homes.[4]

Here as on many other occasions, the blame is on humanism, which "was doomed from the start," says Carroll, "that it carried within its own seed the elements of its destruction."[5] That seed can be understood, as David Ehrenfeld argues, as man's arrogance in replacing God, thus creating a sort of secular religion, of which the core is "a supreme faith in human reason."[6] While Ehrenfeld attacks humanism for its arrogance and blind faith in human rationality, the widely influential postmodern critique not only puts humanism, reason, and the Enlightenment into question, but tries to eliminate the very concept of man as a historical construct drawing close to its end. Michel Foucault's prediction of the disappearance of man perhaps gives the most memorable articulation to this idea. Man, Foucault declares, "is an invention of recent date. And one perhaps nearing its end." It was the invention of the human sciences in the nineteenth century when the modern *episteme* made an abrupt turn to man as the privileged object, with psychology, economics, and philology as the three basic models or paradigms. With a shift of the paradigm in the postindustrial and postmodern age, says Foucault at the end of *The Order of Things*, "one can certainly wager that man would be erased, like a face drawn in sand at the edge of the sea."[7] That surreal picture of man disappearing "like a face drawn in sand" has profound implications for humanity and the humanistic studies in our world today.

It is true that humanism can be traced to the Latin term *humanitas* used by Cicero and other Roman writers to refer to the classical study of arts—language, literature, history, and moral philosophy—and that the term humanist first appeared during the Renaissance to describe a scholar of classical literature and the arts. "Only in the nineteenth century, however," as Nicholas Mann points out, "and probably for the first time in Germany in 1809, is the attribute transformed into a substantive: humanism, standing for devotion to the literatures of ancient Greece and Rome, and the humane values that may be derived from them."[8] In a strictly historical philological sense, then, humanism is closely related to the nineteenth-century paradigm of the human sciences or what in German is known as *Geisteswissenschaften*. With the disappearance of man as Foucault predicted, then, humanism would lose its very fabric and foundation in the postmodern critique.

We may also note Jacques Derrida's remarks on man as the invention of the human sciences, an invention near its end along with the decline of human sciences, or the demise of humanism and metaphysics. "Man is that which is in relation to his end, in the fundamentally equivocal sense of the word," says Derrida. "The transcendental end can appear to itself and be unfolded only on the condition of mortality, of a relation to finitude as the origin of ideality. The name of man has always been inscribed in metaphysics between these two ends. It has meaning only in this eschato-teleological situation."[9] Despite the typically obscure language of deconstruction, Derrida's argument offers yet another example to show that the postmodern critique has turned *la fin de 1'homme* or the End of Man into a sort of slogan or a sign of the times.

Humanism and the very concept of man are indeed facing serious challenges and a profound crisis in the West. Whether we look at the more religiously oriented criticism or the postmodern discourse on *la fin de 1'homme*, the target of criticism is mostly the centrality of man, the privileging of man and human rationality. To put man and human reason at the center indeed constitutes the core of humanism, that is, the intellectual tendency of the Renaissance to move away from the medieval outlook dominated by the orthodoxy of Augustinian theology toward the secularization of social and political life as the first inroads into modernity. Here the Genesis story of the fall of man and its interpretation provide crucial evidence for us to understand the medieval background against which Renaissance humanism emerged as a new trend of thought. The early Christians and their Jewish predecessors, as Elaine Pagels explains, understood Adam's disobedience and its terrible consequences as a story about choice and human freedom, as a warning "not to misuse that divinely given capacity for free choice."[10] In the *City of God*, however, Augustine radically altered Jewish and early Christian interpretations, and turned that biblical story into an allegory of an inherently bad human nature, eventually leading to the doctrine of the original sin. Man's first disobedience was not, according to Augustine, one individual's wrong choice, for Adam was the symbol of all mankind. "In the first man," says Augustine, "there existed the whole human nature, which was to be transmitted by the woman to posterity, when that conjugal union received the divine sentence of its own condemnation."[11] Augustine's powerful symbolic interpretation of the fall of man and the concept of the original sin became, as Pagels observes, "for better and worse, the heritage of all subsequent generations of Western Christians and the major influence on their psychological and political thinking."[12] Under the influence of such a fundamentally misogynic and misanthropic concept, the medieval Church and its theological orthodoxy cast a huge shadow over people's lives in the West for a very long period of time. Despite its complexity and multifaceted nature, the medieval concept of man is thus first and foremost a sinner, whose life is contaminated by the original sin, "as from a corrupt root," even before it begins.[13]

It is against that background of medieval symbolism that some changes started to emerge within Christian theology itself in the thirteenth century when the availability of Aristotle in Latin translation stimulated inquiries into the issue of the relationship between faith and reason and investigations of nature in terms of logical causality. The works of Thomas Aquinas gave the most eloquent articulation to that change, which, as Umberto Eco describes, marked the crucial point where "[t]he symbolical vision turned into a naturalistic vision, which aspired to study causal connections with critical acuity."[14] Instead of being absorbed into a symbolic universe of spiritual meanings, nature was understood as ontologically meaningful in itself with its own formal reality of things. Likewise history was understood as the process of human action, not an allegory of spiritual meanings, which, Aquinas insisted, only the sacred history in the Old Testament imparted. Thus with Aquinas, again as Eco says, "we witness a kind of secularization of postbiblical history and the natural world."[15] The secularization was gradual and on a small scale, but these important changes in the medieval mentality and outlook prepared the way for the advent of humanistic ideas. When the early humanists appeared on the scene, they did not pit human reason against God's omniscience. On the contrary, it was by evoking the idea of divine creation that the humanists first sought to justify the worth and dignity of man as *imago dei*, God's creation in His own image.

In his famous *Oration on the Dignity of Man* delivered in Rome in 1486, Giovanni Pico della Mirandola centered his argument around an imaginary conversation between God and Adam after the divine creation was completed. "We have made you a creature neither of heaven nor of earth, neither mortal nor immortal," God told Adam, "in order that you may, as the free and proud shaper of your own being, fashion yourself in the form you may prefer. It will be in your power to descend to the lower, brutish forms of life; you will be able, through your own decision, to rise again to the superior orders whose life is divine."[16] In contrast to the misanthropic view of the original sin, this is of course a great change, but it is by no means to reverse the Augustinian orthodoxy completely, because man still faces the danger of falling to "the lower, brutish forms of life," though he is also capable of rising to "the superior orders." The possibility of transcending man's condition toward the higher, angelic level is of course enormously encouraging and exciting: "Oh wondrous and unsurpassable felicity of man, to whom it is granted to have what he chooses, to be what he wills to be!" Pico cried out with joy.[17] Perhaps we may say that this is a cry of joy at the birth of the concept of man as fully dignified, which contains a moment of truth of the spirit of Renaissance humanism that tends to get lost or deliberately erased by those critics today who choose to talk about the End of Man, or the disappearance of man like a fading face drawn in sand.

Shakespeare's Hamlet gives a similar expression to the humanist idea when he claims: "What a piece of work is a man, how noble in reason, how infinite in faculties, in form and moving, how express and admirable in action, how like an angel in apprehension, how like a god! the beauty of the world; the paragon of animals" (II.ii.303). But as E. M. W. Tillyard argues, Hamlet's praise of man "is in the purest medieval tradition: Shakespeare's version of the orthodox encomia of what man, created in God's image, was like in his prelapsarian state and of what ideally he is still capable of being. It also shows Shakespeare placing man in the traditional cosmic setting between the angels and the beasts. It was what the theologians had been saying for centuries."[18] That is to say, to affirm human dignity is not a completely new idea of the Renaissance, nor is it opposed to the acknowledgement of man's finitude and limitations, his humility before God. Indeed, Shakespeare's Hamlet immediately continues: "and yet to me what is this quintessence of dust?" (II.ii.308). What is problematic in much of modern or postmodern critique of Renaissance humanism is a mutually exclusive opposition between faith and reason, an absolute dichotomy between man as almost angelic and man as an ideological construct near its end. Such a dichotomous view was actually alien to Renaissance humanism, which conceived of man as capable of both falling down and rising upward, as contrary faculties and capabilities integrated into a unified self.

The Renaissance humanists never dreamed of dethroning God, for they realized that human beings could fall to the lower level of beasts, though they could also rise toward the angelic through the contemplation of God's work in nature and the disciplined study of the *humanitas.* "If, freeing ourselves from active care," says Pico, "we devote our time to contemplation, meditating upon the Creator in His work, and the work in its Creator, we shall be resplendent with the light of the Cherubim. If we burn with love for the Creator only, His consuming fire will quickly transform us into the flaming likeness of the Seraphim."[19] This is just one of numerous examples we can find in Renaissance humanism where the pride of human dignity is closely linked with a strong sense of religiosity. Pico and the other humanists all believed that through the study of philosophy and theology, by abandoning the sensual and bodily desires and living the contemplative life of a philosopher, man could arise above his limitations. That is why humanism has always been closely related to classical learning and humanistic studies, to the idea of liberal education as the cultivating of humanity.[20]

That is certainly a far cry from the kind of "godless monster" that some critics of humanism have blamed it to be.[21] Of course, humanism further evolved as European society became more and more secularized, particularly during and after the Enlightenment, but even modern secular humanism, as Richard Norman argues, does not seek to glorify humanity. "It involves no claims about the inevitability of progress. If it includes a commitment to human rationality, that is not a belief that reason will necessarily triumph, or that human beings can be relied on to act rationally provided only that the influence of those who have a vested interest in keeping us in ignorance can be kept at bay."[22] Secular humanism is just the idea of living one's life rationally, according to principles of reason, justice, and moral good, but true rationality includes a clear recognition of the finitude and limitations of human reason itself.

To come back to the point I raised at the beginning about the historicity of our knowledge and the "imperceptible habits of thought" with which we begin in the process of understanding, it should by now be clear that to blame Renaissance humanism for all the modern problems or problems of all modernity is neither reasonable nor justifiable. It is a gross simplification of humanism to reduce a great deal of its history and meaning to a distorted caricature, and then to blame such a distorted picture of humanism, as some critics do, for the inhumanity of colonialism and imperialism, the horrors of the Holocaust and genocide, and the damage to nature and the environment. It is true that humanism's claim to universality based on limited European or Western experience is partial and limited and should be recognized as such, but that does not mean that we cannot salvage what is valid and valuable from a broader understanding of the idea of humanism, that is, the basic idea that human beings should take priority in considerations of a social and political nature.

From a cross-cultural point of view, that is what I believe that we—scholars in the East—can contribute to in order to have a better understanding of humanism. We can put that basic idea in the context of Eastern culture and philosophy, and reestablish the concept of humanism without the baggage of a rigid Western dichotomy between faith and reason. In East Asia in particular, religious toleration seems to be the norm more than exclusive claims of a predominant religion. In China, for example, the Confucian virtue of benevolence (*ren*) or maintaining a loving and humane relationship with fellow human beings is not established in opposition to god or gods, and the traditional literati have no difficulty in adopting elements from the Confucian, the Taoist, and the Buddhist teachings and moving freely among these different positions. Confucius took religious ritual as a social custom with symbolic meanings rather than a substantial form of religious life, for he once said of performing rituals that one should "sacrifice as if ancestors were present, and sacrifice to the gods as if the gods were present."[23] He almost kept religious belief as a private matter, for he "did not talk about uncanny things, violence, disorder, or deities."[24] Not that Confucius did not have any concept of god or deity, but he put more emphasis on human effort and human responsibility. Religion may still play an important part in people's spiritual life, but human beings must rely on themselves and their own effort to achieve their goals in this world and in their lives. Taoist thinkers like Laozi and Zhuangzi held very different views from the Confucians, but their naturalism, the nondifferentiation of the human from the inanimate, also denies human beings the privilege of being favored by gods. That is to say, in the Taoist cosmos, man is not privileged above nature or other things. "Heaven and earth are not benevolent and treat all things as straw dogs," says Laozi.[25] Thus heaven and earth, or whatever is thought to be superior or divine, do not favor human beings as somehow different from and above all other things. Thus, both the Confucians and the Taoists held that human beings must live their lives based on their own moral understanding of their relationships with nature and the world, not counting on god or gods to take the burden off their shoulders. From the Chinese point of view, then, humanism is not defined against religion, but is understood as man's own effort to manage things in the human world, as ethical, humane, and loving relationships, as the idea of a shared and common humanity, even the effort to achieve a harmonious relationship with the inanimate nature.

Humanism in that sense has nothing to do with hubris or human arrogance, and it does not make any exclusive claim to truth as it realizes the limitations of human understanding. As Gadamer emphasized, the hermeneutic process is modeled on the dialectic of questioning and openness, for "[t]he essence of the question is to open up possibilities and keep them open."[26] When we are truly open to the question of others—not only to the validity of the question, but also the possibility of insight and corrective value of the question—we may then have a genuine dialogue happening among different people, different groups, cultures, and civilizations. For our world today, this is extremely important, because religious systems tend to make exclusive claims, that is, that only my religion is the true faith and the other's is superstition; that only my god is the true god while all others are just so many idols. When we have such mutually exclusive fundamentalist views, dialogue of civilizations would be very difficult, if not utterly impossible. Particularly for our purposes here in celebration of the UN International Day of Peace, to put human beings and human life above everything else promises a far better prospect of world peace and world prosperity than reversing to religious fundamentalism and its exclusive claims to truth. For that, the historical experiences of religious toleration in East Asia (as well as in the West) are valuable spiritual and intellectual resources we can draw on in rethinking of both history and our present times. And for that, Renaissance humanism and its sober realization of both the dignity, the great potential of man and his inevitable limitations may still give us much to ponder and much to learn.

Notes

1 Hans-Georg Gadamer, *Truth and Method*, 2nd rev. ed. (translation revised by Joel Weinsheimer and Donald G. Marshall) (New York: Crossroad, 1989), 282. Emphasis is in the original text.

2 Martin Heidegger, *Being and Time* (John Macquarrie and Edward Robinson, trans.) (New York: Harper & Row, 1962), 195.

3 Gadamer, *op. cit.*, 266-267.

4 John Carroll, *Humanism: The Wreck of Western Culture* (London: Fontana Press, 1993), 1.

5 *Ibid.*, 6.

6 David Ehrenfeld, *The Arrogance of Humanism* (Oxford: Oxford University Press, 1981), 5.

7 Michel Foucault, *The Order of Things: An Archaeology of the Human Sciences* (New York: Vintage Books, 1973), 387.

8 Nicholas Mann, "The Origins of Humanism," in Jill Kraye (ed.) *Cambridge Companion to Renaissance Humanism* (Cambridge: Cambridge University Press, 1996), 1-2.

9 Jacques Derrida, "The Ends of Man," in *Margins of Philosophy* (Alan Bass, trans.) (Chicago: University of Chicago Press, 1982), 123.

10 Elaine Pagels, *Adam, Eve, and the Serpent* (New York: Vintage Books, 1989), 108.

11 St. Augustine, *The City of God* (Marcus Dods, trans.) (New York: The Modern Library, 1993) xiii.3, 414.

12 Pagels, *op. cit.,* xxvi.

13 St. Augustine, *op. cit.,* xiii.14, 423.

14 Umberto Eco, *The Aesthetics of Thomas Aquinas* (Hugh Bredin, trans.) (Cambridge, Mass.: Harvard University Press, 1988), 141.

15 *Ibid.,* 152.

16 Giovanni Pico della Mirandola, *Oration on the Dignity of Man* (A. Robert Caponigri, trans.) (Washington, D.C.: Regnery Publishing, Inc., 1956), 7-8.

17 *Ibid.,* 8.

18 E.M.W. Tillyard, *The Elizabethan World Picture* (New York: Macmillan, 1944), 3-4.

19 Mirandola, *op. cit.,* 13-14.

20 For the concept of liberal education as cultivating humanity, see Martha C. Nussbaum, *Cultivating Humanity: A Classical Defense of Reform in Liberal Education* (Cambridge, Mass.: Harvard University Press, 1997).

21 Ehrenfeld, *op. cit.,* 8.

22 Richard Norman, *On Humanism* (London: Routledge, 2004), 23-24.

23 Confucius, *The Analects*, iii.12; Liu Baonan, *Lunyu zhengyi* (The Correct Meaning of the Analects), vol. 1 of *Zhuzi jicheng* (Collection of Distinguished Philosophical Works), 8 vols. (Beijing: Zhonghua, 1954) 1:53.

24 Confucius, *op. cit.,* vii.21; Liu, *op. cit.,* 1:146.

25 Wang Bi, *Laozi zhu* (Laozi with Annotations), vol. 3 of *Zhuzi jicheng* (Collection of Distinguished Philosophical Works) 3:3.

26 Gadamer, *op. cit.,* 299.

Aesthetics and Communication: The Future of Value

Jérôme Bindé

At the dawn of the 21st century, at a time when attempts to reappropriate ourselves and our civilization seem to have foundered—whether in relation to revolutionary schemes of political emancipation or ventures in the realm of philosophical, spiritual, artistic or political renewal; when certain prophets of doom are proclaiming the advent of a "posthumanity," not to say of the inhuman; when tragic events leave us disoriented and discredit the hypothesis of the "end of History" and when societies are mobilized in the search for new ethical codes, we have to address the question of what we are in the form of a future-oriented philosophical enquiry. Our existence is defined by the way we apprehend and appreciate our inner and outer world—aesthetics—and the way we communicate to form instant or long-term communities: from Paleolithic grottos to personal websites, it is easy to identify those common traits of human activity. Unfortunately, human sites, whether archaeological or digital, do not speak for themselves. We need a frame to understand them, to peer into our past, to grasp our present and to explore our possible futures. The problem with such a frame is that it is not written in stone: it evolves. Thus, before we can discuss future-oriented tools, we have to unearth previous frames and analyze how the Enlightenment invented the original concept of aesthetics only to create intractable paradoxes. When those difficulties are solved we will be in a position to investigate a more adequate frame, values, and ask one key question of our time: what is the future of values?

The Western Enlightenment thinkers invented the Modern conception of aesthetics when they transformed the philosophical interrogation of beauty into a reflection on sensibility. For a very long time, up to the Renaissance, it was widely accepted in the West that beauty had to do with some intrinsic qualities in things. Thus, it was legitimate to hold that people had common criteria to gauge the value of things: discussions on beauty mostly revolved around the concept of harmony and the quest for perfect arrangements and configurations. This implied that cultures, societies and polities were bounded together through their bounds to the self-evident value of the world. This holistic and ordained conception changed dramatically with the emergence of the Modern view, according to which beauty is only in the eye of the beholder. The deep connection established by Plato between the Ideas of Truth, Justice and Beauty was dissolved: beauty, in the Enlightenment conception, is not a path to knowledge and justice, it is, quite to the contrary, the most idiosyncratic shape of our experience.

Thus, beauty became the object of aesthetics, the Greek word for sensibility. Yet, it is a word that the Greeks never thought could encompass the girth of such an immortal and absolute component of reality as beauty. If the aesthetical concept of beauty brought new dimensions to individuality, it also implied a grave problem. The Enlightenment thinkers, having entrenched beauty so deeply into the individual experience, realized they could not explain how aesthetical communities are even possible. If logics can prove that experience is an idiosyncratic phenomenon, experience and history prove that people constantly create esthetical communities. One only has to think of national museums, where nations celebrate themselves through a gathering of what they deem worthy and beautiful. Did the Moderns solve this problem? Not really: they avoided it. According to their concept of community, living together has nothing to do with feeling together. Since we are still a bit modern, we have to read Aristotle again to grasp the implications of this view: to Aristotle, friendship and sympathy for each other are literally the glue holding communities together. The Moderns got rid of that affective glue and replaced it with chains of reasons. This idea that reason is the matrix of communities is evident when one considers the concept of social contract. For instance, a contract is based on a decision that is rational, justifiable and explainable in terms of interests. Aesthetics is concerned precisely with the opposite, because beauty and emotions seize us whether we want them or not. Most of Modernity is a dramatic divorce of sense and sensibility.

The Moderns laboured to find a way out of their paradox. Kant offers one of the most emblematic attempts in that direction. Faced with the problem of reconciling the near idiosyncratic esthetical experience with the obvious existence of esthetical communities, Kant translated the issue into an analysis of conversations. The Modern era was, after all, the Age of conversation. Beauty is not something we can decide or analyze objectively, but it is something we can discuss at length. The sympathy that had prevailed from the Ancients to the Renaissance times had thus been replaced with politeness. Kant found a way to reintroduce the Enlightenment matrix of the social contract in the realm of beauty. There is no aesthetical contract so to speak, since, according to the Moderns, we cannot feel or experience together, but there is a contract of good conversation, a civilized and refined conversation, as elaborate and subtle as a fugue by Bach or a tea ceremonial can be. This solution has the elegance of its time, but it is a fragile one: the aristocratic conversations could not silence the uproar of the Revolutions. Conversation may well be the finest accomplishment of elitist societies, but it is not an accomplishment of democratic communication. If the concept of beauty is defined as an idiosyncratic pleasure rather than the basis for a common world, it is only logical that individuals cannot really communicate. Signing a contract of good conversation cannot guarantee that you will not have a solipsist dialogue of mutual incomprehension.

How are we to understand this paradox Modernity locked itself into? According to Nietzsche, the problem with the Modern view of aesthetics is that, fundamentally, it is dedicated to spectators. Nietzsche's view can be confirmed if we go back to the very word aesthetics: when the Moderns chose this word to define the reflection on beauty, they explicitly reduced beauty and art to matters of receptivity, passivity or experience. Even artists are defined as spectators who happen to have creative skills. It seems logical, in the eye of a Modern thinker, that you can only produce art after you've had an experience of beauty. But this is actually not a very serious way of dealing with art. Art is not just a representation of what we have experienced before: it is an activity, a craft and a production. Nietzsche insists that art is not centred on experience; it is not a spectacle; it is a creation. In *The Birth of Tragedy*, he even wrote that the existence of the world is justified because it is an aesthetical production of phenomenona: Nietzsche reconnected aesthetics to the very nature of reality redefined as a process, not just as being (which is why, try as he may, he is closer to a philosopher like Alfred North Whitehead than to the Greeks). In this postmodern world view, even a spectator is a creator. The landscape we gaze at is neither outside our mind nor inside it; it is an instant cocreation of distinct aspects of reality. It is defined by the value it has here and now. Value is the master concept here: aesthetics, just as politics, economics and, above all ethics, are about the creation and the preservation of values.

But, when he identified values as the foundation of aesthetical creativity and political community, Nietzsche immediately prophesied the advent of nihilism, which he summed up in the formula: "the devaluing of the highest values." Not surprisingly, the talk today is of nihilism, "loss of meaning" and the "disappearance of values," of the "clash of civilizations" and supposedly irreconcilable values. As Nietzsche had foreseen, the question of nihilism, and hence of values, has been central to philosophical enquiry in the 20th century. What is the significance of the absence of any transcendent foundation that enables eternal values to be anchored in an unchanging firmament or received as a final and irrefragable revelation? Does it mean the twilight of values? Or, in a world where cultures encounter one another on a planetary scale, should we anticipate virulent antagonisms, potentially violent clashes between opposing values? Or alternatively, will we see new and unexpected hybridizations between value systems that are currently alien in origin and orientation?

The 20th century has painfully called into question all our certainties concerning society, history and humankind. The contemporary crisis of values affects not only the traditional moral frameworks transmitted by the great religious faiths but also the secular values that succeeded them (Science, Progress, the emancipation of peoples, and humanist ideals of solidarity). The spectre of monstrous evil, which left its mark on the 20th century, seems once again to loom over us. Is there not a risk that technological development—a crucial, unpredictable and uncontrollable factor of change—could render humanity unrecognizable, leading to what some have already disturbingly called a "posthumanity"? In a universe characterized by radical innovations and discontinuities, which will rapidly impact on the human species as a whole and will alter geopolitical balances, how can History continue to be conceived in terms of continuity, and how can the desirable utopia of a better life for the majority be sustained? Can we hold to the vision of a universal project compatible with the multiplicity of our heritages and enhanced by their interwoven histories?

Paul Valéry presciently pointed out that, in a world dominated by speculation, our conception of moral or ethical values was increasingly influenced by the model of the stockmarket. There is no longer any fixed standard of value, any stable and absolute measure, but rather all values fluctuate in a vast market, their quotations rising and falling according to wholly subjective crazes, panics and wagers. The value "mind," he joked, was no different to the value "wheat" or "coal," and it was continuing to fall. In this way, the phenomenon of fashion, which was previously restricted to those sectors where arbitrariness and convention prevail, is permeating our whole conception of values. We live in the realm of the ephemeral, accelerated obsolescence and subjective whim, as if the most sacred values, deprived of any foundation, could enter the great securities market and float in their turn. This speculative view of values as relative to a particular moment and circumstance applies to a great many ethical and aesthetic phenomena in the contemporary world. The role of information and the media reinforce this tendency since the logic of the stock-exchange model of values, like that of fashion and short-term trends, implies taking account of a whole series of ephemeral "indicators," to be seized immediately, instantaneous information replacing a sense of History and recognition of its henceforth indiscernible long-term patterns.

In a context that overwhelmingly seems to privilege a view of values as frivolous, how can we still think of them as serious? How can the crucial question of education find its rightful place in a fluctuating and malleable world subject to the emotional and intellectual influence of ephemeral images? The 21st century could find itself caught in a strange contradiction: never has such value been placed on the ephemeral; yet new values seem to be emerging. They are not so much inherited as invented, not so much reproduced as created, not so much received as transmitted.

Are we then moving towards an aesthetization of values, seeing that the main concern is with their creation—where any new creation involves at least as many destructions? Has aesthetics become the highest stage of economics and ethics? Are we at the threshold of a civilization where aesthetical values are not just another set of values but the core of the concept of value itself? Is it what Nietzsche foresaw when he said that, ontologically, the world is first an aesthetical phenomenon? Today, the antagonism between the artist and the bourgeois, between "aesthetics and political economy" (in the words of Mallarmé), has disappeared. Not only is the artist fully recognized and lauded, but he has possibly never been placed on such a pedestal and never been made the very model of activity productive of meaning and novelty, as he currently is. "Creation" is all about us. We are all—or aspire to be—"creators." All forms of production, enterprise and action are conceived on the model of artistic creation. In our personal lives, in the absence of stable and enduring frames of reference, each of us is obliged to resort to creation, if only of our own existence: we have to invent a "lifestyle." In economic life, innovation is recognized to be the engine of development; market forces place a premium on the seductiveness of the product, on the limitless proliferation of consumer appetites, which can only be sustained through a perpetual dynamic of alluring creations. This pervasive aesthetization affects not only society as spectacle (the media, the advertising world and the visual/aural environment) but the very kernel of ethical principle and of the business dynamic.

May we therefore predict the creation of new values? The 20th century has seen a massive decline in many regions of the world in allegiance to traditional religious dogmas, but also an extraordinary diversification of personal or community quests of a spiritual nature—and, after all, it can be difficult to distinguish between aesthetical and spiritual experiences. Are these minority insights a potential source of strong values that could prove essential for the future? Similarly, while the social cement has been weakened by the rise of an increasingly radical individualism that destroys inherited links and established identities, this is paralleled by an unprecedented growth of new forms of association and the birth of new forms of solidarity. What values will stem from these new networks of affinity, alliance and communication (furthered by technological innovation)? In a world increasingly ruled by economic motives and the materialistic and narcissistic values of consumption, hedonism and short-term satisfaction, can we discern the emergence of alternative values that could be described as "postmaterialist"? These questions are linked to the collapse of patriarchal structures (with their ethical, institutional, cultural and metaphysical dimensions), representing a considerable break with the past and leading to a feminizing of values with far-reaching consequences whose scope is still hard to gauge but which will affect all aspects of the world ahead.

The questioning of values is a symptom of the profound changes that our societies are experiencing under the combined influence of the major phenomena of globalization and the new technologies. Globalization, contrary to what one too often hears, is not reducible to the liberal integration of the markets or the emergence of global thinking. Globalization, understood as a sense of belonging to the world, has a long history that reaches back over the centuries. Was it not under the Roman Empire that philosophers first thought of the concept of cosmopolitanism? As Edgar Morin has pointed out, the history of the first phase of globalization, that of the explorers, the great discoveries and colonization, which saw the prevalence of all kinds of hegemonies and all forms of domination, whether political, economic or cultural, should not make us lose sight of the existence of a second phase of globalization, that of the human conscience, which from Las Casas and Montaigne through NGOs to contemporary global civic movements, informed by the idea of our common humanity and a forward-looking vision of a World citizenship, has been a political, philosophical and spiritual phenomenon as well as a cultural one. Does this lend support to the possibility of harmonious coexistence between cultures, prophesied by those subscribing to an irenic view of globalization? Here, though, we must point to the persistence of flagrant inequalities globally and nationally. Mention must be made here of the role of the new technologies and of the "informational revolution" as adjuncts of globalization. For there is a great risk that the changes taking place will deepen the digital, economic and social divide, which no longer coincides exactly with the North-South split. More than ever, we need to consider how knowledge can be universally shared and how genuine exchanges between cultures can take place.

New challenges call for new responses. This is a measure of how far the new world taking shape before us compels us to rethink totally the social contracts that underpin our societies. UNESCO's role is to be a forward-looking organization, drawing on the talent of leading scientists, researchers, thinkers, creators and international public figures to bring about the marriage of politics with prudent foresight. We now know that science itself, so long as its creativity is not curbed, must also observe the principle of foresight. The consequences of the genetic revolution in particular need to be questioned, both from an ethical standpoint and also from the point of view of the social preferences and discriminatory practices that it has not managed to eradicate. For in the wake of the possible self-domestication of the human species old ghosts and old demons could return to haunt us.

Is there not a risk that too much questioning will induce a kind of disorientation and cause us to diagnose overhastily this loss of meaning we referred to in terms of nihilism? Certainly, loss of meaning is the recurrent context of many of the issues confronting us today. One has only to look at the different forms of modern psychopathologies to see that contemporary societies, having lost touch with time, are also set to lose touch with the soul. It is as if, in the age of short-term returns, we had succumbed to the cult of stress and the tyranny of the emergency.

The global changes described above are evidence of the need for a project for global social and political renewal, which the UNESCO Foresight Programme has tentatively suggested might be centred on the idea of four contracts evoked in the two "21st Century Talks," "Keys to the 21st Century" and "The Future of Values" as well as in "A World Ahead: Our Future in the Making." These four contracts would differ from the uniform social contract of the Enlightenment period: Hobbes, Locke or Rousseau's contracts summarized attempts to justify the monopoly of reason on the polity. The four new contracts are designed with a view to preserving and fostering the diversity of values. This process would take the form of a new social contract founded on lifelong education for all, whose main axes in a global society where the challenges are planetary would be a natural contract, a cultural contract and an ethical contract. Without the provision of lifelong education for all, how is absolute poverty to be eradicated, how are democratic values to be effectively promoted and how are genuine knowledge societies to be built? Without a natural contract under which man would be not the "master and possessor" but the steward of nature, how can we put an end to the excessive exploitation of existing resources, which stands to jeopardize irremediably the possibilities of sustainable development and hence the chances of future generations? Without a cultural contract, which is not the least difficult to conceive, what recourse would we have against the dwindling of cultural diversity based on the idea of our common humanity and on a forward-looking vision of an earth citizenship? Without redefining the ethical requirements that underpin the very ideal of human rights and provide a framework for human security, how can we lay the bases for a forward-looking democracy and a global citizenship? This is a measure of the scale of the task before us.

This is but a partial response to the question implicit in an enquiry into the "future of values." What we should rather be talking about is shifts in meaning and the creation of new meaings. Let us end with a wager: what if the renewal to which we aspire were to spring from knowledge and the spread of knowledge? What if knowledge societies were to take the place of value-based societies? For knowledge cannot be reduced to the questioning of received wisdom and the production of doubt, inherent in the scientific approach. Knowledge is also creation, renewal and keeping abreast of change. There is a clear awareness today that the development of societies predicated on the sharing of knowledge is the best way of waging effective war on poverty and forestalling major health risks such as pandemics, of reducing the terrible loss of life caused by tsunamis and tropical storms, and of promoting sustainable human development. For new modes of development are today within our grasp: these are no longer based, as in the past, on "blood, sweat and tears," but rather on intelligence, the scientific and technological capacity to address problems, intellectual added value, and the expansion of services in all sectors of the economy, which should be conducive to civic development and, in response to the risk society, the growth of a forward-looking democracy. Knowledge societies would thus be based both on a creative or aesthetical experience and network of communications enabling new kinds of communities while reinforcing the diversity of the existing ones. There could be no more admirable goal for all of us than to point the way to this new paradigm.

II

Reason, Ideology and Culture

Beyond Freedom and Equality

John M. Dunn

It is a commonplace of ethical and political reflection across the world today that human beings should live with one another on every scale as equals and in freedom, insofar as the circumstances of their collective life make it possible for them to do so. What remains fiercely controversial and deeply obscure is just how far those circumstances *do* permit anything of the kind. There is, naturally, ample further disagreement about several associated questions: just what it is to be free, which exercises of freedom deserve respect or are entitled to toleration and protection, about which forms of equality are compatible with personal freedom and which necessarily violate it, and about how far (and at what cost) equality itself is a feasible and potentially sustainable condition. None of these controversies is in much danger of definitive solution; and they tend to flow readily into one another, widening and narrowing the space of disagreement as they move through time and space.

It is important to recognize how novel the status of this set of global pieties really is. Two and a half centuries ago, as Jonathan Israel has stalwartly demonstrated in his two massive volumes *Radical Enlightenment* and *Enlightenment Contested,*[1] there were active and spirited proponents of the same judgment in a number of European countries, championing a tradition which he traces back to the renegade Jewish philosopher Benedict de Spinoza and the dynamic commercial capitalism of the cities of the United Netherlands which had sheltered him and helped inspire his political vision. (The proponents themselves, as he also notes, sometimes traced their own lineage back considerably further, to Pre-Socratic Greeks or to the philosophers of Islam's grandest age, amongst other things inventing the history of philosophy as an intellectual genre in their efforts to vindicate the connection.) For Israel, the normative commonplaces of the contemporary globe are above all the heritage of Spinoza's promise. But in 1752, where his second volume ends with the temporary triumph of Diderot and his *Encyclopédistes* over their ecclesiastical persecutors, the full-blooded partisans of freedom and equality were still a tiny band of misfits and transgressives, often harassed mercilessly by the authorities of church or state, forced to live and work for lengthy interludes largely in the shadows, and frequently defenceless in face of what the Abbé Meslier called "*la tyrannie des grands de la terre.*"[2] Only the fickle protection of one or the other of these latter lofty figures, King Frederick the Great of Prussia, Madame de Pompadour, Mistress of France's King Louis XV, could furnish effective protection against the cumulatively overwhelming power of their enemies. To think about the prospects for extending freedom and enhancing equality in the world in which we or our immediate descendants must continue to live, we need first to grasp just how the political fortunes of these values have been transformed so comprehensively, at least at the level of rhetoric and public affirmation, over the last two and a half centuries. We need to see not merely what makes them enticing to us and gives them their current allure, but also what has enabled them to focus and format such huge transformative energies in the intervening years, and spread them so insistently so far beyond the cities of Holland's Golden Age or the boisterous *cafés* of eighteenth century Paris. We need to see not merely what makes them so imaginatively attractive, but also what has given them their startling power. In early eighteenth century Europe, as no doubt in most civilised societies throughout history, many thought and felt that the communities to which they belonged should in many respects be quite different (juster, kinder, safer, less alarming and disagreeable). But very few believed with any confidence that their own communities could actually be made so, and even they, for the most part, not for at all compelling reasons. It is a nice point how far our contemporary expectations have altered in respect of equality, a value which still oscillates ceaselessly between the formal and largely vacuous and the substantive and now totally incredible. But in the case of freedom no one could sanely doubt that many aspects of the lives of very many people in many sharply contrasted parts of the civilised, urban, industrialized world can be plausibly seen as freer now than the lives of all but a handful of their predecessors could ever hope to be even three or four generations ago.

Neither equality nor freedom are clear, univocal or unidimensional values in themselves; and it is far from clear how the two articulate with one another. Each is vigorously disputed in interpretation, and many still suspect that each, for one reason or another, trades off systematically with the other,[3] making them rivals in political, social and economic fact, rather than complementary aspects of a single good for human beings, which it at least makes sense to pursue with closely matched energy and hope. For at least a century and a half the struggle between socialism and capitalism, long over in most parts of the world but still in a caricatured and dangerous form brutally alive on the Korean peninsula, was seen by both parties as a struggle between freedom and equality, with capitalism in socialist eyes normatively disqualified by its open commitment to inequality, and socialism correspondingly poisoned for its political opponents by its blatant indifference to the freedom of the vast majority of those on whom it had been imposed.[4] Now that that struggle is essentially over, with the clear victory of capitalism, the status of freedom as a value is barely challenged, except on religious grounds, but the precise meaning and status of equality remains as murky as it ever was.

At this late stage in that struggle it is hard to take equality entirely seriously; and the real conflicts over human values appear for the moment to have shifted principally to the meaning and normative adequacy of freedom itself.[5] The residual claims of equality are most evocative when they can be presented primarily as prerequisites for freedom, as in the metric of capabilities advocated by the Nobel Prize-winning Indian economist Amartya Sen or by Martha Nussbaum.[6] There is more than one set of good reasons for this outcome, since freedom can at least be envisaged coherently as an end, whereas it is hard to make sense of equality as anything more than an especially consequential type of means (but cf. Williams[7]). We favour equality, those of us who do so (and some crisply don't)[8] partly out of embarrassment (because we find inequality irrational and unjust), and partly in the hope that replacing inequality by equality will yield clear benefits in relation to our other purposes and hopes in living our lives. We favour freedom in our own case because we are agents and have purposes of our own, and since we prefer not to be constrained in pursuing these purposes, against our will and from the outside. Very few human beings are so despondent about their own being in the world that they would willingly surrender to others the opportunity to do as they choose and make that surrender unconditionally and under whatever circumstances happen to be chosen by those to whom they make it. (Perhaps there can be voluntary slavery; but it is infrequent.) In a world no longer confident what else (if anything) is valuable for human beings, over against their own wishes or those of their fellows, the opportunity to live as you wish and choose is as close as we can still get to an evident good in itself. We accept its diminution in our own case reluctantly, and only because of a clear prospective contribution to competing wishes of our own or pressing concerns on the part of others.

We have reached this outcome through a process which the poet Schiller (and, after him, Max Weber) christened the disenchantment of the world. We see its content as human value after superstition (what is left in human valuing after false belief has been extracted from it), the residue of Enlightenment, Spinoza's gift. But that great shift, insofar as it really has occurred (which is quite easy to exaggerate: there are noticeable lags in important sites including Washington, DC), registers simply a transformation in thought and sentiment. It does little to explain why that transformation occurred, and virtually nothing to explain why it has happened as and when and where it has. To grasp these, we need to look not directly at what humans value, or even at how they think and feel about what they value, but at the setting in which most of them now live.

That setting, now as never before in human history, is principally urban. It has been prompted and made possible by the dynamic of modern industry, the vast seething cauldron of global commerce, and the electronic webs which bind us ever tighter together. It was the economic mechanism which generated that world, more than the erratic and dangerous politics which has protected it along its way, which has furnished so many millions of human beings with freer conditions of life than any of their ancestors ever knew. It has been the requirements for and the workings of that mechanism, endlessly reinforcing one another, which have sapped the unabashed power of immemorial inequalities (class, age, gender, cultural condescension), and established in their stead a new and fluidly self-regenerating inequality which issues from the mechanism itself.

Today, in contrast with two thirds of a century ago immensely more people live far more freely in this huge city, and, again in drastic contrast with the past in many respects, the young more deeply, subtly and sometimes flamboyantly so than their still wealthier and more powerful elders. It is capitalism, in all its formidable nastiness, which has built this world and in the end, erratically and largely unwittingly, opened it up to the most vibrant youth culture in Asia and perhaps the world. This is plainly not what Confucius had in mind, any more than it can be what Jesus Christ or Mahomet or the Buddha took the trouble to recommend. But, crucially, it is also not what anyone at all imagined, let alone planned or enacted. It is an unplanned outcome of processes which no one could have clearly conceived in advance, and which can be clearly understood at all only in the deceptive calm of retrospection.

In some ways "Beyond Freedom and Equality" is a curious slogan, suggesting an overoptimistic assessment of where the civilised and successful societies of the world now are and a correspondingly unwarranted presumption that they can readily advance dramatically further if only they choose to do so in the right direction. It is altogether less curious if you hear it instead not as a formula for locating that direction but as a robust expression of the conviction that the values we affirm today and the ways in which we shape our lives together today are each in pressing need of considerable amendment. It does not make sense to suppose that we are in much danger of moving *beyond* freedom and equality unless we have already contrived to reach both. If we take freedom in the unelevated sense employed by Benjamin Constant early in the nineteenth century,[9] the liberty to live as you choose, it is intuitively plausible to claim that all societies in the world which are prosperous today on a non*rentier* basis (and at least one, Norway, which is remarkably prosperous and principally on an evidently *rentier* basis) furnish the mass of their members with a level of modern liberty which Constant himself could scarcely have imagined extending beyond the privileged milieu in which he lived his own life (the salons of Paris, the Chateau of Coppet).

These societies continue to differ from one another in spiritual appeal, cultural composure, and political calm and selfassurance. They also differ, of course, in the clarity and robustness of their economic strategies for maintaining and enhancing their prosperity. But of all of them it can be said at present that their success as societies comes principally from the cumulative effectiveness of those strategies looking backwards, and falters as and when that cumulation for any reason ceases protractedly (Japan in the 1990s for most of its inhabitants,[10] the United States in recent decades for virtually all its working class and most of its middle class).[11] The place of freedom in this record of success is principally the space they allocate to unmolested enjoyment and the opportunity to follow personal whim. Their strongest defence of this provision is that it meets the requirements of justice, leaving the choice of goals in living comprehensively to those whose lives are at stake.[12] So seen, these societies are unpaternalist, undidactic, firmly respectful of the will and capacity of their denizens to choose for themselves, and at least provisionally polite about the choices they prove to make. What cracks the façade of politeness is not merely the virulent malice which some proceed to visit upon others (which can be kept in bounds by the criminal law), but also increasingly the cumulative fiscal burden imposed by individual fecklessness and the political opportunity to pass on to others the costs of picking up the pieces. A striking instance in this case is the global epidemic of obesity and its budgetary impact on societies which continue to fund public health care with any generosity. This is an old space of social conflict, previously fought out principally in the labour market and in the disciplinary counterparts to minimal provision for subsistence. But on a less hasty understanding it pervades the domains of education, health and labour, the core elements of collective social life. I do not know of any society in the world today, whatever its average level of economic prosperity, which is reasonably sanguine about the quality of its systems for educating its citizenry, caring for their health and balancing individual opportunity with consequential contribution in the market in labour. Some societies have tried extremely hard in all three dimensions at once and for many decades on end. Sweden is a notable example. Others switch their attention erratically from one to another. But in none at all, as far as I am aware, is there much current confidence, either amongst the managerial elites of the society or amongst the populace at large, that these central domains of social organization and endeavour both realise a high degree of freedom and put it to a reasonably edifying and prospectively sustainable use.

You can regard this as evidence that human beings at large are less rational and efficacious creatures than we all like to think of ourselves as being, or that the predicament of collective action[13] is inherently harder to solve than the public doctrines of any modern society are willing to acknowledge.[14] But you might also suspect that much of the problem lies elsewhere—in the ways in which we think about what really is of value for human beings and how such value is structured both conceptually and causally.[15] We have, of course, quite a lot of different ways of thinking about that capacious topic, all of them prompted by some aspects of our experience, and none of them, at first sight, so radiantly authoritative that the conclusions they suggest have any claim to be considered incorrigible.

The problems come when we attempt to systematize each of them in turn, and then impose its requirements more or less forcibly on the intimations of the others. How far is it really good for human beings to be free? It is not, by common consent, good for them in general to be free to inflict mortal harm on one another. They should not have licensed opportunity to kill each other gratuitously or for fun, and should only kill any other human for some relevant and very good reason—say, to save others, or because in their own case they have no safe alternative to doing so. But should they, on the same train of thought, be free to inflict some degree of harm on one another? Here, surely, the intuitions are less stable and clear cut, and for very good reason. It is hard to relate to other human beings at all without intermittently doing them at least minor damage, whether deliberately or inadvertently. Very few domestic relationships would survive this particular test: not merely voluntary partnerships between adults, but reproduction and parenting itself, the raising of fresh members of society. If partnerships are built out of freedom, and reproduction happens principally through freedom, much harm within human life (as well as a very large proportion of the benefits which adorn it) must come through and because of freedom. Freedom to act, both conceptually and causally, must always imply the opportunity to damage and even damage badly; and the worst damage may often be inadvertent, or even indiscernible at the time.

Several centuries of strenuous and increasingly secular thinking in Europe and its diaspora have yielded a sophisticated set of competing interpretations of how to split good from bad freedom, or how to capture the miscellany of human values consistently in a way which bypasses the need to make that split accurately. But no one could readily defend the judgment that the outcome of those impressive feats of intellectual construction can show anyone how to judge for themselves in practice what humans really should value, and thus what it would be good for them to be free to aim at or to do anywhere in particular at any given time.

So much for freedom, and where we are left for the present in relation to it. But what about equality? The main quarrels over the dividing line or criterial contrast between good and bad freedom (liberty and licence) arise between those who dispose of coercive power or aspire to direct it, and those who find themselves irksomely subject to it or identify with others in that predicament. Almost invariably, the nub of these arguments lies not in whether in the end it is ever good to limit freedom or ever bad to be subject to coercion, but over what is causally at stake in the particular restrictions or subjections in question.[16] It is hard to overemphasize the political importance of the blunt fact that we have no epistemically reliable means of adjudicating these disagreements. All modern societies are awash with confident judgments about social, political and especially economic causality. But the harsh truth is that we are virtually never in a position to vindicate the validity of any of these judgments, even if we can often show that many (or perhaps most) of them are extremely unlikely to prove true. The principal reason why normative intuitions (especially negative intuitions about human bads or the violation of rights) carry such power in politics is less that humans value their values intensely (though some certainly value some of theirs pretty highly) than that humans today are increasingly nervously aware that they have nothing more reliable to rest their judgments about how the human world does and doesn't work upon—nothing out there within it, independent of and blithely indifferent to what they do happen to value.[17] It would be bad enough if humans were simply addicted to their own passions (as in some measure they rather evidently are). What is really disconcerting is that they have so little else to place their trust in which is stalwartly independent of these passions. You do not need to inspect the shattered streetscapes of Iraqi cities to see that, at least for the present, we lack a coherent cognitive grasp of how to concretize social and political freedom. Downtown Manhattan or suburban Paris will make the point equally well. What we do know is that we ourselves keenly value freedom, and know of no convincing examples of human populations of any scale who fail to share the taste.

It is much harder to judge whether there really is an independent passion or taste for equality as such. What there certainly is is ample room for the workings of envy in all relations of superiority and inferiority. But is envy really a passion to pander to? And even if we acknowledge, and choose to accede to its power, is it really true that it is objective forms of inferiority that furnish most of our occasions for envy? (I intend that as an appeal to the personal experience of every listener, not as the invocation of a presumptively objectively established property of human beings.) The more pervasive an element in human sentiments we see envy as being, the less it makes sense to attribute its power to the external ordering of social, political or even economic activities and the more it comes out as projective and irretrievably pathological.

But, whatever the force, clarity or benignity of our passion for equality, it is at least possible that, in relation to equality, unlike freedom, we do confront ascertainable obstructions in the external world to its practical realisation with any stability, for any length of time, or at a cost that human populations might be prepared voluntarily to bear. The principal political outcome of the last three decades has been the victory of that judgment on a very large scale and in many parts of the world. The overwhelming global political defeat of socialism was caused, prompted and implemented by the passage of that judgment. There is no reason to see the judgment itself as clear, determinate and epistemically secure in ways that other social, economic or political judgments fail to be. But there is by now cumulatively good reason to suspect that obstruction is certainly there, and that it does not issue solely from the inherent recalcitrance of other human beings (the Hobbesian axiom).

The key question for contemporary political judgment, virtually across the world, is just how deep and rigid the obstructions to realising equality truly are within an essentially capitalist economy, both nationally and globally. If they are deep and rigid enough, if the quest for social justice is as Friedrich von Hayek put it, simply a mirage,[18] that conclusion would require the abandonment of any conception of society as a form of common life chosen and shaped over time by its members, in a way well calculated to assist their flourishing severally and together. It would make society as such an improper object for policy, and perhaps even an inappropriate focus for political concern. It would imperil any conception of education as a strenuous venture in nurturing better capabilities and restraining worse ones both in individuals and in groups, privatizing individual life in its entirety, and turning its back on any sense that individuals can only develop and flourish in close mutual dependence and with due concern for one another.

In that sense it would enforce the abandonment of virtually the entire agenda of classical political theory in the west, most of the this-worldly agenda of Christianity as a religious tradition, and, insofar as I understand it, every bit as much the agenda of Confucianism too. The case for repudiating equality as a goal to this degree is essentially the case against the command economy absolutized: that to treat the detailed workings of an economy as a focus of imperative collective choice is to opt for a disastrously ineffectual economic model, and then compound the costs of that choice by imposing willy-nilly a command society and command polity to go along with it. The economic element in this assessment has proved to have considerable negative force.[19] But totalizing the judgment, however much it may augment its rhetorical impact or even its ideological potency, deprives it of any comparable epistemic support; and the implications of accepting it become overwhelmingly destructive. Neither the cognitive impetus behind it nor the human desolation ahead of it suggest that we should bow our necks to this yoke.

If the epochal defeat of socialism has been the product of a real recalcitrance in the structure of human possibilities, there is no reason whatever to take the same view of the temporary outcomes for the present of the political tug of war in any individual territory. Mimesis and impressionability, along with a degree of myopia, are enough together to ensure that politics in neighbouring societies often has many features in common. (What element in our collective life is wider open to the ravages of human superficiality than professionalized political competition?) If you see in electoral politics a strong tendency, prefigured by the economist Hotelling,[20] for competition between two or three main political parties to converge on the midpoint in the local continuum of political taste, where most voters can be acquired at the cost of squandering the fewest,[21] there is nothing strange in recent narrowing in many parts of the world in the scope of political choice. But where the midpoint really lies in such struggles is a perceptual, not a spatial matter. If the professional task for competing politicians is to assemble a coalition of the willing to outnumber any prospective coalition of the unwilling, the distribution of available volitions will depend on the beliefs of those who join or choose not to. So much for rationality and its taut ties to action. But on the issue of just what to believe, rationality finds itself afloat on an altogether wider sea, and with few if any fixed marks from which to take its bearings. There is no reason to believe that the favoured expedients of today will prove any better remedy for the problems we now face than their discarded predecessors have now come to appear.[22]

I suspect myself at this juncture that neither freedom nor equality,[23] for all their political éclat, carry the imaginative potential to show us what we do most urgently need to do to preserve the more precious and immediately endangered elements in our existing ways of life, let alone how to reach boldly beyond them to finer things ahead. To judge how to do better, we need first to position our minds and sensitivities deeper within our existing practices, attain individually and together a less wilful and more attentive appreciation of what really is of value within these, and what is merely dross or actively malignant, and build with due care and patience on and from that appreciation. What we certainly must not do is turn away from all such preexisting habits and institutions, place them defencelessly in jeopardy to the voracious demands of a formula of economic rationalization, and subject them and every other human value (including the peremptory need to preserve a viable biological habitat for our species over time) to the short-term pursuit of increased aggregate wealth.

That political task is as urgent here as it is in London or Washington or Delhi or Beijing or Tokyo. It is a task for all citizens, and I would say more particularly for all would-be social scientists (disciplined seekers of valid understanding of what societies are and what they require). It is also, and more obtrusively, a task for all would-be educators, everyone who tries to teach others to learn how to understand, and especially so for an Academy whose goals are as grand and audacious as yours are. A Renaissance is a re-birth, but a re-birth not merely by iteration and biological destiny, but by imaginative recapture and enhancement of something which had already been born before. It is a synthesis of conservation, recovery, revitalization and reinvention, finding the new within the old and making the old new again. There could be no better rubric for meeting the single most urgent global political and social challenge of our epoch.

Notes

1 Jonathan Israel, *Radical Enlightenment* (Oxford: Oxford University Press, 2000);

Jonathan Israel, *Enlightenment Contested* (Oxford: Oxford University Press, 2006).

2 *Ibid.*, 41.

3 Brian Barry, *Political Argument* (London: Routledge, 1965).

4 Cf. Neil Harding, "The Marxist-Leninist Detour," in John M. Dunn (ed.) *Democracy: The Unfinished Journey* (Oxford: Oxford University Press, 1992); John M. Dunn, *The Politics of Socialism* (Cambridge: Cambridge University Press, 1984).

5 Skinner (1998); Taylor (1979).

6 Amartya Sen, *Commodities and Capabilities* (Amsterdam: North-Holland, 1985); Amartya Sen, *Development as Freedom* (New York: Alfred Knopf, 1999); Martha Nussbaum, "Capabilities as Fundamental Entitlements: Sen and Social Justice," *Feminist Economics* 9 (2003): 33-59; Martha Nussbaum, *Frontiers of Justice* (Cambridge, Mass.: Harvard University Press, 2006); and Andrew Kaufman, Alison M. Jaggar, Keith Dowding, Soran Reader, and Ingrid Robeyns, "Symposium on Capabilities," *Journal of Political Philosophy* 16 (2006): 289.

7 Bernard Williams, "The Idea of Equality," in P. Laslett and W.G. Runciman (ed.) *Philosophy, Politics and Society*, 2nd series (Oxford: Blackwell, 1962); Bernard Williams, *In the Beginning Was the Deed* (Princeton: Princeton University Press, 2005), 97-114.

8 Matt Cavanagh, *Against Equality of Opportunity* (Oxford: Clarendon Press, 2002).

9 Benjamin Constant, *Political Writings* (Biancamaria Fontana, ed.) (Cambridge: Cambridge University Press, 1988), 313-328.

10 John M. Dunn, "Japan's Road to Political Paralysis: A Democratic Hope Mislaid," Third Maruyama Memorial Lecture, Center of Japanese Studies, University of California, Berkeley (2002).

11 Harold L. Wilensky, *Rich Democracies: Political Economy, Public Policy, and Performance* (Berkeley: University of California Press, 2002).

12 John Rawls, *A Theory of Justice* (Oxford: Oxford University Press, 1972); Ronald Dworkin, *Sovereign Virtue* (Cambridge, Mass.: Harvard University Press, 2000).

13 Mancur Olson, *The Logic of Collective Action* (Cambridge, Mass.: Harvard University Press, 1965).

14 John M. Dunn, *The Cunning of Unreason: Making Sense of Politics* (London: Harper Collins, 2000).

15 Bernard Williams, *Ethics and the Limits of Philosophy* (London: Fontana, 1985); Bernard Williams, *op. cit.* (2005); Bernard Williams, *The Sense of the Past* (Princeton: Princeton University Press, 2006).

16 John M. Dunn, *Political Obligation in Its Historical Context* (Cambridge: Cambridge University Press, 1980); John M. Dunn, *Western Political Theory in the Face of the Future*, 2nd ed. (Cambridge: Cambridge University Press, 1993).

17 Cf. John M. Dunn, *Interpreting Political Responsibility* (Cambridge: Polity, 1990); John M. Dunn, *op. cit.* (2000).

18 Friedrich von Hayek, *Law, Legislation and Liberty: The Mirage of Social Justice*, vol. 2 (London: Routledge & Kegan Paul, 1976).

19 John M. Dunn, *op. cit.* (1984); John M. Dunn, ed., *The Economic Limits to Modern Politics* (Cambridge: Cambridge University Press, 1990).

20 Anthony Downs, *An Economic Theory of Democracy* (New York: Harper & Row, 1957).

21 *Ibid.*, and behind him Joseph Schumpeter, *Capitalism, Socialism and Democracy* (London: George Allen & Unwin, 1950).

22 Cf. John M. Dunn, *op. cit.* (2000).

23 Cf. John M. Dunn, *Setting the People Free: The Story of Democracy* (London: Atlantic Books, 2005).

Modern Ideologies

John A. Hall

An English expression tells us that hope rises eternal. This is certainly true in social and political affairs. In 1814 a great French liberal thinker, Benjamin Constant, reflected upon the wreckage of the revolutionary and Napoleonic wars. Conquest had been proved ineffective, he argued, allowing us to look forward to a single and unified modernity within which economic growth based upon extensive trade would play a significant role in ensuring peace. A century later an English writer, Norman Angell, claimed that war was no longer really possible, that it was but a last illusion. History disproved these noble dreams. The twentieth century was marked by great ideologically driven waves of killing. As we look onto the twenty-first century wondering whether we can hope again for peace and a diminution of political passion, it behooves us first to understand why the last century saw so much disaster. Will the same forces be at work? Could it be that the effective end of the Soviet Model means that we inhabit a new world? Must the nonEuropean world follow the pattern of modern Europe? Are there developments in culture and politics that allow us to imagine better times? Equally, are there new problems that will pose challenges in the near future of which twentieth century Europe had no knowledge? These are vast themes, and my claim here can only be that of capturing the leading tendencies of the age. Still, offering a view of our current sense of history may provoke, draw attention to factors omitted, and so enable us to understand our situation.

1. The Dark Continent

There is still much to be said for the view that modern social evolution resulted from two innovations, both of which came to the fore as the eighteenth turned into the nineteenth. One is appreciated less, so should concern us first. A revolution in warfare came with the entry of the people onto the political stage. When citizens of revolutionary France defeated the professional armies of old regime Europe it became necessary, in a Darwinian world of competing states, to change one's society in order to survive. Prussia was representative, abolishing feudalism almost moments after its own disastrous defeats at the hands of Napoleon. Such change was probably a precondition for the second factor that concerns us. No one doubts that the West had a leading edge of power within the world for at least a century from at least 1800 because it was the first civilization to effectively use fossil fuels to escape the limits imposed to that point by an agrarian mode of production. The need for a state to survive of course made it as necessary to industrialize as it was to adapt to the needs of conscription warfare.

If these developments are well known, the ways in which they led to disaster, to Europe becoming the site for a new Peloponnesian war that made it the real dark continent of the twentieth century, are not properly appreciated. In order to understand what mattered we can do no better than to consider Max Weber, the great German intellectual who died in 1920. What matters are his views on socialism and nationalism (that is, the people in their two forms), and on imperialism and the state.

Weber's whole sociology was opposed to the views of Karl Marx, most obviously at an analytical level because of his wholly justified awareness that ideas and power affect the historical record quite as much as do economic factors. But he had very particular reasons for not accepting the views of Marx on political change within capitalist society. Weber disputed the view that socialism was the inevitable ideological product of a singular working class, a transnational force able to create a new world. It had become apparent in his lifetime that there were working classes, that is, that workers had different levels of consciousness in different countries. Something of a range was apparent. One of his friends, Werner Sombart, wrote a book trying to explain why there was no socialism in the United States, as was indeed very largely the case. Contemporary historians have done a great deal to allow us to understand the related British case, in which workers had a measure of class loyalty together with the capacity for industrial action, but virtually no interest in socialism. Weber knew the other end of the scale all too well. In Imperial Germany the workers supported the Social Democratic Party, and had genuine political consciousness tinged with socialist ideals. Where Germans were essentially respectable, Russian workers were, at times, genuinely revolutionary—prepared at times to seize power in attempts to create a new social order.

Weber had no difficulty in explaining this variation. Bluntly, human beings seek to escape fear, and certainly dislike the prospect of being shot on barricades. Workers in the Anglo-Saxon countries were at times militant at the industrial level, but they never took on the state. Why should they have done so? Early democracy and liberalism made it their state—a state moreover, in part in consequence, which allowed them to organize so as to pressure for higher wages from their employers. At the other end of the scale stood states which excluded workers—partially and occasionally in Germany, nearly absolutely in Russia—in such a manner that they had to take on the regime, had to gain political consciousness, precisely because trade union organization was effectively banned. Working classes gained, in other words, their character from the nature of the states with which they interacted. Awareness of this fact made Weber a liberal Ma-chiavellian. Let the workers in, give them a place in society, so as to dilute socialism! This was practical advice, to give up power so as to retain it, but it most certainly was not followed in Russia.

If Weber was, so to speak, ahead of the social understanding of his society in this regard he was entirely of his place and time when considering nationalism—and, as we shall see, even somewhat behind it when thinking about imperialism. His nickname when young was Polish Max, reminding us of his obsession with the entry of cheap Polish labor to the East German Junker estates. He felt that a strong nation—and the nation was his ultimate value—needed to be homogeneous. If this was relatively easy in Imperial Germany, it was of course much harder in the composite monarchies of its rivals. The Tsars hoped that they could so suppress the Ukrainians that they would be mere "little Russians," thereby making Russian-speakers a majority within the empire, able in consequence to homogenize everyone into a genuine nation-state in which cohesion in social and military affairs would be ensured. Austro-Hungary scarcely had this option, at least in the Austrian lands in which German speakers were but a large minority. A general comment is vital at this point if we are to understand the making of European modernity. Secessionist movements are especially likely when nations feel themselves to be threatened. The absence of voice within a polity makes exit an all-too-attractive option. Had the nations been let in, by a liberal Machiavellian regime, they would have behaved as workers eventually did in Europe—for the social psychology is the same—by giving loyalty to something that they could influence. But few rulers realized that giving up some power would have created still more. Such a policy did not appeal given the intensity of geopolitical struggles of the time. And of course, when metropoles found that their centralizing, nationalizing drives bred nationalist resistance, they often came to fear that their enemies would find allies amongst such disloyal subjects. Thus was born the world in which ethnic cleansing became rational politics.

In 1907 Weber visited Vienna and was criticized, after he gave his lecture, by the new marginalist Austrian economists who objected to his imperialist politics. For Weber was a "fleet professor" believing that the wealth of a national economy depended upon the possession of secure sources of supply as well as captive markets. The Austrians resisted this, insisting that empire was expensive, and noting that Germany was becoming the leading economy in Europe without the burden of such appendages. But Weber had a point on his side. Perhaps in the future empires would become rational. To become genuinely interdependent meant opening oneself to the risk of starvation should war come with England, for the Royal Navy might mount—and eventually did mount—an effective blockade.

It is important to pause for a moment. Nationalism has no essence, merely existences. Differently put, nationalism is an especially labile force, taking its color from its surroundings. European modernity saw a close link between imperialism and nationalism. The extent to which this link might be broken will be at the centre of attention when thinking of our future.

If there was much unlit dynamite within late nineteenth century Europe, it is worth stressing again that havoc only came as the consequence of war. Differently put, they reacted to war, rather than causing it. The fourth element about Max Weber that concerns us is his view of the limited capacity of the German state to calculate its geopolitical interests sensibly, to act, in every sense of the words, realistically. Rational calculation is but another word for the setting of priorities. Bismarck knew this, and used his total command of the machinery of state to ensure that Germany never faced the greatest disaster that can befall an inland state, that is, a war on two fronts. Foreign policymaking after Bismarck lost the ability to set priorities. The court society of the Kaiser existed within a newly mobilized social world, in which different groups were bought off by promising something to every single one of them. Specifically, a world policy was developed which suited imperialists, steel magnates, the Navy, and even the social democrats—aware that battleships could not be used on land, so as to put down strikes. At the same time an Eastern policy appealing to the Junkers and the army was endorsed. The result was nothing less than self-encircling, the making of enemies on all sides, united moreover by alliances. Germany started a war to escape from threatening scenarios it had itself done most to create.

Bluntly, socialism, nationalism and imperialism changed the stakes and intensity of war once hostilities began. The first part of Europe's great twentieth-century war saw the destruction of Ottoman and Hapsburg empires, and the creation of a series of weak, nationally homogenizing states in Central Europe, all prone to conflict with each other. But it also witnessed the reconstruction of the Russian empire under new ownership. Without war socialism would never have triumphed, as it did as the result of defeat in 1917 and on the backs of military success in the late 1940s. Just as importantly, defeat in war so destroyed German social institutions as to pave the way for fascism, another of the great ideologies of twentieth century Europe. For war made imperialism more rational, as was evident in Hitler's central European economic model, and this went hand-in-hand with ever-greater allegiance to the view of the nation as an organic ethnic entity. The conflict between the two great revolutionary forces of bolshevism and Nazism of course structured the second part of Europe's great war, leading not just to population transfers and the redrawing of boundaries, but to massive ethnic cleansing and genocide.

The social world of the advanced West at last became more civilized after 1945, and two reasons for this benign, indeed wonderful development need to be clearly stated. Crucially, Europe stopped fighting wars. The security problem was solved. For one thing, Europe wished to be supine beneath an American nuclear shield. For another, Europe itself acted. Crucial defeats in several wars made key French bureaucrats realize that one could deal with Germany by love rather than by violence. In other words, interdependence arrived, as in that founding moment when iron and steel industries became nonnational.

Interdependence increased trade and specialization, and made the holding of overseas territories, which the United States anyway disliked, manifestly irrational. Somewhat to its own surprise, once bereft of empires Europe entered into the greatest period of economic growth in its long history. The second general factor is in part related to this. Peace lowered the necessity for unitary states, thereby allowing for federal and consociational deals that gave sufficient voice to nations to make loyalty to their state-nations attractive. But little self-congratulation is in order here. If such deals have helped in Spain and perhaps in Britain, what matters more is a larger truth. Liberal policies towards nations came, so to speak, after the event. Hitler and Stalin between them massively simplified European space such that the norm did indeed become rule by a dominant ethic group within something like a nation-state. Liberalism was possible when it had almost nothing to do. But any shred of selfcongratulation about European achievements must be abandoned once we think of the Balkan wars of the 1990s. Ethnic cleansing and killing have been very much our present, not just our past.

2. Modernities, Past and Present

Attention has been on the social circumstances that bred the great ideologies, and which gave them power and legitimacy. There is everything to be said at this point for shifting the tone, the angle of analysis, towards a slightly more philosophical stance. Once that is done we can return to the social and cultural possibilities that face us now. We can get the argument under way by noting a recent revisionist trend in academic life suggesting that there were and are "multiple modernities." At the core of this claim for many is revulsion, fuelled by liberal guilt, against Western self-congratulation, dubbed eurocentrism. Thinkers of a different persuasion see a rather similar situation of competing civilizations, with Samuel Huntington going so far as to speak of a clash of civilizations—the presumption being that the West must arm itself to win in this competition. Considering past and present in turn will allow light to be cast on the options and constraints that face us.

As it happens, I am not at all of the intellectual school which suggests that all the world civilizations were at roughly the same stage by the end of the eighteenth century, all equally possessed of rationality and capitalism. To the contrary, my reading of the evidence suggests that Europe was more prone to warfare, thereby able to specialise its military capacities so as to become predators upon the world well before the age of industry. But I am in total accord with the revisionists in refusing automatic and, so to speak, total moral virtue to Europeans for inventing many of the elements that comprise modernity. If one wishes to stress the benefits of modernity, the increase in longevity and the rise in living standards, then one should speak about a miracle that happened in Europe, accidentally and fortuitously, rather than of any European miracle, somehow resulting from plan or virtue. To this must be added the awareness of the cost of European modernity on which I have dwelt to this point. Above all, European development was driven very largely by the competition in war endemic to a multipolar system. Other world civilizations can put on the credit side of any moral ledger their greater capacity to establish peace, especially in the twentieth century where European behavior has been so very brutal.

We cannot leave matters at this point. Extreme positions are no help. Great complexity of course results from the fact that our standards of value are very often entwined with ways of life. That makes one necessary task that of understanding ourselves, so to speak, from the inside. Another task is to attempt the impossible, namely, to imagine a position outside all cultures in which the moral consequences of the varied social worlds of the historical record can be assessed. This is systematic audience hopping, and we should engage consciously in what is ultimately a schizophrenic quest.

Something helpful can be said with this in mind about the twentieth century. The recent revisionist work on multiple modernities misses a banal point. Twentieth-century Europe, quite as much as the great world civilizations, has been witness to great moral worlds. Differently put, European modernity has been multiple not singular—or, if you like, there have been tensions within a particular civilization. Roughly speaking, there have been three contestants—liberalism, socialism and fascism, although imperialism has also mattered with nationalism being an ever-present background condition. It is very important to stress this, for it will make us realize that the liberal world view does not represent some end of ideology; it is rather an option amongst others, whose features need to be understood properly if we are to correctly assess our own life chances.

It is difficult to understand, now that they have been defeated, the extent to which both bolshevism and Nazism were, at least in key moments, genuine moral visions. Both attracted the best and the brightest of their time. Both loathed liberalism, finding it to be morally empty, with such an excess of individualism that human solidarities scarcely existed. This view has deep roots in European thought, and was manifestly present in many thinkers of the romantic counter-enlightenment of the late nineteenth century. It is not hard to understand this appeal. A liberal world view urges us to calculate our interests at all time. Why should we accept such a narrow view? Does love have a price? Is heroism irrelevant? Of course, the success of both bolshevism and Nazism had everything to do with liberal failures in the interwar period. The great depression made state-led social organization seem utterly superior to the passive, despairing view of the liberal world. Still, the two revolutionary forces differed. Nazism was patently nationalist and imperialist, but it was racist too. It was a form of reactionary modernism seeking to combine science with the traditional solidarities of the past. Socialism paid allegiance to universal and scientific ideals, but its appeal very often lay in its dream of moral unity, whilst its plans provided for national economic development, necessary for survival geopolitically.

These critics understood a great deal about the liberalism. One might say that liberalism takes science seriously, so to speak all the way down. The core notion was best expressed by Karl Popper. We cannot be sure of anything, and must constantly subject our knowledge and values to refutation and scrutiny. It is true that this uncertainty principle seems in a sense to be reliable, bringing with it technical power. But there is an opportunity cost to this side of modernity. Technical power is brought at the expense of moral cohesion. The world becomes colder, more disenchanted in the formulation of Max Weber. So here we have an ideology which prides itself on being minimal. This is not a view without some general appeal. A combination of a cold, well-run public world with warmth retained in private life can seem attractive given the appalling record of regimes attempting to reenchant modern social worlds—an ever more difficult task as the division of labor intensifies. Better privacy than Nuremburg rallies! As it happens, the emptiness also appeals to me for idiosyncratic Kantian reasons that are unlikely to have general appeal. Freedom can be defined as being master of one's fate, beholden to nobody—a world of equality and liberty, not one of fraternity. These points are in fact slightly exaggerated. In the background of most liberal societies lies a measure of national sentiment, largely passive at this stage of history. Nonetheless, the appeal of the liberal world view does lack heroism. Its rallying cry at a popular level is essentially not much more than "consumers of the world unite."

Liberalism won the great contest with Nazism and bolshevism. Success was probably not preordained, with the element of luck being particularly apparent in the early 1940s. But a liberal world did have advantages. For one thing, democracy mattered enormously, for it was the most effective way of creating loyalty to regimes. But pure democracy can lead to repulsive outcomes unless it is tempered with liberal institutions. The ability to check and balance, to prevent rulers from making catastrophic mistakes served the West well. Diffusion of power through society moreover enabled social conflict to be milder, indeed beneficial for the society—in contrast to centralized systems which so politicized social forces that visceral conflict came to threaten the very existence of regimes. For another, it has become ever more apparent that state-led industrialization works effectively only for initial economic breakthroughs. Market forces do seem to have proved their indispensability for the running of more complex, late industrial political economies.

Liberalism clearly has enormous power today, with one author—Francis Fukuyama—going so far as to say, in utter contrast to the position of Samuel Huntington, that it has no rival. In contrast to both these authors stand those calling for a world of multiple modernities. This view is essentially relativist, suggesting that every civilization is as good as every other. When such relativism encourages tolerance, on the grounds that many Western standards are questionable customs bereft of real grounding, it is to be welcomed. There is everything to be said for attempting to assess, from an imagined external viewpoint, the costs and benefits of different social worlds, sometimes to protect diversity, sometimes so that best practices can be followed. What this must involve now, given that the great ideologies that marked recent history, socialism and fascism, have been defeated is indeed a dialogue between civilizations—for they are now the great cultural carriers of the contemporary world. Nonetheless, in this area we need to be aware of facts quite as much as of prescriptive norms. At present, it remains the case that some of the social inventions pioneered by the Western world— science, industry, the nation in one form or another—retain their social evolutionary importance. Fortunately, most of those inventions can be transferred—that is, they were created in the West rather than being the preserve of one particular culture. But the inventions do have social impact, tending to bring with them social complexity of every kind. It is very probable that the world civilizations will add their own flavors to a common mode of production, but there can be no doubt but that their own cultures will be transformed in turn. There is probably more to Fukuyama than to Huntington. Still, this new century is likely to revolve around the varied mixtures and bargains that are beginning to be struck, between received culture and the rationalization processes so necessary for the standard of living to which most of humanity aspires.

3. Our Current Sense of History

We live in a world combining novelty with continuity, making our task that of unraveling the nature of the mixture. Let me begin with one very basic consideration that qualifies even further the notion of separate but, so to speak, equal versions of modernity. The idea of comparing different civilizations suggests that each is a complete home unto itself, able to offer a form of life all its own. There is something to this idea, as we shall see, but far less than there used to be. If one thinks of the old adage that one should do what the Romans do, one realizes that it is less and less meaningful. What is involved is more than the simple fact that societies which feel themselves to be behind wish to catch up. Rather societies now interpenetrate each other, so that there is a tendency for each to lose distinctiveness. I myself am British but live in America, swim within the sea of capitalist society, an entity with laws of its own but one heavily influenced by the United States, and might yet find myself killed by involvement in NATO. I have multiple identities. So too do many citizens of the modern world. It is very noticeable that many elites of the developing world wish to join the centre of world power, rather than retreat from it. They wish to be part of the action.

This leads directly to a key change that has taken place within the world polity. The point can be approached by means of a contrast drawn from the ending of the socialist world in Central Europe. The nationalist card was played by "failures" such as Milosevic, unable to exist within a new world. In contrast, by the 1980s the Hungarian communist party had all but ceased to exist. The elite there realized that advantage was to be found in the market, preferably with an international dimension. There is, to get at what is going on in another way, something to be said for the notion of globalization.

This is a sea change in human affairs. Nazism was against the market fundamentally, requiring empire and always insistent on geopolitical and ideological goals, even though private ownership was maintained. Socialism obviously stood in total opposition to market forces, believing nonetheless that an increase in social solidarity would release such energy that it would soon be able to outstrip the productive capacity of capitalism. Complete retreat from the market these days seems like madness, a recipe for backwardness. The link that was so present in European history between nation and empire now seems almost broken. Rich countries are those with brains rather than those with territory. Denmark has a claim to be the richest country in the world: it became such by losing war after war after 1800, so that it is small and homogeneous—free from nationality problems, determined to make its way by increasing its human capital. Of course, not everyone realizes this. Perhaps Vladimir Putin genuinely believes that the retention of Chechnya will aid the Russian economy. But he is wrong. There is everything to be said for downsizing territory so that there is a better fit between nation and state. Doubtless there will be more leaders like Putin, but there will be many more who take the opposite path.

Breaking the historic link between nation and empire may well allow for a diminution of conflicts concerning national minorities. Naturally one must pray that the developing world, in which so many countries contain diverse populations, does not follow the European route of forcible homogenization of peoples. This is a crucial area in which it is rational to entertain hope. Let us consider India, and more particularly the question of language—around which so much nationalism has been built. The American theorist of nationalism David Laitin has suggested that an Indian citizen needs facility in three plus or minus one languages in order to have decent life chances. The presence of two languages is easy to explain. Nehru was not in a sufficiently powerful position at the time of independence to force Hindi upon all Indians, not least because his own civil servants valued the cultural capital they possessed as the result of their excellent command of the English language. So Hindi and English both became state languages. One needs a third tongue if the language of one's province is not Hindi—and a fourth if one is a member of a linguistic minority in such a province. The final linguistic repertoire is that of an Indian living in a Hindispeaking province; facility in merely two languages is all that is needed in this case. The point to be made about India, and about several African countries as well as newly liberated countries such as Ukraine, is that they seem to work. Differently put, the European ideal of the nation-state may be replaceable at times by loyalty to a state nation, that is, to a political unit guaranteeing respect to different nations within it. Social cohesion can come from homogeneity, as is perhaps true of Korea; but where such homogeneity is lacking, there may still be a way in which cohesion can be created and maintained without mass violence. There are counter examples, perhaps most notably that of Rwanda, in which European style behavior is all too obvious. But one can hope for more. A precondition for such hope is that of peace, for it is the fear of fifth columns which encourages ethnic cleansing and the fog of war which makes it possible. That is why it is so important that the link between nation and empire has been at least partially severed. If owning territory is no longer the sure route to success, then nations can be respected through federalism and consociationalism—and sometimes even allowed to secede in peace.

It is important that these points about nationalism are not misunderstood. To begin with, one must have ambivalent feelings about elites so concerned to join a larger world that they are prepared to leave their peoples behind. There is the positive side to this, already noted, in the possibility that an alternative avenue of social mobility might allow dictatorial leaders to exit quietly. But there is also a negative side to the equation. In the advanced West, nationalism has changed it colors again, with resentment amongst those left behind by greater interdependence perhaps having sufficient force to prevent further development of the European Union. But that scarcely matters, given the success of the European Union, compared to the situation in the developing world. If the elite leaves, will there be sufficient leadership to ensure that a new state and society is built? In this area it is extremely important to stress how misleading are some of the ideas that come from the core of the advanced world. Neoliberal ideology argues for lessening the power of states. This may make sense in the advanced West where peace rather than a return to the jungle can be taken for granted given that nation-building is complete and states in full possession of adequate bureaucracies. But to impose this view on the developing world, often desperately in need of solutions to basic Hobbesian problems of order, is very dangerous. Many West African states have been so weakened in recent years that their leaders scarcely know what is happening outside their capital cities. In these circumstances regimes can be toppled by the very few, armed with Kalashnikovs. The West's lack of awareness of the preconditions of its own existence—of its own history of the establishment of national cohesion and state capacity—is very worrying indeed when it translates into dangerously misguided policy. What is necessary is the creation of policies to help nation-building, to help establish nonpredatory states capable of leading development efforts. The West has scarcely any tools with which to engage in this key political task.

Nothing that has been said to this point should be taken to suggest that the great world civilizations have lost all their power. One detects very different social patterns. The rate of Chinese expansion is of course stunning, and its increasing nationalist drive somewhat reminiscent of the European past. There are worries here. Foreign policy-making is most rational when in the hands of authority or when subject to the critical scrutiny of an open society. Imperial Germany caused disaster because it so uneasily combined authority with semi-mobilization of the people. That is the Chinese case today. India at last seems to have turned to the world market, and it has on its side the institutions of liberal democracy. There is much to hope for here. In contrast, the classical heartland of Islam presents great, all too obvious worries. One should be very careful not to take fundamentalism at its word, that is, as a return to the past, as a rejection of the modern world. To the contrary, the stress on Puritanism and scripturalism within Islam is best seen as its high tradition seeking to undermine backward folkways so as to prepare for the modern world. Sadly, the record of Islam as ersatz puritan ethic remains very poor, especially in Arab countries. Development is stalled, democracy denied, and the position of women appalling.

In these circumstances what form would a dialogue between civilizations take? The developing world—which will include all three civilizations just mentioned for years to come—is already a part of such a dialogue. They wish to catch up, and are often exceptionally adept at imitating the leading edge of power. There is a real sense in which the absence of genuine dialogue derives from the fact that the greatest of all powers in the history of the world, the United States, does not wish to listen to the requests and desires of other parties. This is true in economic terms. The advanced world all too often talks of the need for free trade, but is hypocritical in its actions within this realm. American interests desire the opening of markets when and where its economy is strong, but often protects itself on other occasions in areas where it feels itself to be weak. How can much of the world develop if its comparative advantage in agricultural products is stymied by American and European protectionism? Further, the current informal system on which the world economy depends—in which the United States borrows most of the excess capital of the world in return for either military protection or for the maintenance of relative openness of some of its markets—is certainly wasteful. Curiously, this system is not immediately unstable. For there is nothing like the overlap between military and economic power that once made Imperial Germany a genuine challenger to the hegemony of Great Britain. But if listening to the world in economic matters is recommended here for moral reasons, something stronger can be said in the political terms. The United States is not an empire, nor is it likely to become one—at least in the classic sense of seeking to hold territories overseas. Nonetheless, both its military interventions and its rewriting of the rules of the world political economy in its own interest create enormous resentment in the rest of the world. This may seem to matter little given that no state seeks to knock the United States off its perch as world leader. But resentment leads to a refusal to share burdens; this increases the financial costs of American policy in a very dramatic way indeed. No system lasts forever, and we may be witnessing the beginning of the end of American supremacy—an end caused by the follies of the leader rather than by challenges coming from others. Imperial Germany chose to behave in a "heroic" manner when it could have achieved more by acting as a trading state. The same might yet be true of the United States.

4. Conclusion

I have stressed the presence of some real reasons to allow hope—whilst not wishing to hide tremendous continuing difficulties involved in forced industrialization and in nation-building. But all this is to hope that the world can share a material civilization, within which some measure of cultural difference can prosper. It is only proper to end with a huge question, namely that of the very sustainability of this model. The West rose to power on the back of dirty industry, whilst the United States consumes an astonishing proportion of the resources of the world. Why should the rest of the world be denied the chances from which current leaders benefited? Resources can be discovered, and certainly better utilized. But the industrialization of the globe, so desirable on moral grounds, may not be possible without genuine change. Social peace as well as decent living standards was in part the result of the creation of a larger pie to share, that is, the escape from the politics of redistribution. The thought of redistribution on a world scale is literally mind-boggling. Hence, one must long for the creation of fusion power. There is little good news in this area, however, and something more dramatic, and horribly difficult, may have to be tried—so as to try to stabilize the situation. At present we tend to reward those with the most inherently interesting jobs with very high salaries. Our future may depend upon the breaking of this link between status and income. Those with miserable jobs may need to be paid to do them, whilst those with intellectually challenging professions may well do them for less. The point is perfectly illustrated by academics. It would be possible to lower the price of academic salaries in the United States whilst maintaining scholarly standards—as has, in effect, been done in some European countries, albeit by stealth rather than transparent design.

The fact that such thoughts have to be entertained suggests that the twenty-first century will not be lacking in severe challenges, to our minds as much as to our institutions.

Reason and Culture Today: Transversality and Transculturality

Wolfgang Welsch

I am very honored to have been invited to this demanding and important conference. If I understand correctly from the organizer, the central question is: How in future can we come to find a cooperative form of cultures? How can one overcome the cutting off of individuals within a culture and of cultures among one another, how can one come to find more commonality and reciprocity?

To achieve this objective, according to the organizers, emotion is more expedient than reason. For emotion is to form the basis of culture and to link people, whereas reason establishes compulsive rules and draws separative boundaries.

I share the general view that we ought to create a more cooperative and reciprocal form of culture. But I would like to set a somewhat different accent concerning the role of reason. I think that in today's situation of merging cultures precisely reason can fulfill a connecting function. One must, however, distinguish between reason and rationality. It is the latter that separates, whereas the former connects. Rationality imposes rules that differ from culture to culture and thus separate them; reason, on the contrary, is a power of transition between different sets of rules and represents a potential for connecting them. Hence, my conclusion will be that reason (properly understood) is a means (and not an obstacle) to the desired bridging and merging of cultures.

I will present my view in two parts: First, I will discuss the current merging of cultures—the emergence of a condition that I have called "transcultural" and in which every culture is intrinsically characterized by crossings and transitions. Second, I will explain how in its very core reason has a transversal nature, by virtue of which it opens up transitions and is therefore well suited to foster the bridging of cultures.

1. Transculturality

1.1 The Traditional Concept of Cultures as Closed Spheres

The traditional concept of culture thought of cultures as national cultures and as closed spheres, homogeneous in themselves and in opposition to other spheres (cultures).

It goes without saying that this traditional concept (which in Europe became dominant towards the end of the eighteenth century) does not provide space for intercultural or crosscultural or transcultural blending as we experience and advocate it today. The concept is intrinsically opposed to that. Herder articulated this trait very clearly when, in his *Another Philosophy of History for the Education of Mankind* from 1774, he stated that "every nation has its *centre* of happiness *within itself* just as each sphere has its centre of gravity," and then concluded that cultures conceived like spheres can only "*clash with one another*."[1] (This, by the way, is the historical origin of the idea of a "clash of civilizations.")

1.2 Obsoleteness of the Traditional Sphere Model

It is obvious that today's cultures can no longer be described as closed spheres, or in terms of inner homogeneity and outer separation. Rather, they are characterized by manifold mixing and permeations. The traditional sphere model of cultures has become obsolete.

I designate the new form of cultures "transcultural." The term is meant to express that the form of current cultures *transcends* the traditional concept of cultures and that cultural features today *pass through* traditional boundaries as a matter of course. In the following, I want to briefly summarize the main points of this concept of transculturality, which I started developing a couple of years ago.[2]

1.3 Transculturality at the Macrolevel

a. Hybridization

At the macrolevel contemporary cultures are characterized by multiple permeations and by *hybridization*.

This obviously applies in terms of population, merchandise, and information. Worldwide, in most countries, live citizens of most other countries of this planet. Any piece of merchandise, as exotic as it may once have been, is more and more globally available. And the global networking of communications technology makes all sorts of information available virtually everywhere. The medical sector provides another example of cultural mixing: Western medicine is on the advance in Asian countries, whereas in the West people are increasingly turning to acupuncture, Qigong or Ayurveda.

Similarly, lifestyles no longer end at the borders of national cultures but go beyond these and are increasingly found in a similar way in other cultures too. The way of life for an economist, an academic or a journalist is no longer French or American or Japanese, but rather global in tone.

The effects of permeation even affect basic cultural questions. Today the same basic problems and similar modes of consciousness appear in cultures once considered to be fundamentally different—think, for example, of human rights debates, feminist movements or ecological awareness. They are powerful unifying factors across the board culturally.

b. Dissolution of the Own-foreign-difference

Put tersely: As a result of the increasing interpenetration of cultures *there is no longer anything absolutely foreign*. Accordingly, *there is no longer anything exclusively own either*. The own-foreign-difference—once so decisive for the old concept of culture—is more and more becoming superficial.[3]

Let me illustrate this with an anecdote. Fifteen years ago, when I visited Japan for the first time, friends took me to a restaurant where everything (so they said) was supposed to be genuinely Japanese. But I was quite surprised when I entered and saw the chairs—they looked familiar to me. So I asked my companions whether everything, including the chairs, here was really completely Japanese. They seemed astonished by the question, almost annoyed, and hastily assured me that everything (including the chairs) was completely Japanese. Well, I knew the chairs: the model name is "Cab," they were designed by Mario Bellini and are produced by Cassina in Milan, and I have these chairs at home in Berlin. Later, when our plates were brought, I experienced the next déjà vu: the crockery was also the same as I use at home: plates from the Suomi series produced by Rosenthal in Germany. (But this time I didn't even dare to ask whether the crockery is genuinely Japanese.) What is astonishing is not that European furniture and crockery should be found there, but that the Japanese held them to be products of their own culture. The case exhibits a distinctive feature of transculturality: the foreign and own are becoming more and more indistinguishable.

1.4 Microlevel: Transcultural Formation of Individuals

Transculturality is gaining ground not only at the macrolevel of societies, but also at the microlevel of individuals' lives. For most of us, multiple cultural connexions are decisive in our cultural formation. We are cultural hybrids. Today's writers, for example, emphasize that they are shaped not by a single homeland, but by differing reference countries—by Russian, German, South and North American, or Indian literature. Their cultural formation is transcultural. Or think of young people and how they are influenced by pop and music culture: their role models can no longer be sorted nationally at all.

In this way transculturality is today determining the formation of individuals' cultural identity in the most natural manner. As the American philosopher Amy Gutmann put it: "Most people's identities, not just Western intellectuals or elites, are shaped by more than a single culture. Not only societies, but people are multicultural."[4] And this is likely to become even more so in the future.[5]

1.5 Transculturality in a Historical Perspective

In a historical perspective, two things should not be overlooked:

First: Transculturality is not something absolutely new. Rather many cultures have in fact already been transcultural in their genesis and history—shaped by mixing, fusion and acquisition. It is just that there was often a tendency to keep quiet about or not to recognize this. The fiction of purity and the claim to superiority often formed a couple. At the factual level, however, most cultures were mixed cultures. One could even argue—as Edward Said or Jacques Derrida did—that cultures never "consist of a homogenous fabric" but always imply a "difference towards themselves."[6]

Second: In the European tradition in the 19th and 20th century there were not only nationalist tendencies, but also the idea that cultural oddities ought to be transcended in the direction of a world culture. The future was supposed to be characterized by transculturality. Goethe got things started with his appeal for a "world literature"[7] (and Marx followed him in this[8]). In the 20th century Scheler looked forward to a "global age of adjustment" that would bring together and reconcile the potentials of all cultures.[9] And Jaspers predicted a "new Axial Age" in which the identity "humans = commonality" was finally to be fully developed.[10]

The "Family of Man" is an old ideal. The current development towards transculturality—although it is often the effect of economic or capitalist dynamics—corresponds to this cultural aspiration to greater cosmopolitan human commonality in the future.

1.6 The Relevance of Cultural Conceptions —They are Active Factors in Respect of Their Object

We should be clear that cultural ideas also take on a formative power with respect to the factual constitution of culture. The "reality" of culture is, to some extent at least, also a consequence of our conceptions of culture.

If one tells us (as the old concept of culture did) that culture is to be a homogeneity event, then we practice the required coercions and exclusions. We seek to satisfy the task we are set—and will be successful in so doing. Whereas, if one tells us or subsequent generations that culture ought to incorporate the foreign and do justice to transcultural components, then we will set about this task, so that corresponding feats of integration will belong to the real design of our culture. Again: The "reality" of culture is also a consequence of our conceptions of culture.[11]

This is what makes exchanging and sharpening ideas about the future path of culture—as we are doing here—so important. Here lies a possibility for the humanities to influence the future of culture—and indeed an obligation for them to do so.

1.7 Uniformization?

Before turning to the role of reason, I should respond to a popular concern about transculturality: that it amounts to uniformization. Some intellectuals lament that the current change in the form of cultures will result in straightforward uniformization, in the loss of cultural difference.

However, that is obviously wrong. Consider just how transcultural identities are formed. Different groups or individuals will draw partly on the same, but partly on different sources. So the resulting identities are already partly different in their inventory. And even if people draw on the same set of cultural elements, they will probably give those elements different weight and a different overall arrangement, so that even in this case differences arise, not uniformity.[12]

So diversity is not vanishing. Rather its *mode* is changing. Diversity, as it traditionally existed between single cultures, certainly is diminishing. Instead, differences between transcultural networks arise.

But this new type of difference has a great advantage over the old one. It is open to connections and communication, because transcultural identity networks always have some elements in common while differing in others. There is always some overlap between them (they are, to use Wittgenstein's term, characterized by "family resemblances") that allows for connections and understanding between them. And on the basis of initial commonalities, a second range of commonalities can be developed, which may even comprise elements that hadn't previously seemed capable of being agreed upon.

2. Reason

If we now ask ourselves what force is actually driving the processes of permeation of cultures, then it is certainly not reason—and just as little is it emotion—but the economy. The latter is undoubtedly the motor of this whole development. Now if reason does not have a founding or productive function in this new constitution of cultures, is it then completely without relevance, or does it nonetheless fulfill an important role?

2.1 Distinguishing Reason and Rationality

Let us first be clear what is to be understood by "reason." Reason is, of course, (firstly) a cognitive faculty. Within the field of cognition it (secondly) stands on the side of spontaneity as opposed to receptivity: reason does not take in information as sensation and perception do; rather, reason acts on its own, is reflective, is brainwork. And finally (thirdly) within the group of reflective powers reason distinguishes itself from rationality in being more strictly self-reflective while rationality is more content-oriented.

The philosophical tradition of the West has always distinguished between reason and rationality. In Greek this was the distinction between *nous* on the one side and *dianoia* or *logos* on the other, in Latin that of *intellectus* versus *ratio,* in German that of *Vernunft* versus *Verstand*, and in current English it is that of *reason* versus *rationality*.

The distinction appeared indispensable for a number of reasons. The business of proof-giving and argumentation (which is typical of rationality) cannot by itself guarantee the validity of the premisses and first principles it relies upon (such attempts lead into an infinite regress or into a circle); rather, for that purpose a different capacity is required that, as distinct from rationality, does not proceed by way of conclusion but by means of induction or evidence, and this capacity, more powerful than rationality, was traditionally identified as reason. Another motive for distinguishing between rationality and reason was the following: Our mental powers obviously comprise not only discursive but also intuitive faculties, and this duality too was rendered as that of rationality and reason.

I cannot here go into the details and the historical subtleties of the distinction. One can summarize it by saying that "rationality" (*dianoia, logos, ratio, Verstand*) refers to the standard procedures of our reflective capacity: to argumentation, proof, scientific method, to the establishment of rules and a corresponding ordering of things. "Reason" (*nous, intellectus, Vernunft*), on the contrary, refers to more extraordinary activities like questioning the procedure of argumentation and proof, providing elementary principles, comparing and evaluating different sets of rational rules, or suggesting a new order of things. Rationality, one could say, does the weekday labor, reason is for the Sunday enjoyment. Or to put it more seriously: Both capacities are, as I said before, reflective, not receptive activities, yet rationality is more object- and content-oriented while reason is more self-reflective. The tasks of reason begin where those of rationality end; rationality explains how the various spheres of being and knowledge are structured, whereas reason asks how things are related on the whole. Reason enquires more deeply than rationality and asks questions that are holistic in type.[13]

2.2 Transversal Reason: The Capacity for Transitions

Traditional conceptions of reason have focused on reason's power to deliver first principles. A modern conception of reason highlights a different trait as typical of reason: the capacity for transitions.

While rationality erects various rational buildings—theories, institutions, specific types of rationality (like cognitive, practical, esthetic rationality), and different modes of communication—, reason creates bridges and pathways between those buildings. Its main activity consists of performing transitions between the manifold of rational complexes. It opens up connections, effects comparisons, stimulates modifications between the rational complexes, which without these interventions of reason would remain closed on themselves. Without the transitional activities of reason the field of rationality would be frozen and paralyzed. Reason is, so to speak, rationality's *élan vital*. And it is so exactly because it performs transitions. When you start exploring what constitutes the most basic activity in all your mental procedures, you will find that this is the activity of transitions—between concepts, objects, experiences, views, memories, theories, assumptions, reflections, and so forth. It is this transitional and connective activity which constitutes the core of our mental life. Reason, in its very heart, is "transversal reason."[14]

2.3 Transversal Reason and Transculturality

Given these features of reason, it should be clear why I think reason has an important role to play in cultures' current and future move from a monocultural to a transcultural condition.

Transversal reason, I said, enables us to effect transitions between different rational complexes. Now in a sense cultures *are* such rational complexes: they are characterized by specific rules of communication, behavior, knowledge-acquisition and so on. Hence transversal reason—the genuine capacity for transitions—is able to perform transitions not only between rational complexes, but between cultures as well. Using the potential of transversal reason we are able to understand the specificity of cultural rules, or to uncover their one-sidedness and limitations, or to imagine modifications, to follow or create new links, and to explore novel patterns arising in the course of transcultural merging.

To reiterate: I am not saying that reason is the driving force in the contemporary permeation of cultures, I am only urging that it represents one of the best pieces of equipment we have for coming to terms with this new, transcultural situation. People can only really participate in changes in the design of cultures if they are able to carry these out *with understanding.* And today such understanding no longer requires, as was previously dominant, adopting the standards in a culture considered as holding for everyone, but comprehending *different* and sometimes rapidly *shifting* cultural standards. It is the transversal character of reason that makes us capable of this.

It should also be borne in mind that the situation of transculturality includes not only objective, but also subjective changes. The outward plurality and hybridization of cultural patterns leads, as I previously set out, at the same time to an inner, a subject-internal pluralization and hybridization. As individuals are cast by differing cultural references, the linking of their transcultural components with one another becomes a specific task in identity-forming. Work on one's identity is increasingly becoming work on the integration of components of differing cultural origin. That is why people today need the power of transversal reason not only to understand others, but also to understand themselves. Only in this way can they bring about the coherence in themselves that prevents them from simply going crazy or cracking in view of the manifold complexities that besiege them.[15]

3. Concluding Remarks

Let me summarize my argument as follows: 1) The present situation is characterized by increasing cultural merging; we are moving more and more into a transcultural condition. 2) In this situation it is increasingly important for people to be able to carry out transitions between different social and individual cultural patterns. 3) Transversal reason is the faculty that enables this to be done generally. 4) Hence, transversal reason is something that we have need of precisely in the current cultural change: in order to be able to perform transitions between various cultural patterns, and equally in order to achieve the goal of further bridging cultures and of attaining greater reciprocity. And it seems to me that people are indeed practicing transversality more and more, that they are making use of the potential of reason in order to cope with current transcultural challenges and to move towards greater reciprocity.

Let me conclude by expressing my gratitude to the organizers. I developed the concepts of transversal reason and of transculturality rather independently of each other about 15 and 20 years ago respectively. The topic of this conference gave me the opportunity to connect these two concepts for the first time. I am very grateful for this opportunity—and would be even happier if you were to find my perspective helpful in coming to terms with the problems we are facing in our world.

Notes

1 Johann Gottfried Herder, *Auch eine Philosophie der Geschichte zur Bildung der Menschheit*, vol. 4 of *Werke* (Frankfurt am Main: Deutscher Klassiker Verlag, [1774] 1994), 9-107, here 39. To be sure, Herder's conception also contains elements that we may still value: the emphasis on everyday culture, or the equitable recognition of all cultures, so different from the Enlightenment's unificatory and Eurocentric assessment. The sphere model, however, is something we ought to get rid of.

2 The conception was first presented in 1991 and published as "Transkulturalität—Lebensformen nach der Auflösung der Kulturen," *Information Philosophie* 2 (1992): 5-20. More detailed renderings are found in Italian: "Transculturalità. Forme di vita dopo la dissoluzione delle culture," *Paradigmi. Revista di critica filosofica*, Special edition "Dialogo interculturale ed eurocentrismo" X/30 (1992): 665-689; in English: "Transculturality: The Puzzling Form of Cultures Today," in Mike Featherstone and Scott Lash (eds.) *Spaces of Culture: City, Nation, World* (London: Sage, 1999), 194-213; in German: "Auf dem Weg zu transkulturellen Gesellschaften," in Günter Seubold (ed.) *Die Zukunft des Menschen—Philosophische Ausblicke* (Bonn: Bouvier, 1999), 119-144; and in Spanish: "Transculturalidad: la forma cambiante de las culturas en la actualidad," in Cristina Camachos Ramos, Miriam Calvillo Verlasco, and Juan Mora Heredia (eds.) *Democracia y ciudadanía en la sociedad global* (Aragón: Universidad Nacional Autónoma de México, 2001), 191-218.

3 Cf. The following statements by sociologists Anthony King and Ulf Hannerz: "People belong to many different cultures and the cultural differences are as likely to be *within* states (i.e., between regions, classes, ethnic groups, the urban and rural) as *between* states" (Anthony King, "Architecture, Capital and the Globalization of Culture," in Mike Featherstone (ed.) *Global Culture: Nationalism, globalization and modernity, A Theory, Culture & Society Special Issue* [London: Sage, 1990], 397-411, here 409); "Cultural diversity tends now to be as great within nations as it is between them" (Ulf Hannerz, *Cultural Complexity. Studies in the Social Organization of Meaning* [New York: Columbia University Press, 1992], 231).

4 Amy Gutmann, "The Challenge of Multiculturalism in Political Ethics," *Philosophy & Public Affairs* 22.3 (1993): 171-206, here 183.

5 Sociologists have been telling us since the seventies that modern lives are to be understood "as a migration through different social worlds and as the successive realization of a number of possible identities" (Peter L. Berger, Brigitte Berger, and Hansfried Kellner, *The Homeless Mind. Modernization and Consciousness* [New York: Random House, 1973], 77) and that we all possess "multiple attachments and identities"—"cross-cutting identities," as Bell put it (Daniel Bell, *The Winding Passage. Essays and Sociological Journeys 1960-1980* [Cambridge, Mass.: Abt Books, 1980], 243). What once may have applied only to exquisite subjects like Montaigne, Novalis, Whitman, Rim-

baud or Nietzsche—major advocates and prophets of a pluralistic identity—seems to be becoming the structure of almost everybody today. Montaigne had stated: "I have nothing to say about myself absolutely, simply, and solidly, without confusion and without mixture, or in one word. [...] we are all patchwork, and so shapeless and diverse in composition that each bit, each moment, plays its own game." See Michel de Montaigne, *The Complete Essays* (Donald M. Frame, trans.) (Stanford: Stanford University Press, 1992), 242 and 244 (II 1); Novalis wrote that one person is "several people at once," since "pluralism" is "our innermost essence." See Novalis, *Schriften* (Paul Kluckhohn and Richard Samuel eds.), vol. 3 of *Das philosophische Werk II* (Stuttgart: Kohlhammer, 1983), 250 (63) and 571 resp. (107); Walt Whitman declared: "I am large ... I contain multitudes." See Walt Whitman, *Leaves of Grass* ("Song of Myself") (New York: Penguin Books, [1855] 1985), 84 (1314-1316); Rimbaud stated "JE est un autre." See Arthur Rimbaud, Letter to Paul Demeny, 15 May 1871, in *Œuvres complétes* (Paris: Gallimard, 1972), 249-254, here 250. And Nietzsche said of himself that he was "glad to harbour [...] not 'one immortal soul,' but *many mortal souls* within." See Friedrich Nietzsche, *Menschliches, Allzumenschliches. Ein Buch für freie Geister. Zweiter Band*, vol. 2 of *Sämtliche Werke. Kritische Studienausgabe in 15 Bänden* (Giorgio Colli and Mazzino Montinari, eds.) (Munich: Deutscher Taschenbuch Verlag, 1980), 386 (II 17); he also coined the formula of the "subject as a multitude." See Nietzsche, *Nachgelassene Fragmente. Juli 1882 bis Herbst 1885*, vol. 11 of *Sämtliche Werke. Kritische Studienausgabe in 15 Bänden*, 650 (August-September 1885). On the issue of the plural subject see both my "Subjektsein heute—Überlegungen zur Transformation des Subjekts," *Deutsche Zeitschrift für Philosophie* 39.4 (1991): 347-365 and my *Vernunft. Die zeitgenössische Vernunftkritik und das Konzept der transversalen Vernunft* (Frankfurt am Main: Suhrkamp, 1995), Second Part, Chapter XIV: "Transversalität und Subjektivität," 829-852.

6 Cf. Edward W. Said, "Kultur und Identität—Europas Selbstfindung aus der Einverleibung der Welt," *Lettre International* 34 (1996): 21-25, here 24; and Jacques Derrida, "Das andere Kap," in *Das andere Kap. Die vertagte Demokratie—Zwei Essays zu Europa* (Frankfurt am Main: Suhrkamp, 1992), 9-80, here 12 f. Similarly J. N. Mohanty states "that talk of a culture which evokes the idea of a homogeneous form is completely misleading. Indian culture, or Hindu culture consists of completely different cultures. [...] A completely homogeneous subculture is not to be found" (Jitendra N. Mohanty, "Den anderen verstehen," in R. A. Mall (ed.) *Philosophische Grundlagen der Interkulturalität* (Amsterdam: Rodolpi, 1993), 115-122, here 118. Mohanty also notes generally: "The idea of cultural purity is a myth" (ibid., 117).

7 In 1827, he stated "National literature does not now have much to say, it is time for the epoch of world literature, and every one must now act to expedite this epoch." See Johann Peter Eckermann, *Gespräche mit Goethe in den letzten Jahren seines Lebens* (Munich: Beck, [January 31, 1827] 1984), 198.

8 Cf. Karl Marx and Friedrich Engels, "Das Kommunistische Manifest (1848)," in S. Landshut (ed.) *Karl Marx, Die Frühschriften* (Stuttgart: Kröner, 1964), 525-560, here 529.

9 Max Scheler, "Man in the Era of Adjustment," *in Philosophical Perspectives* (Oscar Haac, trans.) (Boston: Beacon, [1927] 1958), 94-126.

10 Cf. Karl Jaspers, *Vom Ursprung und Ziel der Geschichte* (Munich: Piper, 1949).

11 Hence critical reflections on cultural concepts, such as I undertake here, are—from time to time at least—necessary. No one would claim that an alteration of the concept *eo ipso* already alters reality. That would be overly simplistic idealism. But, conversely, the way in which the conscious and subconscious efficacy of cultural terms codetermines cultural reality should not be overlooked. The subcutaneous and officious efficacy of the old concept of culture (one thinks automatically, or even states explicitly that culture is to be homogeneous, national, etc.) contributes to separatisms and particularisms of the obsolete sort. Work on conceptual enlightenment is called for to counter this.

12 And even with regard to some phenomena of uniformization one should not only see

gray. Whereas uniformization brings with it cultural losses on the one hand, greater communicability between people of different origins (as is seen particularly in the younger generation) ensues in its wake. Understanding each other is becoming more a matter of course, and it is becoming easier to get on with each other in everyday life than was the case in any earlier generation. So ongoing processes of transculturality might lead us close to the old dream of a Family of Man and a peaceful global society. And *for this* one might very well accept some loss of diversity.

13 Ultimately, however, reason and rationality are not two separate faculties, but rather signify different layers and functional modes of our reflective activity altogether. Reason is in play in every step of rationality as well. It is like the fluid substance of all our reflective or mental activity. This fluid substance or framework comes explicitly to the fore when we ask ultimate questions, while remaining comparatively hidden in the normal, object-oriented procedures of rationality.

14 Cf. Wolfgang Welsch, *Vernunft: Die zeitgenössische Vernunftkritik und das Konzept der transversalen Vernunft*, 4th ed. (Frankfurt am Main: Suhrkamp, [1995] 2007). A short exposition of the concept is to be found in my "Rationality and Reason Today," in Dane R. Gordon and Józef Niznik (eds.) *Criticism and Defense of Rationality in Contemporary Philosophy* (Amsterdam/Atlanta: Rodopi, 1998), 17-31, or on the Internet: "Reason and Transition: On the Concept of Transversal Reason" (http://www2.uni-jena.de/welsch/).

15 See my *Vernunft: Die zeitgenössische Vernunftkritik und das Konzept der transversalen Vernunft*, especially 829-852.

The Crisis of Modern Society and Critical Rationality*

Nam-In Lee

Husserl and Habermas agree on the diagnosis of modern society. Contrary to the positivistic philosophy that considers the modern society to be the highest achievement of mankind, they declare that modern society is pathological. In the last work published in his lifetime, *The Crisis of European Science and Transcendental Philosophy*, Husserl claims that European culture and humanity is in a total crisis that has its origin in the crisis of philosophy.[1] In his major work published in 1983, Habermas also claims that modern society is in a critical situation with "the pathology of the life-world"[2] that has its origin in "the colonization" (TKH 2, 293) of the life-world by what Habermas calls system.

They also agree on the prescription to overcome the crisis of modern society. Contrary to some irrational philosophers who claim that reason or rationality has limitations in overcoming the crisis of modern society, they claim that reason and rationality are the only means; this does not mean that the concept of rationality pursued by them is the same as the positivistic concept of instrumental rationality. According to them, the positivistic concept of instrumental rationality

* This paper was published in *Revue Internationale de Philosophie Moderne* (2008): 97-122. Special Issue for the XXIInd World Congress of Philosophy.

is too narrow and it could not overcome the crisis of modern society. It is in this context that Husserl calls positivism "the old rationalism" (Crisis, 298) or "an absurd naturalism" (Crisis, 298). Husserl as well as Habermas pursued a true rationalism that could overcome "the old rationalism" of the positivistic philosophy.

In my view, the core of the true rationalism that Husserl and Habermas pursued is critical rationality. Critical rationality means the rationality that has the critical potential in a true sense and is able to overcome the pathology of modern society. In his later phenomenology, Husserl laid emphasis on "a heroism of reason" (Crisis, 299) and "the genuine sense of rationalism" (Crisis, 16) as a means to overcome the crisis of modern society and was on the way to developing a theory of critical rationality.[3] But we do not find in Husserl's phenomenology an explicit theory of critical rationality. However, it is different in Habermas' case. Developing his theory of communicative action as "a critical theory of society," Habermas proposes a theory of critical rationality. The theory of communicative rationality, as the central part of his theory of communicative action, is nothing other than a theory of critical rationality.

In my view, however, Habermas' theory of critical rationality has serious problems and, therefore, cannot be called a theory of critical rationality in a true sense. It is the aim of this paper to sketch out a theory of critical rationality in a true sense. I would like to call the theory of critical rationality discussed below a phenomenological one, since it claims to be a theory that deals with the given matters themselves (Sachen selbst). In my view, it is the very theory that Husserl had in mind when he tried to found his phenomenology as a type of rationalism.

In order to develop a phenomenological theory of rationality, I will critically assess Habermas' criticism of Husserl's theory of evidence (sections 1-2). Developing his theory of communicative action, Habermas criticizes Husserl's theory of evidence. But his criticism on Husserl has serious problems and it is the task of sections 1-2 to assess it. After I assess Habermas' criticism on Husserl, I will develop the concept of intuitive rationality (section 3). Then, finally, I will try to develop a phenomenological theory of critical rationality (section 4). Let me first delineate Habermas' criticism of Husserl's concept of evidence.

1. Habermas' Criticism on Husserl's Theory of Evidence

Habermas develops his theory of communicative action as "a critical theory of society" (TKH 2, 548). The theory of communicative action is critical in the following twofold senses. First, it is critical to the modern society that is pathological due to the colonization of the lifeworld through instrumental reason. Second, it is critical to contemporary social sciences that, being blind to the pathological character of modern society, they are unable to solve various problems confronting it. According to Habermas, the pathology of modern society has its roots in the distortion of the system of communication that is proper to lifeworld; and such pathology could be overcome by recovering that system. The recovery of the system of communication proper to lifeworld means the recovery of communicative rationality that has the power to criticize the pathologies of modern society as well as the problems of the contemporary social sciences.

Developing the theory of communicative action, Habermas criticizes Husserl's theory of evidence. Husserl's theory of evidence is one of the most important targets of Habermas' criticism on Husserl. Habermas claims that Husserl's theory of evidence is solipsistic,[4] since evidential experience that a person has at a moment is conceived of as something that has nothing to do with other persons. Habermas believes that evidential experience in Husserl is an experience that has a mere "subjective validity" in the Kantian sense. Kant makes a distinction between the subjective and the objective validity.[5] According to Kant, not being accompanied by the transcendental unity of apperception, a perceptual judgment (Wahrnehmungs-urteil) has a mere subjective validity, whereas an experiential judgment (Erfahrungsurteil) that is accompanied by the transcendental unity of apperception has an objective validity. An example of the perceptual judgment with a mere subjective validity is the judgment that "I have the feeling that the stone is hot"; and, on the other hand, an example of the experiential judgment could be the judgment that "The stone is hot." The difference between perceptual and experiential judgment lies in the fact that, making an experiential judgment, a person raises truth claims with respect to what he believes to be true. For this reason, she/he is ready to ask other persons to check whether what she/he believes to be true is also acceptable to them, whereas it is not the case with the perceptual judgment. Making a perceptual judgment, a person does not raise any kind of validity claim, but she/he merely expresses her/his subjective feelings.

According to Habermas, a person who has an evidential experience in Husserl's sense does not raise any kind of truth claim with respect to what he believes to be true, since evidential experience has only subjective validity in the Kantian sense. Thus, Husserl's evidential experience has nothing to do with the problem of truth. This is the reason why, commenting on Husserl's concept of perception as a typical example of evidential experience, Habermas maintains that, "in a certain sense, perception [in Husserl] cannot be false" (VE, 152) or that "the problem of truth cannot be raised with respect to perception, since perception cannot be false" (VE, 152). Since evidential experience has nothing to do with any truth claim, it is not by recourse to evidential experience, but through communicative actions with other persons that a person can decide if any truth claim is really acceptable or not. The key to the solution of the problem of truth is not the evidential experience, but the communicative action. It is not the evidential experience, but the communicative rationality as the formal pragmatic property of discourse that makes the truth claim of a statement acceptable. Here, communicative rationality means the rationality that makes communicative action rational. For example, a communicative action performed by a person could be called rational, if that person obeys grammatical rules and uses clear expressions and right statements that other people could understand.

Habermas ascertains that Husserl's theory of evidence, which cannot contribute to solving the problem of truth, should be replaced by his own theory of communicative action. He maintains that it is not the evidential theory of truth, but the consensus theory of truth that is compatible with his theory of communicative action. "The consensus theory of truth that has the merit of being able to make a distinction between intersubjective validity claim and an experience with a mere subjective certainty" (VE, 150) is able to solve the problem of truth, whereas the evidential theory of truth that, dealing only with evidential experience equipped only with subjective validity in the Kantian sense, cannot solve the problem of truth. Habermas maintains that "the condition under which a statement can be called true is the consensus of all persons" (VE, 137) and the consensus of all persons cannot be achieved without communicative rationality. Thus, communicative rationality turns out to be critical rationality that, making the discovery of truth possible, could be critical to the pathological aspect of modern society and to the contemporary social sciences.

2. Critical Assessment of Habermas' Criticism on Husserl's Theory of Evidence

Habermas' criticism on Husserl's theory of evidence totally misses the mark, since the concept of evidence that Habermas criticizes as the Husserlian one is not actually Husserlian at all. Contrary to what Habermas maintains, evidential experience in Husserl does not have a mere subjective validity in the Kantian sense. For example, if a person has a perception and makes a judgment that a tree on the street is green, she/he is not claiming that she/he has a mere subjective feeling that it seems to be green, but she/he is making a judgment that it is green. It is not the case that "perception cannot be false" or that "the problem of truth cannot be raised with respect to perception." There are endlessly many cases in which perception could be false. Since perception can be either true or false, the problem of truth can be raised with respect to perception. In fact, the problem of truth in perception is one of the most important topics in Husserl's phenomenology and Husserl was deeply engaged with the problem of truth in perception in his later phenomenology, as shown in the *Lectures on Logic* from the 1920s.[6]

Thus, evidential experience in Husserl does have an objective validity in the Kantian sense. When I perceive a tree on the street and say that it is green, I am ready to ask other persons to check if the tree is really green for them. I am claiming implicitly that the fact is valid not only for me, but it could be valid for all normal persons who could perceive that tree. This implies that a person who has an evidential experience of a certain fact needs to check whether other persons have the same kind of evidential experience with respect to the same fact. The constitution of a fact in an evidential experience is not a process that is carried out in the private chamber of an individual person, but it is open to intersubjective connection with other persons, as indicated in the following passage from the Fifth Cartesian Meditation.

> At any rate, in me, within the realm of my transcendentally reduced pure consciousness-life, I experience the world together with the others, in its experiential meaning, not as my so-called private synthetic product, but as something foreign to me, as something intersubjective, as something that is there for everybody [. . .].[7]

Since the constitution of a fact by an evidential experience is open to intersubjective connection with other persons, it is necessary to investigate the intersubjective dimension of constitution to clarify the condition of the possibility of that constitution. This is the reason why, dealing with the problem of evidential intuition, Husserl develops the "phenomenology of intersubjectivity" as an indispensable part of his phenomenology. If Husserl had believed that it would be possible to clarify the problem of truth only with the help of the evidential experience equipped with subjective validity in the Kantian sense, he would not have been engaged with phenomenology of intersubjectivity so intensively.

Since evidential experience of a person is open to intersubjective connection with other persons, evidential experience is closely connected with communicative action. On the one hand, an evidential experience of a person should be supplemented by communicative action with other persons so that it could be changed from an experience that is valid for that person into an experience that is also valid for other persons. On the other hand, communicative action should be further supplemented by the evidential experiences of individual persons so that it should be able to contribute to the discovery of truth. One might say that evidential experience without communicative action might be blind, whereas communicative action without evidential experience might be empty. For this reason, the theory of evidential experience and that of communicative action cannot be divorced from each other.

With respect to the close relationship between the theory of evidence and that of communicative action, I would like to point out the following two points.

First, Husserl is also aware that he has to develop a theory of communicative action as a supplementary part of his theory of evidence. Contrary to what Habermas claims, it is not the case that, being a kind of solipsism,[8] Husserl's phenomenology has nothing to do with the theory of communicative action. The theory of communicative action is a constitutive part of Husserl's phenomenology and, in a later manuscript from the 1930s, Husserl attempts to develop "a phenomenology of a communicative society"[9] as a theory of communicative action. In fact, his attempt to develop a phenomenology of communicative action can be traced back to the time when he was working on his *Ideas*, as the following passage from *Ideas II* shows.

> The sociality is constituted through the specifically social, communicative acts, acts, in which the I turns to the others and the others are also known to the I as those whom it turns to and who, moreover, understand this turn [...].[10]

Secondly, even though Habermas is extremely critical of Husserl's theory of evidence, he also admits tacitly that his theory of communicative action needs a theory of evidence as its supplementary part. He maintains that, carrying out a communicative action, each person should give "a valid ground" for what she/he is claiming to be true. Only in this case would it be possible for each person to experience "the power of the better argument that is rationally motivated[.]"[11] To the best of my knowledge, there is no passage where Habermas is engaged with the problems of "the valid ground" for what a person claims to be true. However, he admits that "the valid ground" in this context is the evidential experience, as he maintains that only those could be called rational who are able to ground any validity claim "by giving a corresponding evidence to it" (TKH 1, 35). In this sense, one can see that the evidence, which Habermas considers to be the valid ground for what a person claims to be true, is not actually different from the one dealt with in Husserl's theory of evidence.

3. The Concept of Intuitive Rationality

In order to develop the concept of intuitive rationality, I would like to clarify the concept of evidence in more detail. Evidence is a kind of experience of an object, whether it might be an empirical object such as a tree on the street or a mathematical, essential or transcendental object. Here, experience means the intentional relation of the ego to the object in the widest sense. In this context, it should be noted that there are two kinds of experience, namely the "original experience" (Hua III/1, 11; *Ideas I*, 6) and the "non-original experience." An original experience of an object posits it in its living presence, whereas the non-original experience does not. A typical example of the original experience is a perception of a tree on the street. A typical example of the non-original experience could be an expectation of bad weather that I have not seen yet but could perceive in its living presence in the future.

In Husserl's phenomenology, evidence means the original experience (die Selbstgebung) as the experience of the matter itself. With respect to the concept of evidence, I would like to point out the following two points.

1) Evidence as an original experience means the intuition of the matters themselves. To have an evidence of something is the same thing as to have an intuition of something. Evidence and intuition are interchangeable concepts.

2) Evidence as the original experience of an object is the validity-foundation for the non-original experience of the same object. The evidence of an object is just the foundation of validity to which we have to appeal in order to justify the validity-claim of the non-original experience of the same object. Let me suppose that I have a non-original experience of something, namely an empty expectation of something that I have never seen, but tend to claim that it is a thing that has such and such properties. In this case, in order to justify the validity-claim that I have of the same thing, I have to appeal to the perception that I could have of it—I go to it and see it with my own eyes. Why does the evidence of an object play the role of the validity-foundation of the non-original experience? It is because the evidence is none other than "the experience of truth" as "the actual carrying out of an adequate

identification" (Hua XIX/2, 652; LI 2, 263). As "the experience of the truth," evidence is the source of rationality as an ability to distinguish the true from the false.

I would like to call the rationality founded on evidence *intuitive rationality*. It is called intuitive, since evidence is the same thing as the intuition of an object, as discussed above.[12] Intuitive rationality is the property peculiar to a belief that is formed on the basis of evidence.

Let me clarify some important traits of intuitive rationality.

1) As mentioned above, intuitive rationality is the property peculiar to a belief that is formed on the basis of evidence. The belief formed on the basis of evidence can be called rational in a peculiar sense. As such, it is distinguished from the belief that, having been formed without any recourse to evidence, can be called irrational. There are other sorts of belief distinguished from the rational belief par excellence, on the one hand, and from the irrational belief, on the other hand, and these other forms of belief could be also considered to have intuitive rationality to a certain degree. In this respect, it should be noted that, between the evidential experience and the empty experience of an object, there are various kinds of experience of the same object that are neither evidential nor totally empty. The belief that is based on the empty experience of an object could be called irrational, whereas the belief that is based on the evidential experience could be called rational in a peculiar sense. The belief that is based on the experiences that are neither evidential nor totally empty can be called less rational than the belief that is fully based on the evidential experience. Of course, among the beliefs that are based on the experiences that are neither evidential nor totally empty, some beliefs could be more rational than other ones. Thus, intuitive rationality is a concept with respect to which it is possible to observe different degrees.

From the genetic standpoint, the most original form of intuitive rationality can be called subjective. This means that the intuitively rational belief that a person has at a moment with respect to a certain fact could be considered to be valid only for that person.[13] We can name this kind of intuitive rationality "subjective intuitive rationality." A belief that a person has at a moment can be changed into a belief that is valid not only for that person but also for others with whom that person can communicate. In this case, the rational belief can be called rational in a higher degree and the intuitive rationality observable in this kind of belief can be called intersubjective intuitive rationality. Needless to say, there are various degrees of intersubjective intuitive rationality. The highest form of intersubjective rationality is objective rationality. We can say that a belief can have objective rationality if it could be acceptable to all possible participants who could perform communicative action with respect to that belief.

2) The concept of intuitive rationality is pluralistic. This is due to the fact that the phenomenological concept of evidence is itself pluralistic. It should be noted, furthermore, that there is a basic difference between the phenomenological concept of evidence and the Cartesian one. As it is well illustrated in *Meditationes de Prima Philosophia,*[14] the Cartesian concept of evidence allows only one kind of evidence, namely apodictic evidence with which the object is given to the experiencing ego in an indubitable mode. Contrary to the Cartesian model of evidence, that of the phenomenological evidence is a pluralistic one.[15] There are various kinds of evidence according to the phenomenological model of evidence. Accordingly, it should be noted that there are various regions of objects such as the regions of physical objects, biological objects, psychological objects, cultural/historical objects, mathematical objects, *eidos* or essences. It should be also noted that those various regions of objects are not experienced in the same way but in many different ways of their own. This is the reason why the essential structure of evidence varies from one region of objects to another. For example, the essential structure of the evidence of physical objects is totally different from that of the *eidos*. The evidence of the experience

of the categories as universal essences could be adequate, since it is possible in principle to grasp their structure without remnants,[16] whereas the evidence of the experience of physical objects cannot be adequate because it is impossible to perceive a physical object in its entirety without remnants. Thus, there is an essentially correlative relationship between the categories and the mode of their evidence, on the one hand, and between the physical objects and the mode of their evidence on the other. The passages from *Ideas I* and FTL certify this:

> Whether or not this or that evidence is possible in a given sphere depends on its generic type. It is therefore a priori prefigured, and it is countersense to demand in one sphere the perfection belonging to the evidence of another sphere (e.g. that of eidetic relationships) which essentially excludes it. (Hua III/1, 321; *Ideas I*, 333)

> Category of objectivity and category of evidence are perfect correlates. To every fundamental species of objectivities—as intentional unities maintainable throughout an intentional synthesis and, ultimately, as unities belonging to a possible "experience"—a fundamental species of "experience," of evidence, corresponds, and likewise a fundamental species of intentionally indicated evidential style in the possible enhancement of the perfection of the having of an objectivity itself. (Hua XVII, 169; FTL, 161)

There are so many different kinds of evidence, as there are so many different kinds of regions of objects. It is one of the tasks of descriptive phenomenology to make distinctions between different kinds of evidence. Husserl makes, for example, distinctions between adequate and inadequate evidence, between assertoric and apodictic evidence, formal and material evidence, and so forth (cf. Hua III/1, 317 ff.; *Ideas I*, 329 ff.).

Since there are many kinds of evidence that correspond to different kinds of region of objects, we can say that there are also many different kinds of intuitive rationality. Intuitive rationality that is observable in one region of objects is different from that observable in other regions of objects. We have to make a distinction between different kinds of intuitive rationality (e.g., physical scientific rationality, mathematical rationality; still further moral, economic, political, cultural, aesthetic, religious rationality, the rationality of the life-world, etc.). It is the task of the theory of intuitive rationality to clarify the structure of various branches of intuitive rationality in more detail.

3) From the genetic-phenomenological point of view, intuitive rationality is conditioned by the cultural tradition. In this respect, it should be noted that the evidence of the life-world is the genetic phenomenological origin of all kinds of evidence. Intuitive rationality is conditioned by cultural traditions, since the life-world as the genetic-phenomenological origin of all kinds of evidence is nothing other than the cultural world itself. The thesis that intuitive rationality is conditioned by cultural traditions should not be understood as a kind of sheer relativism advocated by the proponents of postmodernism. Even if intuitive rationality is conditioned by cultural traditions, it does not endorse a sheer relativism. This is due to the fact that some kinds of intuitive rationality could transcend the limitations of cultural traditions and be developed into objective rationality. It should be noted that, after all, different fields of the subject matter have different structures of intuitive rationality. For example, the field of natural scientific research has a structure of intuitive rationality different from that of history. In some fields, such as art or religion, it could often be the case that intuitive rationality can not be developed from its subjective or intersubjective phase into an objective one. In this case, cultural relativism has its validity. In other fields, such as mathematics, logic, natural sciences and partly in ethics, intuitive rationality can be developed into higher objective rationality. Cultural relativism has no place in these fields. It should be decided, through phenomenological analysis, whether or not intuitive rationality in a field could be

developed from its subjective or intersubjective state into the state of objective rationality.

4) One might claim that the concept of intuitive rationality is an oxymoron. The distinction between intuition and inference in Descartes' *Regulae*[17] might motivate one to believe that intuition has nothing to do with rationality, whereas inference as a rational process imbibes rationality. The concept of intuition that Bergson distinguishes from intelligence[18] might also motivate one to believe that intuitive rationality is impossible. But that is not the whole story. In the long history of philosophy, one can also find the tradition that considers reason to be intuitive. A typical example is Platonism. Plato defines *nous*, that is, reason, as the intuitive faculty that receives the ideas in the soul.[19] In this sense, the attempt to develop the concept of intuitive rationality could be defined as an attempt to rehabilitate the tradition that considers reason to be intuitive.

5) Some proponents of the theory of communicative rationality, like Habermas, would maintain that intuitive rationality has to be discarded, since it is subjective in its most original form and thus has limitations in explaining the process of gaining access to the intersubjectively valid truth. In this way, they will point out that it will be impossible for us to find out the intersubjectively valid truth with respect to a certain matter, if each of us sticks to what he considers to be intuitively rational and does not accept what other persons consider to be intuitively rational. In fact, there are cases in which it is impossible for the participants performing communicative action to find out the intersubjectively valid truth. Exemplifying these cases, some people might persistently maintain that the concept of intuitive rationality should be renounced after all.

This kind of criticism on the concept of intuitive rationality is, however, off the mark. First, we actually see many cases in which, basing their statement on intuitive rationality, the participants performing communicative action find objectively valid truth. Secondly, it is also needless to say that there are cases in which, again basing their statement on intuitive rationality, the participants performing communicative action cannot find any intersubjectively valid truth. These latter cases, however, do not show that the concept of intuitive rationality should be discarded. Rather, they show that intuitive rationality is an irrefutable concept that reflects the matter-of-course finitude of the human being. The concept of intuitive rationality has the merit of explaining not only why it is possible for us to find out the intersubjectively valid truth in some cases, but also why it is impossible in other cases.

6) Some critics might raise a basic question whether the concept of intuitive rationality is a tenable one at all, since it might be impossible for us to make a distinction between a belief with subjective intuitive rationality and an irrational belief like illusion. I believe that this kind of criticism is a valid one, for it is impossible for us to make a distinction between them in advance. If a person having an illusion maintains that his belief is a rational one, it would be impossible for us to check whether the person has an illusion or not. In this case, we have to reserve the possibility that the person's belief might have a subjective intuitive rationality. What we need in this case is tolerance. Of course, it should be examined intersubjectively whether the person really has a belief with intuitive rationality. We should not exclude the possibility that the person's belief could have intuitive rationality, even if it might seem to be irrational to common sense. Any kind of belief that a person considers to be rational should have the right to be examined intersubjectively. The concept of intuitive rationality is coupled with the premise that even those beliefs that seem to be totally irrational to common sense could be intuitively rational. It should be remembered that important discoveries of truth in the past were possible on the grounds of beliefs that might have seemed, at first sight, to be totally irrational to common sense. Therefore, we empha-

size that tolerance is an essential component of intuitive rationality. Intuitive rationality and tolerance should always go hand in hand with each other. Intuitive rationality without tolerance could not be called rationality in a true sense.

4. The Structure of Critical Rationality

As mentioned at the outset, Habermas identifies critical rationality with communicative rationality. In doing so, he tends to ignore the role of intuitive evidence or formal-logical rationality as the constitutive moments of critical rationality. Apropos of this he states:

> The expectation that the correctness of an argumentation should be based on logical consistency and empirical evidence results from the false premise that an argumentation consists of a series of statements. (VE, 161)

As this passage shows, Habermas seems to claim that intuitive evidence and formal rationality might have nothing to do with critical rationality. In my view, Habermas' position is highly problematic. I do not deny that critical rationality contains communicative rationality as its constitutive moment; however, critical rationality should not be identified directly with communicative rationality, since the former consists not only of the latter but also of other kinds of rationality. For example, critical rationality should have formal-logical rationality as one of its constitutive components referring to formal consistency amongst statements. If a belief that a person has at a moment lacks formal logical rationality, it cannot be called critical. Moreover, critical rationality should also have intuitive rationality as its constitutive moment. If critical rationality does not contain intuitive rationality in itself, it cannot be critical in a true sense, either.

Thus, critical rationality has at least three components, namely communicative rationality, formal logical rationality and intuitive rationality. Among these three components, communicative and formal logical rationality are the formal components of critical rationality, whereas intuitive rationality is its content. In my view, intuitive rationality is the most important among the components of critical rationality. It is the core of critical rationality. Critical rationality could not be critical in a true sense and overcome the crisis of modern society, if it does not have the component of intuitive rationality. Let us suppose that, even though all members of a society are equipped with perfect communicative rationality and communicate with each other perfectly, they are so stupid as not to have intuitive rationality. In this case, they would not have any chances to overcome the crisis with which they are faced. Thus, contrary to what Habermas claims, communicative rationality alone would not be able to truly criticize modern society and overcome its crisis. The fact that communicative rationality functions perfectly in a society does not guarantee that the society could be free of crisis and pathology.

Since intuitive rationality is the core of critical rationality, no critical theory whatsoever can be thought to be truly critical, if it does not take account of the critical power of intuitive rationality. It is also the case with Habermas' theory of communicative action that claims to be a critical theory. Even though Habermas does not deal with intuitive rationality, he also would have to admit that intuitive rationality has its own critical power. For example, he develops his theory of communicative action with the observation that modern society is pathological. The question that can be raised in this regard is how he could diagnose modern society as pathological at all. In my view, it is not communicative rationality but intuitive rationality that enables him to "see" the pathological feature of modern society. Thus, without the power of intuitive rationality, the theory of communicative action cannot even be launched as a critical theory.

Moreover, it should be noted that intuitive rationality can be conceived as the condition of the possibility of communicative rationality at all. Communicative rationality, in a true sense, cannot function prior to intuitive rationality. If the participants in communication could not experience a world in advance and do not have intuitive rationality with respect to that experience, it would be meaningless for them to take part in a communication concerning any matters of the world. For example, it would be meaningless for those who are totally blind to the religious world to take part in a communication concerning religious matters. This should be the case not only for the religious world, but also for any worlds, might it be the physical, historical or social world or the world of art.

Intuitive rationality, as the condition of the possibility of communicative rationality, determines the types of communication. Even though Habermas makes a distinction between different kinds of communication such as theoretical, practical and aesthetic discourse (criticism), he does not discuss why they could be distinguished from each other. He seems to hold the view that the difference between various kinds of discourse is inherent to the structure of communicative rationality itself. In my view, such difference is due to the fact that different kinds of world yield different structures of intuitive rationality that also condition the structures of communicative rationality itself.

Since intuitive rationality is the condition of the possibility of communicative rationality, the constellation of the latter is crucially influenced by that of the former. In order to shed light on the entire constellation of communicative rationality, it is necessary to analyze the structure of intuitive rationality. It is the future task of a phenomenological theory of critical rationality to clarify the constellation of critical rationality by describing the various ways in which communicative rationality is influenced by intuitive rationality.

The concept of intuitive rationality as the condition of the possibility of communicative rationality shows that Habermas' theory of communicative action is highly problematic in many respects. In this regard, I would like to make the following two points.

1) The concept of the ideal situation of discourse that Habermas considers to be the condition for the discovery of truth is not so obvious as Habermas claims it to be. Habermas claims that, in an ideal situation of discourse, everyone should have the same right to give opinions concerning a fact.[20] Only in this case would it be possible for the participants in a discourse to get consensus on a fact that could transcend the social and historical restrictions. However, the exposition of intuitive rationality as the condition of the possibility of communicative rationality ascertains that Habermas' claim is highly problematic. The ideal situation of discourse should not be provided unconditionally to all persons, but only to those who can have intuitive rationality of a fact to be discussed. The person who is blind to the given fact should not be allowed the same right in communication as the person who does have intuitive rationality concerning that fact. In certain circumstances, for example, the discourse performed could be extremely irrational if laymen have the same right as experts on a certain special topic.

2) As discussed above, one of the most important aspects of intuitive rationality is that it is essentially conditioned by cultural traditions. For this reason, communicative rationality is also conditioned by cultural traditions. Habermas' theory of communicative action has serious problems, since it does not take account of the fact that communicative rationality is conditioned by cultural traditions. For example, Habermas' conception of a universal pragmatics thereby turns out to be very problematic. Habermas develops his universal pragmatics as a discipline dealing with the universal conditions of the possibility of communication that should go beyond the limitations of cultural traditions. In this line of thought, Habermas talks about "understandability" as one universal condition for communication. Understandability means that each person participating in a communication should use grammatically correct sentences and clear expressions so that other persons can understand correctly what she/he is claiming.

Yet, contrary to what Habermas maintains, understandability cannot be claimed to be a universal condition of the possibility of all kinds of communication. There are some kinds of communication that could be called rational, even though they do not fulfill the condition of understandability. A typical example might be the communication that is carried out by the monks in Zen Buddhist temples. As is well known, they make intentional use of difficult, dubious sentences and solecisms. The ideal ways in which communicative rationality functions can differ from one cultural tradition to another.

In my view, Habermas' universal pragmatics is not universal at all, but is conditioned by the Western cultural tradition, especially by the tradition of positivistic philosophy. Even though Habermas aims to criticize positivism, he also falls a victim of positivism in one way or another. Habermas attempts to criticize the rationality that is defined too narrowly by positivism, that is, instrumental rationality, and seeks to restore "a wider conception of rationality" (VE, 605) than that of instrumental rationality. Needless to say, the wider, original conception of rationality that Habermas attempts to restore is communicative rationality, which is the central cornerstone of his theory of communicative action. However, his communicative rationality could not be an original one, because, dealing with communicative rationality, he did not take intuitive rationality into account and instead derived the concept of communicative rationality from what he calls theoretical discourse.

Even though Habermas criticizes positivism and its cognitive instrumental rationality, there exists an affinity between rationality of this kind and his own conception of rationality, that is, communicative rationality. There is a positivistic and universalistic trait in his conception of communicative rationality and this trait is corroborated by the fact that he does not deal, for example, with religious discourse in his theory of communicative action. His conception of communicative rationality has, after all, nothing to do with religious rationality that is heavily conditioned by cultural traditions.

I do not deny the possibility of developing a universal pragmatics in a true sense. Yet, the universal pragmatics in this sense cannot be the same as the Habermasian one that is developed on the soil of the cultural tradition of the European sciences. The universal pragmatics in a true sense should be developed on the basis of intercultural dialogues between various cultural traditions. In these intercultural dialogues, Habermas' conception of a universal pragmatics turns out to be one that does not have objective rationality but rather subjective or intersubjective rationality. The components constitutive of this universal pragmatics could not be so rich as those of Habermas' universal pragmatics. For this reason, it should be noted that "understandability" cannot claim to be a constitutive component of the universal pragmatics in a true sense. Of course, one should not imagine that the universal pragmatics in a true sense might be totally empty in its contents. One possible component of our true universal pragmatics would be, I presume, like the following: have a good will to find out what truth is.

Notes

1 The passage reads as follows: "Thus the crisis of philosophy implies the crisis of all modern sciences as members of the philosophical universe; at first a latent, then a more and more prominent crisis of European humanity itself in respect to the total meaninglessness of its cultural life, its total 'Existenz.'" E. Husserl, *The Crisis of European Science and Transcendental Philosophy* (D. Carr, trans.), 12. In this paper, this work will be cited with the abbreviation Crisis.

2 J. Habermas, *Theorie des kommunikative Handeln,* Bd. II (Frankfurt/M.: Suhrkamp, 1988), 29. In this paper, this work will be referred to with the abbreviation TKH 2.

3 In this sense, Husserl's phenomenology could be defined as a practical philosophy. See Nam-In Lee, "Practical Intentionality and Transcendental Phenomenology as a Practical Philosophy," *Husserl Studies* 17 (2000).

4 J. Habermas, *Vorstudien und Ernzungen zur Theorie des kommunikativen Handeln,* (Frankfurt/M.: Suhrkamp, 1986), 15 f. In this paper, this work will be referred to with the abbreviation VE.

5 Kant makes a distinction between subjective validity and objective validity in I. Kant, *Prolegomena zu einer jeden zukunftigen Metaphysik* (Hamburg: Felix Meiner, 1976), 53 ff.

6 See E. Husserl, *Analysen zur passiven Synthesis. Aus Vorlesung—und Forschungsmanuskripten 1918–1926* (Den Haag: Martinus Nijhoff, 1966).

7 The German text runs as follows: "Jedenfalls also in mir, im Rahmen meines transzendental reduzierten reinen Bewusstseinslebens, erfahre ich die Welt mitsamt den Anderen und dem Erfahrungssinn gemäß nicht als mein sozusagen privates synthetisches Gebilde, sondern als mir fremde, als intersubjektive, für jedermann daseiend [...]" E. Husserl, *Cartesianische Meditationen und Pariser Vorträge* (Den Haag: Martinus Nijhoff, 1973), 123.

8 I have shown that Husserl's phenomenology is not solipsistic in the following works: Nam-In Lee, *Edmund Husserl's Phänomenologie der Instinkte*, Phaenomenologica, Vol. 128 (Dordrecht: Kluwer Academic Publishers, 1993), 197 ff.; Nam-In Lee, "The Static-Phenomenological and Genetic-Phenomenological Concept of Primordiality in Husserl's Fifth Cartesian Meditation," *Husserl Studies* 18 (2002); and Nam-In Lee, "Problems of Intersubjectivity in Husserl and Buber," *Husserl Studies* 22 (2006).

9 One of Husserl's later manuscripts from 1930s carries the title: "Phänomenologie der Mitteilungsgesellschaft" (Phenomenology of Communicative Society). See E. Husserl, *Zur Phänomenologie der Intersubjektivität. Texte aus dem Nachlass*, Dritter Teil 1929-1935 (Den Haag: Martinus Nijhoff, 1973), 461.

10 The German text runs as follows: "Die Sozialität konstituiert sich durch die spezi-fische sozialen, kommunikativen Akte, Akte, in denen sich das Ich an Andere wendet, und dem Ich diese Anderen auch bewusst sind als die, an welche es sich wendet, und welche ferner diese Wendung versteht [...]" E. Husserl, *Ideen zu einer reinen Phänomenologie und phänomenologischen Philosophie. Zweites Buch: Phänomenologische Untersuchungen zur Konstitution* (Den Haag: Martinus Nijhoff, 1953), 194.

11 J. Habermas, *Theorie des kommunikative Handelns,* Bd. I (Frankfurt/M.: Suhrkamp, 1988), 70. In this paper, this work will be referred to with the abbreviation TKH 1.

12 Analyzing the "intuitive foundation of rationality," Rosemary R. P. Lerner also deals with the problem of intuitive rationality. See Rosemary R. P. Lerner, "Intuitive Foundations of Rationality," in C.-F. Cheung et al. (eds.) *Essays in Celebration of the Founding of the Organization of Phenomenological Organizations* (webpublished at www.o-p-o.net, 2003), and Rosemary R. P. Lerner, "Husserl versus Neo-Kantianism Revisited: On Skepticism, Foundationalism, and Intuitionism," in *The New Yearbook for Phenomenology and Phenomenological Philosophy IV-2004.* With respect to the inseparable relationship between intuition and rationality, Lerner writes as follows: "Phenomenology's revolutionary approach to the problem of reason consists in proposing a radical reform of the meaning of logos, which was traditionally reduced to the sphere of validating inferences, whether demonstrative, deductive, or argumentative. Husserl extends rationality to include the domain of phenomenological experiences wherein the formerly "rational" procedures are themselves "validated"—the ultimate source of which is "originally giving intuition." Rational, indeed, is the subject's life as a whole—whether perceptive, axiological, or normative." (R. R. P. Lerner, "Husserl versus Neo-Kantianism Revisited: On Skepticism, Foundationlism, and Intuitionism," 207).

13 One should not confuse this kind of belief with the belief based on a mere subjective validity in the Kantian sense, since it is open to intersubjective connection with other persons.

14 R. Descartes, *Meditationes de Prima Philosophia, Oeuvres de Descartes* VII (C. Adam & P. Tannery, eds.) (Paris: Librairie philosophique J. Vrin, 1973).

15 I have dealt with the phenomenological concept of evidence in Nam-In Lee, "Experience and Evidence," *Husserl Studies* 23 (2007). I have borrowed some passages below from this paper.

16 In this context, Husserl writes as follows: "Every category of object [...] is a universal essence which of necessity can be brought to adequate evidence in principle [...]" (Hua III/1, 330; *Ideas I*, 341).

17 R. Descartes, *Regulae ad directionem ingenii, Oeuvres de Descartes* X (C. Adam & P. Tannery, eds.) (Paris: Librairie philosophique J. Vrin, 1974).

18 H. Bergson, *L'Evolutiom créatrice*, in *Œuvres* (Paris: Presses Universitaires de France, 1984), 645 ff.

19 Plato, *Politeia,* 511d.

20 For example, VE, 177.180

III

Global Civil Society and Governance

Global Governance in the Post-Cold War Era

Takashi Inoguchi

1. Governance

Governance is a new English word, meaning steering, handling, directing or ruling. Governance is used most frequently when one wants to avoid the traditional top-down approach and flavor inherent in the word *government*. Governance is defined here as the state of affairs in the relationship between *the governing* and *the governed* in terms of (1) transparency and accountability of the relationship from the angle of processes; (2) legitimacy and efficacy of the governing from the substantive angle; and (3) deliberation and decision of the governed from the participatory angle. First, the relationship between the governing and the governed is two-directional. Therefore, my definition may not be a good one. But in order to clarify the somewhat ambiguous concept, I use this definition. Second, transparency and accountability have to do with the processes of interactions between them. In order to reduce the potentially hierarchical and authoritarian nature of the relationship and to enhance the jointly undertaken nature of governance, preventing the processes of interactions from degenerating into opaqueness and inaccessibility is of utmost importance. Nurturing the sense of shared information, shared norms and values is an absolute must. Third, as long as good governance means good results, one must instill the sense of comfort in delegating the task of governing to the governed and of contentment with the positive outcomes of public policy. Without the former component, good governance can be bumpy. Without the latter component, good governance can be hollow. Fourth, participation in the process of governing is of critical importance to good governance. Individual action associated with deliberation and decision is positive because it reinforces the identity of participants with the amalgam of what would be otherwise the two separate bodies of the governing and the governed.

Governance, a somewhat foggy word, is most pertinent when used in the context of global management after the Cold War. A world government as dreamt by Esperanto speakers remains something that cannot be touched at the dawn of this century. Yet something short of it is there. That is often called global governance. The tightly demarcated line between the capitalist and communist blocs is gone forever. The earth has flattened. The earth has been flattened by two forces: globalization and democratization. Globalization has flattened national economies, their borders, their organic integration, their policyeffectiveness. Thomas Friedman[1] argues most illustratively how the earth has flattened. Democratization has fragmented national electorates, their allegiance to the national government, their stake in the national government, their loyalty to the nation. Samuel Huntington[2] is the earliest analyst of the Third Wave tide of democratization in the last quarter of the 20th century. Yet the whole picture is bereft of an overarching political authority. There is no world government. Rather global governance is the most pertinent expression to describe global politics at the dawn of the 21st century.

2. Four Versions of Governance

Governance is such an elusive concept that characterizing the current state of affairs in global governance is bound to give rise to a huge diversity. Let us examine briefly the following authors on global governance: David Held,[3] G. John Ikenberry and Ann-Marie Slaughter,[4] Michael Mandelbaum[5] and Robert Kagan.[6] Held envisages a social democratic version of global covenant. Ikenberry and Slaughter envision a liberty under law prevailing among democracies and beyond; Mandelbaum contends that the United States government is a world government; Kagan argues that Americans sought power and asserted ideology even before they founded their United States. All the four are more or less optimistic about how their versions will prevail. Let us examine them one by one.

Mandelbaum sees global governance as something nobody takes care of as seriously as the United States government. After all, it is only the United States that possesses such formidable military power. It is everyone's knowledge, for instance, that the number one air force in the world is the United States Air Force. Which air force is the number two air force? It is that of the United States Navy. Furthermore, US military predominance is likely to continue for the next two to three decades unless some extraordinary circumstances are created to subvert it. The United States overwhelms all the rest by taking a lion's share of 85% of the world's R&D expenditure on new weapons and weapons systems, which *ceteris paribus* would ensure that the United States would remain the number one superpower in twenty to thirty years' time as well.

Furthermore, it is only the United States that has the will to exercise its force. The events subsequent to 9/11 have so vividly demonstrated that it is the United States that has passed the test of will to exercise its force almost at any costs. It is precisely here that the divide came out between the United States and the European Union on how to confront the attacks of 9/11. Robert Kagan characterizes the European Union as a cowardly parasite on the United States with whom the European Union shares democratic values and free capitalist spirit, but not the will and power to defend them by force if necessary. It is the United States that spearheaded a series of military operations from Afghanistan in 2001 to Iraq in 2003 and onward. It is the United States that has organized the whole range of antiterrorist and antinuclear proliferation operations the world over including the Interior Ministers' meeting of the Group of Eight in Scotland since 2004. The "coalition of the willing" was so nicely assembled in 2001 with the global outrage directed at global terrorism. Yet by 2006 the coalition of the willing would have more accurately been called "the ad hoc coalition of the temporarily willing." Not only was the bulk of troops sent to Iraq and Afghanistan returned home, but also the antiterrorist spirit seemed to subside somewhat, judging from the Gallup International's Voice of People polls.[7] The most ardent antiterrorist spirit, in relation to the Hizbollah's terrorism in Israel/Pal-estine/Lebanon, was expressed by Indians, but not necessarily by West Europeans. Indians have even surpassed Americans in this regard.

Mandelbaum believes in realism, which acknowledges a major role of coercion. Mandelbaum does not play down the importance of networking and persuasion. But without the force and will to use it, no world government is possible. The fact that the United States government has the force and will to use it enables the United States government to become a world government. Mandelbaum acknowledges the primary importance of Leviathan in building a world government just as Thomas Hobbes believed in the prerequisite of building a Leviathan, an absolute monarch, in England in the 16th century. The United States has been enabling a world government to achieve a fledgling entity, according to Mandelbaum.

G. John Ikenberry and Ann-Marie Slaughter believe in liberalism. They believe in freedom, democracy, human rights and free market capitalism. They envisage global governance under the banner of "liberty under law." They envision a global governance primarily led by the PAR (popular, accountable and rights-regarding) governments all over the world and, needless to say, the leader of leaders is the United States. The task of the United States is to wave the banner of democracies under law in order to enhance the shared norms and values of PAR governments and thus to steadily build a democratic union under law, which would bring global governance closer to a primitive world government. In carrying out this task, the United States' resurrection of moral leadership, steadfast socialization of norms and values through all the networks—governmental and nongovernmental, civil, military, and transnational—and pragmatic joint undertakings and handling of global issues together with an eye at producing good results, would be the most necessary items of action.

Their voice is to get out of the primitive stage of using naked force in building global governance. Rather, inculcating shared norms and values through networks of professionals across countries and jointly tackling global issues would be necessary. Going beyond naked force is their voice. Departing from unilateralism in the use of force and making use of multilateralism in deliberating issues and possible solutions is their message. Their argument is that the United States has the tradition of respecting freedom, human rights and democracy, without the utilization of which the United States would not be able to stand tall in running global governance: Because the costs of the unilateral use of force is immense and because the spirit of unilateralism reduces the legitimacy of leading the world. In this regard, Michael Mann's[8] argument that utilizing military force too single-mindedly would bring the United States down is resonant with the one of Ikenberry and Slaughter. Also, Niall Ferguson's[9] argument that power must be used deftly in order to prolong the leadership of the United States in global governance is no less resonant with the one of Ikenberry and Slaughter. The beauty of Ikenberry and Slaughter is that their argument appeals to the liberal tradition of the history of the United States, especially in an atmosphere of angst in the prolonged antiterrorist war and its possible consequences.

David Held[10] makes his argument for a socially-democratically inspired global covenant especially with an eye on the income gap between the rich North and poor South and at measures that are to be taken up by rich democracies and international institutions like the United Nations, the World Bank, the International Monetary Fund and the European Union. This is not an American centered vision of global governance. Rather, it is a European-centered vision of global governance. However, Held is not dissimilar to Ikenberry and Slaughter in that both believe in the power of ideas. Whether it is social-democratic or liberal-capitalistic does not matter too much in this respect.

Robert Kagan[11] is different from both realists like Mandelbaum and from ideationists like Ikenberry/Slaughter and Held. Kagan regards both force and ideas equally strongly and believes that they are tied to each other. Kagan portrays America as a dangerous nation bent on expansion and extension with ideology attached. Kagan differs qualitatively from many ideationists in that his American ideology is most closely tied with the often unilateral use of force to put forward and promote itself. Kagan dismisses the whole bunch of American clichés about America and its conduct in the world arena. Kagan contends that America has never been isolationist but steadfastly internationalist and expansionist. Kagan contends also that the American polity has evolved in a similar fashion with many other countries and that the liberal portrayal of the United States as a liberal state from the very beginning is not quite accurate. His contention is provocative: he argues that the United States, before the abolishment of the institution of slavery, is best called a rogue state, that the Civil War is the first large-scale ideological conquest of a defeated nation (the Southern Confederation), and reconstruction is best called "nation building."

With these admittedly cursory summaries of the four authors on global governance, let me move on to a systematic examination of the four in terms of the processual angle of global governance, the substantive angle of global governance, and the participatory angle of global governance.

Table 1. Competing Versions of Global Governance

Areas of Comparison↓	Mandelbaum	Ikenberry/Slaughter	Held	Kagan
Two components:				
Force and ideology	force	ideas	ideas	force-cum-ideas
Four angles:				
Legitimacy	not concerned	stressed	stressed	innate
Efficacy	preoccupied	preoccupied	optimistic	high
Participation	never thought	keen on	keen on	optimistic
Accountability	never thought	preoccupied	preoccupied	fine

2.1. Legitimacy

As long as good governance needs to acquire some legitimizing power on the part of the governing, say, those bodies manned by professional elite corps across nations, legitimacy cannot be left undiscussed. Essentially, Mandelbaum is not too much concerned about this as long as the issue of legitimacy comes up, sharply jeopardizing the United States-led global governance. Legitimacy comes along with the success of the United States, he contends. Ikenberry and Slaughter are quite concerned about legitimacy. They argue that the unilateral use of force undermines American ideas and subverts American power. Instead, argue Ikenberry and Slaughter, the coalition of the willing in terms of advancing the banner of liberty under law needs to be constructed both to instill legitimacy and increase efficacy. Only those schemes well-grounded on such concerns can hope to spread the American ideals as well as good global governance. Held stresses the importance of legitimacy in reference to the incredible gaps between the rich North and poor South and the critical importance attached to bridging the gap through the social democratic scheme written large on a global scale. Without installing a modicum of legitimacy by addressing seriously the issue of the North-South inequality, good global governance would fail, argues Held. In contrast to Held, Kagan sees innate legitimacy in a United States-led global governance. Legitimacy is endogenous to the endeavor of the United States. In contrast to Ikenberry and Slaughter, Kagan sees the beauty of unilateralism in that the American spirit is not watered down.

2.2. Efficacy

Mandelbaum sees efficacy in the United States-led world government. He is positive and optimistic about the United States. His belief in this stems from his strong belief in the supreme military power of the United States. Ikenberry and Slaughter see efficacy possibly eroding somewhat due to the less-than-solid commitment to liberty under law (meaning antiunilateralism as well) and popular, accountable and rights-regarding governments. Held is most concerned about the gap and inequality of income and all others between the rich North and the poor South. To bring about the policy measures by international institutions and member states, he is most emphatic that his scheme be accepted, giving legitimacy and enhancing efficacy. Kagan sees the strength of the United States lying in the combination of force and ideas put forward relentlessly. Legitimacy and efficacy would come along with this unusual and dangerous nation.

2.3. Participation

Mandelbaum addresses the American participation in global governance with high remarks. The fact that the United States government virtually runs a world government assures Mandelbaum. It is like the tenacious American belief that only under an American commander-in-chief can United States troops feel assured that fighting will go safely and victoriously. Ikenberry and Slaughter underline the critical importance of participation in joint undertakings by popular, accountable and rights-regarding governments. Held sees participation of critical importance since the poor South has not been well represented by international institutions proportionately to its demography or counterproportionately to its income level. Kagan does not see much merit in participation. Participation seems to him to represent a marginal increase in returns. Participation is important. But participation by the United States makes a primary difference to legitimacy or efficacy, he contends.

2.4. Accountability

Mandelbaum does not see much importance beyond what American law and practice require: accountability of global governance conduct. As long as American law and practice is one of the most stringent in the world in terms of accountability, Mandelbaum does not see much in this term. Ikenberry and Slaughter see this differently. They envisage the participation of many popular, accountable and rights-regarding governments in global governance; therefore, they are emphatic on this matter. Held sees participation of critical importance as only through participation in concluding a global covenant in terms of wealth transfer and income generation can a historic deal between the North and the South be given the hope that the gap will be reduced and justice be brought to bear on inequality. Kagan does not pay much attention to this matter as he focuses on the United States and on its innate strength.

3. Conclusion

We have examined four versions of global governance: Mandelbaum's, Ikenberry/Slaughter's, Held's and Kagan's. Mandelbaum is a realist in the sense of regarding force as of critical importance. His realistic version of global governance is that of *Pax Americana*, phase three (The third phase runs from 2001 through year X; the first runs from 1945 through 1975; the second runs from 1975 through 2000), meaning it is assisted by allies and friends. Ikenberry and Slaughter are liberal in the sense of regarding ideas of primordial driving force. Their liberal version of global governance is that of *Pax Consortis* or *Pax Democratica.*[12] Held is a social democratic in the sense of reducing inequality by policy actions and passions. His social democratic version of global governance is that of *Pax Socio-Democratica.* Kagan is a neocon in the sense of seeing ideas and force as inseparable. The Kagan version of global governance is that of *Pax Americana Unilateral.* It is clear that the contents of global governance are in the eye of the beholder.

Notes

1 Thomas Friedman, *The World Is Flat: A Brief History of the Twenty-first Century* (New York: Simon Schuster, 2006).

2 Samuel Huntington, *The Third Wave* (Oklahoma: University of Oklahoma Press, 1993).

3 David Held, *Debating Globalization* (Cambridge: Polity Press, 2004).

4 G. John Ikenberry and Ann-Marie Slaughter, *Forging a World of Liberty under Law: U.S. National Security in the 21st Century* (Woodrow Wilson School of Public and International Affairs, Princeton University, 2006).

5 Michael Mandelbaum, *The Case for Goliath: How America Acts as the World's Government in the Twenty-First Century* (New York: Simon Schuster, 2006).

6 Robert Kagan, *Dangerous Nation: America's Place in the World from its Earliest Days to the Dawn of the Twentieth Century* (New York: Knopf, 2006).

7 Gallup International, *Voice of the People* (London: Gallup International, 2006).

8 Michael Mann, *Incoherent Empire* (London: Pluto Press, 2005).

9 Niall Ferguson, *Colossus: the Rise and Fall of the American Empire* (New York: Basic Books, 2002).

10 David Held, *Debating Globalization* (Cambridge: Polity Press, 2004).

11 Kagan, *op. cit.*

12 Takashi Inoguchi, "Four Japanese Scenarios for the Future," *International Affairs* 65.1 (Winter 1988/1989): 15-28.

The World as One: In Search of the Norms and Principles of Universalism, Cosmopolitanism, and Global Civil Society

G. John Ikenberry

1. Introduction

The world today has become global. We live in a global society, at least measured in terms of the scale, scope, and intensity of human interaction. Since the end of the world wars of the last century, the globe has become a single entity. There is a world economy, global institutions, and transnational groups and associations. In this age of globalization, it is even possible to talk about the rise of global civil society and citizenship.

But what are the sources of commonality and agreement that unite people on a global scale. Put bluntly, is there anything that the world actually agrees upon? In this age of clashing nations, reli gions, and civilizations, are there any norms or principles that come close to receiving universal assent? Is this growing conglomeration of people—increasingly connected and interdependent—simply an aggregation and little more? Or is there some underlying agreement on the principles and norms of the global system that is also emerging?

These questions are particularly important when the question is posed: is there an emerging global civil society? This is because the notion of a global civil society invokes the idea that people are actually "members" or "citizens" in a worldwide community.

It is not inherently necessary for a globalized world system to be based on shared norms and principles about world political order. The world can experience growing interdependence without a commensurate growth in a shared embrace of what is just or right. States and peoples can interact simply on the basis of social exchange—a primitive social institution in which the only necessary agreement is the mutual recognition of the possibility of market exchange. Likewise, the global system could simply be based on the balance of power among states. Here the interaction is based on an equally primitive notion of coexistence. Each state simply musters enough state power to block the advances of other states, resulting in a balance or stalemate of power. The actual societies that make up these "balanced-states" do not need to agree on anything else—culture, politics, ideas, religion. In neither of these instances—market exchange and balance of power—is there anything necessarily more elaborate in the resulting relationship. Neither is there really a "community" in any meaningful sense.

But it is clear that the world today is moving well beyond these primitive social institutions. Market exchanges actually have emerged with the rise of social institutions—both within particular societies and across longer distances.[1] Likewise, balance of power systems of states have also developed more elaborate shared understandings of state, power, interest, and order. Shared expectations and political institutions have developed over the centuries even as the underlying mechanism of power balancing remains the essential component of order.[2]

So it is not surprising that one can discern some of the traces of universal norms and principles in today's globalizing world. But what are they? We are obviously interested in both normative and causal ideas about the way the world works and should work. We are interested in any agreements that may exist about the "terms" of international order. If the global system is to be built around an agreed upon set of norms and principles about international order, what might those norms and principles be?

There is clearly a vast realm of politics and society where disagreement on principles and norms would remain illusive. Culture, tradition and authority are all orienting aspects of human life that create and reinforce distinctive groups and societies. Global society today is moving in both directions—toward greater integration and universal forms of interaction and toward separation and difference. Through this dialectical process of integration and separation, what might a future global civil society look like?

In this paper, I explore the possible terms of international order that is established around agreed upon universal norms and principles. It is out of this discussion that the shape and character of an emerging global civil society can be grasped. The obvious starting point is the "liberal ascendency"—the rise over the last two centuries of a liberal vision of global order. As we shall see, this is not, in itself, sufficient as the embodiment of global order— but it is a starting point. After this, I explore various possible principled bases of universal order. In the end, I argue that the best way to identify norms and principles that might be universally embraced is to engage in a Rawlsian exercise of selecting rules and institutions under a "veil of ignorance." This yields a procedural set of principles that protect differences but also provide a global environment for progressive development.

2. Universalism, Cosmopolitanism, Global Civil Society

What is it that ties the world together? One can answer this question by looking at norms and principles of society and politics, at the impulses that lead peoples to join together across cultural and national borders, and at the actual functioning of an emerging global society. Three concepts help introduce this perspective—universalism, cosmopolitanism, and global civil society.

Universalism refers to norms and principles that purport to apply across the whole of human relationships. When architects of global rules and institutions seek to establish comprehensive and inclusive principles of order, they are engaged in universalism. Philosophical arguments about the "rights of man" or the "global principles" of justice are universalistic statements of what ought to be. Global social theories that advance notions of a deep and worldwide developmental logic as work are universalistic statements of the way the world works. Universalism—in these various guises—involves efforts to show the unified character of the human experience. Universalistic impulses and claims can be contrasted with the particularism of individuals groups and countries.

The vision of a single unified global system founded on the universal rights and dignity of humankind makes its appearance in the early European enlightenment. Its political manifestation is set forth in various philosophical statements and political declarations, including the 1789 "Declaration of the Rights of Man." Groups and societies around the world were seen to be composed of individuals, each possessing an inherent worth and respect, and together they were united as a single people.

Cosmopolitanism is the disposition of people to identify with other people across borders and boundaries, grasping and appreciating the identity of humanity as a whole. It is the antithesis of nationalism or particularism. Kwane Anthony Appiah reaches back in history to define it: "Cosmopolitanism dates at least to the Cynics of the fourth century B.C., who first coined the expression cosmopolitan, 'citizen of the cosmos.' The formulation was meant to be paradoxical, and reflected the general Cynic skepticism toward custom and tradition. A citizen—a *polites*—belonged to a particular *polis,* a city to which he or she owed loyalty. The cosmos referred to the world, not to the sense of the earth, but in the sense of the universe. Talk of cosmopolitanism originally signaled, then, a rejection of the conventional view that every civilized person belonged to a community among communities."[3]

Global civil society is a way of describing an emerging social order organized on a global scale. In it, peoples not only interact within a global world economy, but they also participate as "citizens," as participants with rights, roles, and obligations defined in complex global relationships. Individuals around the world occupy a transnational civil space in which they voluntarily enter into extended relationships outside the spheres of the state and power politics. Building on the notion of civil society, global civil society has several aspects. One is that the "civic space" that it emerges in is transnational—or global. It is a realm beyond the reach of the state and traditional structures of power. Another is that individuals enter into this space in voluntary ways—pursuing interests, promoting values, building coalitions, buying and selling. Yet another is the notion that global civil society is, in some sense, bringing justice and community within the larger global system. That is, there is a sense that global civil society is a movement—it is a "project." As John Keane argues: "There is general agreement that talk of global civil society is a response to rising concerns about the need for a new social and economic and political deal at the global level."[4]

The question is: what are the terms for an emerging global political order that is grounded in agreement on its fundamental norms and principles? What universal and cosmopolitan vision is sustainable by widespread assent from peoples and societies worldwide? Cosmopolitans aspire to a universal order—even a global civil society—but what is its logic?

3. The Liberal Ascendency

The first and most sustained effort to build a global political order emerged in the 19th century with the "liberal ascendency"—carried forward, first by Great Britain, and brought into the 20th century by the United States. This is the "liberal project"—a vision of a liberal global order in which all the peoples and societies of the world would be joined together in a single system of trade, law, security, and democratic community.

Indeed, the most profound transformation of world politics over the last two hundred years has been the rise in the power, influence, and global scope of liberal international order. Rising to global power during the industrial revolution, Britain built an empire—but it also pioneered in organizing global relations around open markets and international law. Through the Victorian era and into the 20th century, the fortunes of liberal democratic great powers flourished—and with the growth and expansion the core and organizing principles of world politics increasingly took on a liberal internationalist cast. This liberal ascendency took a dramatic jump forward in the hands of the United States after World War II, when America built a global order on explicit liberal principles. A system of free trade and global institutions were constructed and the democratic world was bound together in alliance and institutionalized partnerships.

This liberal democratic world expanded massively in the postwar decades and by the 1990s, in the aftermath of the Cold War and the collapse of the last great challenge to this order, it dominated the world. Under the cover of the Cold War, a revolution in relations between the Western great powers took place. It was a Western order built around cooperative security, managed open markets, multilateral governance, and American liberal hegemonic leadership. The Cold

War facilitated the building of this order—particularly the strategic bargains between the U.S. and Europe—but the project began before the Cold War and survived its end. Indeed, the Cold War ended as it did in large part because this Western order was so integrated, dynamic, and cooperative. This liberal international order did not come to life automatically. It was built around hegemonic bargains.

Daniel Deudney has described this liberal ascendence—"the rise to an historically unprecedented preeminence of the 'free world' composed of the United States of America and its democratic allies. Republics (polities based on political liberty, popular sovereignty, and limited government) have been historically precarious and rare, generally poor, and massively compromised. They now constitute a zone of peace, freedom, and prosperity far greater than any other in history. For most of history, republics were confined to small city-states where they were insecure and vulnerable to conquest or internal usurpation, but over the last two centuries they have expanded to continental size through federal unions and emerged victorious from the violent total conflicts of the twentieth century. In contrast, their major despotic and imperial adversaries have failed spectacularly. The American-led 'free world' overcame the reversals of the 1930s and early 1940s, expanded with the reconstruction of Western Europe and parts of East Asia as capitalist, liberal, constitutional, and federal democracies, and has built a dense network of international institutions."[5] The 19th century started as a moment when the democratic countries were a distinct minority threatened by autocratic and imperial states across the great power world. The 20th century ended very differently—with the global triumph of liberal democracy and a liberal international order that bound them together.

The liberal democratic world was more than simply an assembly of powerful and dynamic capitalist democracies. They established and operated within an expansive international order. It is a liberal international order with universal aspirations. The norms and principles of this order are several. First, it is built around free trade and open markets. Countries are invited to join into this capitalist world economy—and, indeed, this global economy has continued to expand and deepen and draw new countries into its orbit. Second, the liberal order is built on shared institutions of governance. Countries jointly command and operate a set of multilateral institutions that provide governance for the larger order. These rules and institutions are both substantive and procedural. That is, they proscribe and prescribe policies for states within the order—policies relating to trade, security, and the environment. But these rules and institutions are also procedural. They provide mechanisms for dispute resolution and the adjudication of conflicts. Third, the liberal international order also provides security partnerships that are meant to jointly defend against threats. NATO and the bilateral security pacts in East Asia are the cornerstone of this liberal security zone. Finally, there is a thriving informal world of democratic community and transnational civil society. The liberal order is infused with nongovernmental organizations and activist groups that cooperate across great distances and lobby governments on behalf of various policies and aspirations.[6]

Together this liberal order offers the world a set of principles and rules for universal global order.

4. Liberal Order and Global Order

This vision of liberal international order has two sides to it—impulses toward both "liberal internationalism" and "liberal imperialism," an awkward and problematic duality that persists today within the liberal tradition. The liberal internationalist impulse was embodied in Woodrow Wilson's Fourteen Points address and his ambition to forge a postwar order built around law, the consent of the governed, and the organized opinion of mankind. It is embodied in the efforts to launch the United Nations and build global relations around rules about the use of force. Liberal internationalism is a vision of democratic community and the rule of law.

But the "liberal imperial" impulse is also on display in the great liberal ascendency. It can be seen in British imperialism throughout the 19th century and into the middle of the 20th century. It can be seen in America's early 20th century impulse toward imperialism in Latin America and the Philippines. Woodrow Wilson's interventions in Mexico in 1914 and 1916 signaled this impulse. Wilson said that America's deployment of force was to help Mexico "adjust her unruly household." Regarding Latin America, Wilson said: "We are friends of constitutional government in America; we are more than its friends, we are its champions. I am going to teach the South American republics to elect good men."

But the most salient feature of liberal order—manifest in particular in the postwar era—is its capacity and tendency to expand outward and integrate disparate peoples and societies. Liberal order began as a Western order—but today it is global and globalizing.

In this regard, the postwar liberal international order is remarkably unique in a comparative historical perspective. It is more open and rule-based and deeply institutionalized than past international orders. All international orders dominated by a powerful state have been based on a mix of coercion and consent. But the American-led postwar order has been distinctive in that it has been marked more by liberal than imperial characteristics. This has made it more accessible, legitimate, and durable. Its rules and institutions are rooted in and reinforced by the evolving global forces of democracy and capitalism. It is expansive. It has a wide and widening array of participants and state-holders. In all these ways, in comparison with past international orders, it is easier to join and harder to overturn.

In particular, three features of liberal international order seem distinctive—features that have contributed to its success and longevity. First, more so than with imperial systems of the past, the liberal international order is built around rules and norms of nondiscrimination and market openness—creating conditions for rising states to participate within the order and advance their expanding economic and political goals within it. Across history, international orders have varied widely in terms of whether the material benefits that are generated accrue disproportionately to the leading state or whether the material benefits of participation within the order are more widely shared. In the liberal system, the barriers to economic entry are low and the potential benefits are high. Non-Western countries such as Japan, Korea, and (most recently) China have already discovered the massive economic returns that are possible through operating within this open market system.

A second feature of the liberal international order is the coalition-based character of its leadership. This is an order in which a group of advanced liberal democratic states work together and assert collective leadership. It is not just an American order; a wider group of states are bound together and govern the system. These leading states do not always agree but they are engaged in a continuous process of give and take over economics, politics, and security. This too is distinctive— past orders have tended to be dominated by one state. The stake holders in the current order include a coalition of status quo great powers that are arrayed around the old hegemonic state.

A final feature of the liberal international order are its unusually dense, encompassing, and agreed upon rules and institutions. International order can be rigidly hierarchical and governed by coercive domination exercised by the leading state or it can be relatively open and organized around reciprocal, consensual and rule-based relations. The postwar liberal order has been more open and rule-based than any previous order. State sovereignty and the rule of law are not just norms enshrined in the United Nations charter. They are part of the deep operating logic of the order. To be sure, these norms are evolving, and America itself has historically been ambivalent about binding itself to international law and institutions, and at no time more than today. But the overall system is remarkably dense with multilateral rules and institutions—global, regional, economic, political, and security. These institutional creations are one of the great breakthroughs of the postwar era: establishing the basis for greater levels of cooperation and shared authority and governance of the global system.

Together these features of liberal international order give it an unusual capacity to accommodate rising powers. Its sprawling landscape of rules, institutions, and networks provide newer entrants into the system with opportunities for status, authority, and a share in the governance of the order. Access points and mechanisms for political communication and reciprocal influence abound.

But the question remains: is liberal international order the most basic and enduring set of norms and principles around which global order can be built—or is it still incomplete and ultimately Western? If it does offer some deep foundation for an agreed upon global order, what precisely are the norms and principles that do—or can—gain universal assent?

5. Nationalism and Self-Determination Movements

It is worth recalling that the liberal ascendency in the late 19th and early 20th century triggered counter movements. These oppositional movements were not simply efforts to stop the globalization of liberal order (and the liberal imperial impulses that came with it). They themselves were also global movements, and their efforts had the effect of expanding the global character of politics and society as the decades of the 20th century advanced.

The first oppositional movement involved struggles from inside (and to a lesser extent outside) of the Western liberal order to reform itself. These efforts have been called “subversive internationalism”—struggles by various groups that tried to build on liberal order and make it better. These included philanthropic movements, international socialist and other working class movements, women’s organizations, and world parliaments of religion. The 1927 Congress of the

Suppressed Nations in Brussels, which included the participation of Jomo Kenyatta, Kwame Nkrumah, and Ho Chi Minh, was a particularly explicit effort to challenge the dominance of the Western powers while still operating within the existing order.[7]

A second reaction was a wide-ranging array of nationalist moments that erupted at the turn of the century in opposition to colonial empires that coexisted with the emerging liberal international order. The liberal "project" gave voice to subjected peoples and societies that rose up to challenge imperial control. The result was a globalization of nationalism. Nation-states sprang up in places such as New Zealand, Australia, China, Persia, and Siam. But the rise of "mass nationalism" also appeared in Latin America, the Habsburg Empire, and multiethnic polities inside and outside of Europe. Nationalist movements developed strong ideological tones and eroded wider transnational identities in places such as Egypt, the Balkans, and India. This movement continued well into the 20th century, and new struggles for independence and national self-determination emerged after World War II. American foreign policy after the two world wars gave voice to these far flung movements. The spread of nationalism and movements for self-determination involved, in effect, the taking of ideas from the West about the primacy of the nation-state and self-rule to challenge the imperial and colonial formations that Western powers had constructed.

A third movement aimed at reforming the international order was the rise of regionalism. One of these tendencies was among the advanced countries. In the 1930s, there was a movement among many of the great powers to construct regional empires—Great Britain, Russia, Japan, and Germany all sought to create and expand regional orders, and the United States had the Western hemisphere as its protectorate. A different sort of regionalism was advocated by the "Pan movements," which sought to build regionalism around cultural and ethnic commonalities. These included the Pan-Islamists, Pan-Arab, and Pan-Asian movements—and all expressed anti-Western sentiments and made efforts to protect their cultural and religious traditions from the assaults of modernization.

A final movement during this era was the widespread movement toward traditionalism and fundamentalism. Conrad and Sachsenmaier argue: "Less an organized movement than a cultural and political trend and mentality, traditionalism in a broad (and not party-political) sense posed the antithesis of modern, European civilization allegedly devoid of true and inner meaning and a fuller, less alienated form of communal life to be found in the golden past, or outside the West."[8] The image was to invoke the traditional values—in places such as Africa, China, India, and Japan—as remedies for the challenges posed by Western globalism.

While these movements were, at least in the first instance, animated by an effort to slow or mute the expansion of Western modernity, these oppositional movements were themselves agents of globalization. In each instance, the result of the struggle was to increase the consciousness of groups and societies around the world to the reality of the power and reach of Western-led globalization. In some cases, the goal was to moderate and redirect the forces of the market and Western political control. In other cases, the goal was to stop it altogether. But in the dialectics of this struggle across the 20th century, the liberal international order itself expanded and evolved.

6. Universal Norms and Principles

What norms and principles might gain near-universal agreement as the "terms" for international order? There are a range of possibilities. These would include norms and principles that both protect individuals and societies and that provide the basis for cooperation among groups and peoples that facilitate the provision of social benefits.

Individual Rights and Protections. The most elemental norms are those that ascribe rights to individuals. These are the first principles of the Enlightenment age—individuals are endowed with fundamental and inalienable rights as human beings that cannot be subverted or abridged by others. John Locke, of course, is the most famous theorist of this view of liberal individualism. Man is the "master of himself and the proprietor of his own person."

Conceptions of the role of individuals in society vary widely around the world, but some elemental agreement would seem to exist regarding respect for life and the dignity of individuals—These sentiments are enshrined in modern documents such as the United Nations charter— expressed in the preamble statement about the "dignity and worth of the individual."

The universal rights of individuals can be simple, as expressed in the United Nations charter, or they can be more expansively detailed, as in the UN Universal Declaration. In this more comprehensive articulation of individual rights, modern social protections are added—rights not to be tortured or subjected to inhumane treatment, and so forth. In a sequence of declarations and protocols that followed in the postwar decades, additional social and political rights have been elaborated—rights of women, children, and basic social welfare and protections. In these ways, the norms of individual rights have traveled from basic rights of the individual as a free and worthy creature to negative and positive freedoms.[9]

Group rights and self-determination. These are a bundle of norms and principles that suggest that societal groups and nations have some fundamental rights of self-determination and autonomy. These ideals begin with the view that individuals do exist within social and cultural groups. Individuals are not simply autonomous agents but are social entities that have some fundamental right to remain tied to these identity groupings.

These rights and protections are manifest in the modern norm of national self-determination. This sentiment—that a people had a right to their own self-government—was expressed in the American Declaration of Independence and it was argued in philosophical terms by thinkers such as John Stuart Mill. As a doctrine, national self-determination became an ideological tool against colonialism and imperialism. The UN Universal Declaration also states that peoples have a right to a nation. In effect, the norm of self-determination is what recognizes the legitimacy of nationalism as an aspect of international order.

Procedural Norms. There are a wide variety of procedural norms and principles that have wide support around the world. These include specific dispute settlement mechanisms—such as those associated with peace and security issues that come before the UN Security Council and procedures for the settlement of disputes in the World Trade Organization. In these cases, procedurals are agreed upon that set out how various parties are to be given hearing and disagreements adjudicated. Parties may not be able to agree on the substantive merits of the issues, but there is some basic agreement on the rules and institutions through which the disagreements are settled.

All these procedural norms and principles come with an assumption about the fair and impartial settlement of disputes. This is an assumption that even within the international system it is possible to get a fair hearing. The results of these dispute settlement procedures are not accompanied by any enforcement mechanism. In this sense, there is not an expectation that the world will be governed with the full array of judicial and law enforcement authority. Quite the opposite—there is a general agreement that enforcement and authority will and should remain decentralized. But the dispute settlement mechanisms are established with the idea that findings have some normative weight that even powerful states will have incentives to respond to.

Modernity. There is a more complicated set of norms and principles about the progressive development of society and politics. But the basic sentiment—widely shared—is that each generation has some obligation to make life better for those who follow. Or, to put it in more individualistic terms, that parents want their children to have advantages and opportunities that they did not have—to improve the life chances of their family.

This commitment to what might be called progressive modernization is manifest in various ways. It can be seen in the explosive growth of the postwar global human rights movement—and the growing willingness of groups to go beyond support for "negative freedoms," such as free speech and equal protection, to "positive freedoms," such as rights to education and health care. The world has moved, in effect, from libertarian sensibilities to social democratic sensibilities, at least in a very general way. But the commitment to progressive modernization can also be seen in the spread of world opinion against slavery in the 19th century and opposition to apartheid in the 20th century. The rise of the environmental movement is also part of this commitment to a progressive vision of modern life.

Taken together these norms and principles do evince a certain Western liberal character. They are all universal ideas that emerged out of the rise of Western power and the liberal ascendency. But they are not inherently Western—they offer rights and protections to widely divergent types of societies and cultures. These norms and principles also embody a tension between activism and protection. On the one hand, the universal rights norms and principles effectively empower the international community to get involved in the safeguarding of individuals—even if this involved intervening inside of sovereign states. On the other hand, the norms and principles of self-determination and national autonomy offer protection against outside interference. It is the balancing of these different aspirations that bring us back to procedural mechanisms that create legitimate and widely acceptable forms of global order.

7. Behind a Veil of Ignorance

In the search for norms and principles that can unite the world as one, it is useful to engage in the hypothetical exercise of architecture and order building. If we could start anew, what sort of rules and institutions could be established on a global level that would receive the wide agreement of divergent peoples and societies?

We might call this the great "neo-Rawlsian" question of our era. It was the famous political philosopher John Rawls who suggested that political institutions should be designed behind a "veil of ignorance"—that is, under conditions where the architects of the institutions did not know precisely where they would be within the resulting socioeconomic system.[10] This thought experiment forced the institution builders to design institutions that would safeguard his interests regardless of where he or she ended up—weak or strong, rich or poor. The world community would do well to engage in a similar thought experiment. What institutions should we try to put in place today that will safeguard our interests in future decades when we are uncertain whether we will have the power to protect our interests and way of life on our own?

It seems that we would construct a world based on norms and principles along the lines sketched above—emphasizing protection and procedural precepts. This would be a world in which rights and protections would infuse the global order. Rights would ensure that regardless of who you are—or where you are in the global socioeconomic hierarchy—you have some minimal legal-political capacity to live and be free. And the protections you would want would be ones that ensure that other states were not able to invade and dominate your society.

Such a world order would provide for respect for differences—different cultural and religious systems. Norms of selfdetermination and national sovereignty would be utterly necessary in a newly designed global order. But to safeguard individuals from the worst outcomes—violence and oppression visited upon them by their own government—the order would also need to have a legitimate right for the "international community" to intervene to provide rescue and protection. The critical issue is: what mechanisms will ensure that sovereignty is respected and only violated when fundamental rights are in jeopardy? This is the dilemma that the global system today faces. The problem is this: the norms and principles that establish the legitimacy and moral obligation for the international community to intervene in troubled countries far outstrip the capacity of countries to act—and this serves to erode the legitimacy of the liberal order that upholds these norms and principles. There are a cluster of thorny issues. There is the problem of who is to act on behalf of these norms and obligations. There is the problem of when and how to act. And there is the problem of making choices when states cannot respond to them all.

Because there is no neutral and independent global government that determines when and where interventions will take place, major states themselves decide—and they inevitably act when their more parochial or strategic interests are at stake. Bosnia and Kosovo were on the doorstep of Europe, and so NATO acted. Rwanda suffered mass killings but the international community did not respond. The weakly established international arrangements to deal with humanitarian emergencies and the selectivity of the interventions threaten the legitimacy of the norms and principles themselves.

In the end, the most difficult mechanism to establish at the global level—but the mechanism most necessary for the functioning of a legitimate and effective global order—is a decision-making institution that allows for these dilemmas to be settled in a just and consensual way. This is the heart of global governance and it is the fundamental requirement of a well ordered international order. The world has become one. A global world order has emerged. But the interconnectedness of that order has far outpaced the development of political mechanisms that can defend and support the glimmerings of universal norms and principles that are slowly emerging.

Notes

1 Karl Polanyi, *The Great Transformation: The Political and Economic Origins of Our Time*

(Boston: Beacon Press, 1957).

2 Hedley Bull, *The Anarchical Society: A Study of Order in World Politics* (New York:Columbia University Press, 1977).

3 Kwane Anthony Appiah, *Cosmopolitanism: Ethics in a World of Strangers* (New York: Norton, 2006).

4 John Keane, *Global Civil Society* (New York: Cambridge University Press, 2003), 3.

5 Daniel H. Deudney, *Bounding Powers: Republican Security Theory from the Polis to the Global Village* (Princeton: Princeton University Press, 2007).

6 See G. John Ikenberry, *After Victory: Institutions, Strategic Restraint, and the Rebuilding of Order After Major Wars* (Princeton: Princeton University Press, 2001).

7 This section draws on Sebastian Conrad and Dominic Sachsenmaier, "Introduction: Competing Visions of World Order: Global Moments and Movements, 1880s-1930s," in Sebastian Conrad and Dominic Sachsenmaier (eds.) *Competing Visions of World Order: Global Moments and Movements, 1880s-1930s* (New York: Palgrave Macmillan, 2007).

8 Conrad and Sachsenmaier, "Introduction," 12.

9 Jack Donnelly, *Universal Human Rights in Theory and Practice* (Ithaca: Cornell University Press, 1989).

10 John Rawls, *A Theory of Justice* (Cambridge, MA: Harvard University Press, 1971).

Beyond National Identities and Global Civil Society

Bob Jessop

Humans can only achieve the status of masters of the world when they maintain mutuality. In this sense, the new human kind that will carry on the 21st century can be called Homo reciprocus.
– Presentation of Conference theme

In its citation, the Norwegian Nobel Committee said the United Nations panel and Mr. Gore had focused 'on the processes and decisions that appear to be necessary to protect the world's future climate, and thereby reduce the future threat to the security of mankind.'
– Citation for the 2007 Nobel Peace Prize

In the year when a former US-American Vice-President, Al Gore, and the Intergovernmental Panel on Climate Change, a United Nations-sponsored network of more than 2,300 scientists, shared the Nobel Peace Prize for their political and scientific contributions to the understanding of climate change, it may seem odd that a conference to commemorate United Nations Peace Day has not explicitly put human-nature interactions on the agenda. Peace and the desire for "perpetual peace" are clearly important in the light of a bellicose and murderous 20th century with its innumerable hot and cold wars and its contest for land and resources. But humankind scarcely has a better record as "masters of the world" in relation to first and second nature, that is, "raw" nature and, ever more significantly, nature as it has been modified by the human species, than it does regarding their mutual relations. But perhaps the organizers want me to look forward some decades into a 21st century when the values and conduct of a reformed *homo reciprocus* might dominate the inclinations of *homo bellicus* and *homo economicus*. In this future era, sustainable reciprocal relations over several generations between humankind and (second) nature in an integrated world community would inform shared economic strategies, political projects, and hegemonic visions. This is a collective more than individual challenge and my presentation will focus on national identities and global civil society through the optic of the state and its transformation. But it will also move beyond this broad, but still limited, concern to include reflections on political ecology and political economy as well as on political science. It concludes with a call for a wisdom-based society.

I first consider national identities and global civil society but proper answers about global reciprocity require us to go beyond this topic. A second step takes us to political economy and moral economy and then to political ecology. This will involve reflections on the status and meaning of "society" in the context of the world market and a tendentiously emerging, but highly differentiated, world society. In particular, I ask whether the world market, global politics, and cyberspace require or facilitate a 21st century global civic society. Finally, I return to democratic governance and global solidarity and the pre-requisites of a sustainable social and natural order.

1. Nation-States and National States

We can distinguish two forms of modern organized political community, namely, national states and nation-states. The former is the classic

"Westphalian state," which is organized around a clearly demarcated territory and recognized by most other states as having juridico-political sovereignty in its own territory. The subjects of such states are subordinate to common laws and should, ideally, recognize the national state (and, perhaps, its lower tiers) as the legitimate authority within its sovereign territory. It took more than three centuries from the initial treaties inaugurating the peace of Westphalia, signed in 1648, for the great majority of states to acquire this "classic" form[1] and not all contemporary states are full Westphalian states, whether because of inadequate state capacities and/or continued foreign intervention. National states are analytically distinct from nation-states. Three types of nation-states can be identified: (1) an ethno-national community (*Volksnation*), which rests on an—imagined—common ancestry, consanguinity, and ethnic identity (e.g., Germany); (2) a *Kulturnation* based on a shared national culture that is often defined and actively promoted by the state itself (e.g., France); and (3) a *Staatsnation* (civic nation) based on patriotic commitment to the constitution and to fellow citizens in a system of representative government (e.g., the USA) (table 1). These types may exist in relatively pure form, be combined in mutually reinforcing or contradictory ways, and may support or weaken national states. In all cases, nationhood typically institutional-

Table 1. Typology of Imagined Political Communities Linked to Nation-States

Type of Nation	Simple National Community	Basis of Community Membership	Multiplex Form of Community	Form Taken by Nation When Decomposed
Volksnation	Ethnos	Blood ties or naturalization	Multiethnic	"Melting Pot Society"
Kulturnation	Shared Culture	Assimilation, Acculturation	Multicultural	Postmodern Play of Identities
Staatsnation	Constitutional Patriotism	Test of Political Loyalty	Nested Political Loyalties to Multi-Tiered Government	"Dual State" in Given Territory or Transnational Diasporas

izes exclusion as well as inclusion, within or beyond the boundaries of the national state. National identities are also subject to gendering, "racializing," and other identitarian divisions; and there are also important differences in terms of class relations and uneven national development.

Forms of national state and "nation-state" vary widely and the conference organizers are presumably most interested in the future(s) of the national territorial states that have developed successively following World War II, national independence, and the collapse of the Soviet bloc. Despite significant differences, they all tend to be organized in terms of national economies, national territorial states, nation-building efforts, and, in some cases, national welfare states. Examples include advanced West European, North American, and Australasian welfare states, Latin American import substitution states (whether authoritarian, bureaucratic, or military dictatorships), South Asian national states, East Asian developmental states based on export-led growth, or various national states in the Soviet Bloc, seeking national self-determination after 1989. Concentrating on nation-states (especially those based on ethno-nationalism) or treating all national states as if they were pure nation-states, would divert attention from the more important issue of the future of national states in the 21st century, whatever their bases of nation-building.

2. Three Main Trends in National States

Various scholars have identified at least three trends in the restructuring and reorientation of national territorial states. First, there is the tendentious denationalization of statehood. Specifically, whilst the national state retains a large measure of formal sovereignty rooted in the mutual recognition of national states and remains an important site for political struggles, its substantive capacities to project its power domestically (let alone abroad) have generally been decisively weakened both by the shift towards more internationalized, flexible (but also regionalized) production systems and by the growing challenge posed by global ecological deterioration induced by human action (and inaction). This trend involves the "hollowing out" of national states with old and new state capacities (including rule and decision-making powers as well as the capacity to mobilize resources and penetrate society) being reorganized territorially and functionally on subnational, national, supranational, and translocal levels. We find some state capacities increasingly transferred to a growing number of pan-regional, plurinational, or international bodies with a widening range of powers; others are devolved to restructured local or regional levels of governance in the national state; and yet others are being usurped by emerging horizontal networks of power—local and regional—which by-pass central states and connect localities or regions in and across several nations. Paradoxically, this also extends the scope for the national state itself to mediate between the supra- and sub-national.

Second, there is a general trend towards the destatization of politics based on a shift from the centrality of government to more decentralized forms of governance on various territorial scales and across various functional domains. Whilst the first general trend concerns the territorial dispersion of the national state's activities, the second affects the functional reorganization of state activities in the broader political system on whatever territorial scale it operates. It involves movement away from the primacy of official (typically national) state apparatuses towards the assumed need for quite varied forms (and levels) of partnership between official, parastatal, and nongovernmental organizations in the management of economic and social relations. It also involves a shift from the top-down hierarchical political organization that is a formal characteristic of sovereign states to emphasis on promoting and/or steering the selforganization of inter-organizational relations. In this expanding range of networks, partnerships, and other models of economic and political governance, official apparatuses remain first among equals. For, although public money and law underpin their operation, other resources (such as private money, knowledge, or expertise) would also be critical to the success of state projects. Hence the state's involvement tends to be less hierarchical, less centralized, and less dirigiste than in previous periods. Although this involves a loss of decisional and operational autonomy by state apparatuses (at whatever level), it could enhance their capacity to project state power and achieve state goals by mobilizing knowledge and power resources from non-governmental stakeholders.

Third, there is a general trend towards the internationalization of policy regimes. On the one hand, there is the increased strategic significance of the international context of domestic state action and governance practices; and, on the other, the national state's field of action for domestic purposes has expanded to include an extensive range of extraterritorial or transnational factors and processes. This dual strategic reorientation is reflected in many fields of state policy. For example, the prime object of economic and social intervention by national states has changed in almost all types of national state from well-balanced domestic performance of the "national economy" to its "international competitiveness" understood in very broad terms. This is associated with diverse policies to promote permanent innovation, an enterprise culture, and labour market flexibility as well as to subordinate social policy more generally to the "imperatives" of international competition. Neoliberalism is only one empirical manifestation of this trend and its long-term effectiveness has not yet been proved superior to other approaches.

3. Three Main Trends in Civil Society

I find the concept of "civil society" problematic, especially when defined as a specific institutional space with its own structured coherence. It is hard to separate "civil society" fully from the economy (which is always socially embedded, although the forms of this embedding vary) and the state (defined by Gramsci, 1971, e.g., as "political society + civil society"). This raises the question whether "civil society" is an autonomous domain of social life with its own logic or comprises no more than a heterogeneous set of social relations that are not (yet) dominated by other institutional orders. Habermas advances the former approach in identifying the democratic potential of the "public sphere." In contrast, I see civil society as relatively formless—but argue that it is this very formlessness that makes it such a significant (if imaginary) stake in so many different struggles. Not only are there what Habermas calls "colonizing" attempts to penetrate civil society and subordinate it to the requirements of specific institutional orders (e.g., market, law, science, education, healthcare, politics, foreign or homeland security) but civil society also serves as a site of struggles to resist such colonization in defense of identities and/or interests that lie outside and/or crosscut the relevant institutional orders (e.g., in defense of class, gender, race, nationality, generation, stage in the life-course, citizenship, human rights, the natural environment). This makes "civil society" an essentially contested space for representatives of very different types of interests, norms, and values. It serves as a target for strategies to secure the dominance of particular institutional orders through expansion into this space; and as a reservoir of antagonistic "instincts" (rooted in other identities) and social resources for resisting this.

This said, what are we to make of the alleged resurgence, recovery, resistance, or revenge of civil society on the market economy and/or national territorial states and of the countless calls from many quarters to promote a "global civil society"? The former trend is linked to the crisis of state socialism in the Soviet bloc and the initial construction of postsocialist societies; and the latter trend is evident in the heartlands of advanced capitalism as well as the "global South." This does not entail that "civil society" has become materially and socially unified—let alone on a global scale. But it does indicate major changes in the "selfunderstanding" and "self-description" of societies that are reflected in the renewed discussions on "civil society." In particular, growing structural and social complexity together with the processes of time-space distantiation and compression entailed in the development of world markets, global politics, and world society have increased the significance of a growing plurality of values, identities, and interests as means to cope with the disorienting effects of complexity by providing social anchoring and meaning.

These changes are linked to three trends in contemporary "civil society" as defined above. First, just as a de-nationalization of statehood is occurring relative to the heyday of the national territorial state—which occurred from 1945-1980 and, indeed, even later in the case of post-Soviet states, we are now witnessing the "denationalization" of civil society. This is reflected in the increased importance of cosmopolitanism, "tribalism" (i.e., the rediscovery or sheer invention of primordial, affective identities at the expense both of liberal individualism and of civic loyalty to an "imagined" national community), and expansion of diverse social movements that operate across national boundaries. Second, particularly in the "West," where civil society had its firmest (albeit fragile) roots, several major changes have affected the principles and practices of civil society considered as a (residual) social sphere. These include rejection of classbased egalitarianism (with its associated redistributive politics); greater concern with empowerment or social inclusion (via measures to secure lifetime access to participation in different institutional orders, e.g., the promotion of employability, entitlement to essential legal services, lifetime education in the "learning society," subsidiarity in the political system, access to scientific assessment of individual and collective risks); growth in identity politics (with its emphasis on respect, authenticity, and autonomy); and expansion of the so-called "third" sector (operating outside both the pure market and the bureaucratic state). The first two trends are linked in contradictory ways both to more nationalist, populist, and authoritarian discourses and to a more cosmopolitan, neoliberal demand for "more market, less state" in a more open economy.

Third, although national citizenship is still important in many established national states, there is increasing emphasis on (transnational) human rights that can be invoked even where an individual is not a citizen of a given state and/or where the state resists the enforcement of human rights by external agencies. In part, the development of human rights is related to the globalization of the legal system, the economy, and the political system. But it also represents the development of a cosmopolitan "public sphere" in which liberal principles can be extended beyond national boundaries and thereby challenge the bases of purely national citizenship and the rise (or re-invention) of liberal humanitarian intervention.

4. Counter Trends and Limitations

Having considered recent trends in the reorganization of the national state and civil society, I now comment on some important countertrends and limitations. First, the tendentious denationalization of statehood is being countered by an increasing role for stronger national states in managing the transfer of old and new state capacities upwards, downwards, and sideways. For individuals and organizations still expect that, however complex the real world may be and however global the world's functional systems may become, there should somewhere be a social power (typically the state) capable of managing crises and securing social cohesion despite the tendencies towards uneven development that inevitably occur in a modern social formation. Paradoxically, the state is an interdependent part of a more complex system but is held responsible for that system's overall performance. This paradox is reinforced by the residual significance of the national state as a focus of political loyalties. Indeed, national identities help to block the development of a supranational state or global governance system with powers equivalent to those of national states. There are important asymmetries among national states in this regard with the United States seeking, especially since its rise to single superpower status and the broadening of its claims to exercise "extraterritorial" power, to pursue something close to what Noam Chomsky calls a "single standard," that is, the principle that whatever is in the interests of the United States as currently perceived should be pursued and that no state, international organization, or set of foreign economic interests should be permitted to interfere with this.[2] Whether this makes the US more effective internationally or intensifies the risks of "blowback" is, of course, another matter.[3] Nor is the United States alone in seeking to implement such a standard—it is simply better placed to do so.

Second, while there is a steady shift from government to governance, there is a countervailing shift from government to meta-governance. This involves the role of states (especially, but not exclusively, national territorial states) in organizing the framework for self-organizing governance regimes. States' control of organized coercion and their constitutional right to treat any activity as politically relevant tends to give them greater authority to engage in governmental, governance, and meta-governance activities than any other organizations within their territory. Hence social relations are typically organized and conducted "in the shadow of [state] hierarchy." Moreover, even when state managers try to reject responsibility for specific fields of action, social forces tend to hold the state responsible for the effects of withdrawal and to call for reengagement in one form or another. The response may be renewed direct intervention by the state and/or modifications in attempts to modify the rules of the game and/or the balance of forces as the state seeks to organize self-government through its continuing role in meta-governance.

Third, as international regimes grow more important across a widening range of policy and issue areas, local, regional, national, and supranational states engage in increasing struggles over the form and content of such regimes and the extent and timing of their adoption and implementation in particular territorial states. This holds as much for the emerging global civil society as it does for formal economic and political regimes. Indeed, global civil society is becoming another terrain for interstate struggles as well as for class hegemony.

Fourth, the "de-nationalization" of civil society prompts state policies to deal with the challenges to many of the traditional bases of national citizenship and mutual solidarity that arise from multiethnicity, multiculturalism, and divided political loyalties—whether these latter features stem from or are inherited from the earlier stages of state formation or are the product of more recent regional or global shifts in population and/or are from other economic, political, and sociocultural transformations. This is where the issue of national identities and global civil society begins to emerge—whether in terms of their potential opposition or reconciliation. For example, growing individualism weakens national identity; a "melting pot society" may also do so but, in states like the USA, it could also reinforce identification with the *Staatsnation* and promote patriotism; multiethnicity is potentially threatening to the *Volksnation*; multiculturalism could weaken the *Kulturnation* or reinforce identification with global civil society; cosmopolitanism and nested political loyalties may promote identification with supranational regimes (e.g., the European Union); and, when tied to plural identities, cosmopolitanism may promote global civil society.

Fifth, "civil society" comprises a heterogeneous set of institutional orders, many of which are operationally autonomous and structurally resistant to control from outside—whether through top-down command or through horizontal networking. It is also the site of identities and interests that are not grounded in any specific institutional order but crosscut them by virtue of their relationship to the experience and "lifeworld" of whole persons. Indeed, people with multiple roles and complex personal identities and, in addition, complex multifunctional organizations often attempt to integrate their personal and organizational lives by retaining autonomy and resisting state intervention. This is where demands for empowerment and capacity-building become relevant. But identity politics and empowerment could become just another opportunity for capital to appropriate more flexible labour power, to commodify other institutional orders, to restructure consumption even as its tendencies towards economic polarization continue on a global scale, to seek legitimacy through the domestication of calls for corporate social responsibility, and so forth. This would limit attempts to ensure the inclusion of all citizens within each order.

Sixth, the promotion of human rights by transnational social movements and parts of the legal profession is still best seen as a secondary rather than dominant feature of political and social organization. Humanitarian intervention risks becoming another means of inter-state conflict with the rationale, timing, extent, and purposes of such intervention being contested and the incidence of intervention explained more in terms of reasons of state than universal principles.

5. A New Form of Civil Society?

Some of the countertendencies that prevent a complete destatization of politics in favour of market forces and/or civil society and that prevent a complete "governmentalization" (state absorption) of the economy and civil society could also enable a partial transcendence of the opposition between state and civil society or, a fortiori, between a plurality of national states and an emergent global civil society. Here I would particularly identify: (1) the decomposition of different forms of national identity associated with nation-states, which creates the space for transnational and/or cosmopolitan identities as well as for localist, "tribal," or other particularisms; and (2) the continuing importance of state power, in the sense of state capacities and strategic resources rather than formal territorial sovereignty, for the realization of major objectives of the social forces active in an emerging global civil society. What brings these two factors together is "meta-governance," that is, the organization of the conditions for self-organization and the reflexive search for the appropriate balance between different modes of coordination in achieving global economic, political, social, and cultural objectives.

In this context, "global civil society" would have a dual significance. First, it would develop as a "public sphere" based on dialogue not only among individuals but also among organizations or associations as representatives of a wide range of personal, interpersonal, organizational, interorganizational, systemic, and intersystemic interests. The development and expansion of social forums, either independently of or in parallel with intergovernmental or business forums, illustrates this. Such forums could be seen as a new form of associational democracy with its own autonomous logic based on dialogue in the context of solidarity. As such they would provide crucial transversal networking mechanisms among social movements on different scales with a view to building new forms of transnational solidarity. Their aim would not be to replace all forms of coordination through the market (though emphasis would go to fair trade rather than free trade) and/or through statal and other hierarchical organizations. Instead, they would aim to provide forums for shaping the appropriate balance among different coordination mechanisms and to provide flanking and supporting devices for solidaristic initiatives. Thus the overall challenge is to connect particular local struggles, generalize them, and link them to a universal project of socioecological transformation, against the socially and ecologically destructive universalization of a globalising neoliberal capitalism as the regulator of society and nature.[4] As such, it would also be grounded in the heterogeneity of social relations and the openness of a space for dialogue, subject to agreed rules for participation in that dialogue.

Second, it would be crucial for the emerging global civil society to have the resources, capacities, and collective will to resist hegemonisation, domination, or colonisation by the institutional logics associated with one particular functional system (e.g., the profit-oriented, market-mediated logic of the capitalist economy, the authority of science, the fetishism of law, the prioritization of military security) or by the power interests of one superpower or bloc of states. Only then could it serve as a space for dialogue between different systemic and organizational logics with a view to developing mutual understandings and sustain negative and positive coordination among different organizations and systems. This dialogue might lead to consensus on hegemonic values, axial principles of societalization, and procedural roles for system integration and social cohesion without the need for an increasingly impossible top-down government or blind coevolution of anarchic market forces.

What practical principles might underpin the development of this kind of global civil society? First, disregarding questions about specific fields and scales of government or governance, four factors affect the capacity to build effective self-reflexive government or governance mechanisms of the kind that a global civil society needs:

- Simplifying models and practices that reduce the complexity of the world but are still congruent with real world processes and their governance.

- Developing the capacity for dynamic interactive learning about various causal processes and forms of interdependence, attributions of responsibility and capacity for actions, and possibilities of coordination in a turbulent world.

- Building methods for coordinating actions among different social forces with different identities, interests, and meaning systems, over different spatiotemporal horizons, and over different domains of action. This depends on self-reflexive self-organization to sustain exchange, negotiation, hierarchy, or solidarity as well as on the specific nature of the coordination problems engendered by operating on different scales and over different time horizons.

- Establishing both a common world-view for individual action and a system of meta-governance to stabilize key players' orientations, expectations, and rules of conduct. This allows for a more systematic review and assessment of problems and potentials, of resource availability and requirements, and of the framework for continued commitment to negative and positive coordination.

Presented in these terms, it might seem that these are purely technical matters that can be left to relevant "experts" or the "leading" states as the final arbiters of good governance issues. Effective decision-making involves not only institutional design but also "cultural" governance. Whereas there has been much interest in issues of institutional design appropriate to different objects of governance, less attention has been paid to the reform of the subjects of governance. This poses basic questions not only about institutional compatibility of different modes of governance in a global governance regime but also about the complementarity among the individual and collective capacities and individual and collective orientations needed to sustain them. The conference proposal highlights this in its reference to *homo reciprocus* over *homo economicus* or *homo hierarchicus*. But how can we encourage the development of *homines reciproci* and their primacy in decision-making? I address this in terms of democratic renewal and "romantic public irony."

6. Democratic Renewal

Representative democracy involves a plebiscite of a state's citizens to elect deputies who will make decisions on their behalf. It is premised on the relation between individual citizens and territorial states based on the rule of law. The ruler-ruled relation always tends towards oligarchy and representative democracies are no exception. “Natural parties of government” insert themselves into this space to reconcile the formal logic of electoral majorities with the substantive logic of the effective exercise of state power. Moreover, while representative democracy enables responsibility to be formally attributed to named officials and bodies and to change those held accountable in this way, it does not follow that actual political responsibility is located at specific points or with specific persons. Power circulates through wider and more complex sets of social relations both within and beyond the state and these circuits become increasingly complex in a period of globalization affecting many different institutional orders and social worlds. There is typically a chaotic multiplicity of directly political and politically-relevant networks in which effective political responsibility is impossible to locate, even if it can be said to exist. At most, then, loss of office (or its threat) may encourage other political agents to take greater account of public opinion and political legitimacy; at worst, it may lead to a cynical symbolic politics to hold on to power and a shift to more authoritarian forms of government, governance, and meta-governance.

Complicating these issues further is the growing disjunction in an increasingly integrated global economy between the formal structures of political power in sovereign states and transnational circuits of power. Yet, with the development of world society, national states (plus supranational states like the EU) may become even more important addressees of political communications. This does not mean that national states can effectively exercise power as increasing complexity makes it harder for any state to exercise effective power. If representative democracy is based on territorial representation, it is rendered problematic by the relativization of scale (the loss of primacy of the national scale), by de- and re-territorialization (the territorial rescaling of government powers and authorities), the resulting increase in variable geometries and tangled hierarchies of political power (the loss of territorial congruence and/or of neatly nested hierarchies of power across a growing range of fields of government action), and the challenge to many of the traditional bases of national citizenship and mutual solidarity in some national states that come from multiethnicity, multiculturalism, and divided political loyalties. It is also rendered harder by the growing complexity of the tasks that hierarchical, sovereign states are expected to resolve through the traditional means of imperative coordination. Given everincreasing interdependence among functionally differentiated systems with their own operational codes, logics of appropriateness, temporalities, spatialities, and so forth, it becomes harder for one system (even the state as the core of the political system) to control the operations of other systems from outside and above. This is an important factor, as we have seen, behind the shift to governance.

Representative democracy can also rest on inclusion within a system of indirect functional representation rather than on individual citizenship of a territorial state. Examples include syndicalism, corporativism, corporatism, the negotiated economy, and the "stakeholding society." But indirect functional representation is made harder by more rapid and often unpredictable changes in the nature and relativities of the functional bases of representation (e.g., through sectoral shifts, occupational changes, the increased importance of the space of flows and mobilities at the expense of place-bound activities and relative fixities), the contestability of functional and institutional boundaries, uncertainty about relevant stakeholders, and problems of externalities. This explains why institutionalized and even constitutionalized forms of functional representation have given way to more flexible, informal social pacts and/or proliferation of short-term public-private partnerships and strategic alliances. This poses many issues around the legitimacy, inclusiveness, and consistency of functional arrangements in and across different fields and scales of action as well as about the participation of social forces anchored in identities, interests, and values that are not directly rooted in different functional systems (or, to put the same point differently, social forces anchored in civil society). To this we must add the more general problem of functional as well as territorial representation, namely, the potential division of interests between leaders and led (e.g., trade union leaders versus the rank-and-file members).

Direct democracy faces even more difficulties. In its ideal form, in a decentralized world with adequately resourced and empowered local communities or other inclusive, self-organizing bodies, local organs of direct democracy would propose, ratify, and implement policies in a complex system of self-management, taking account as far as possible of the repercussions of their decisions on legitimate interests beyond the borders of their respective local communities. But even in these conditions there are real risks of parochialism, more or less subtle forms of discrimination and social exclusion, and neglect of externalities. With growing complexity, increasing inequality in local resources and capacities, these problems and threats become even greater. In addition, the general problems of securing legitimacy, inclusiveness, and consistency characteristic of an increasingly fragmented and disjointed system of indirect functional representation are reinforced in the case of direct democracy. This is why some theorists suggest that the difficulties of coordinating dispersed and fragmented democratic organs at the base should be resolved by linking them organically to representative democracy. Thus the superordinate tier of government would be responsible for ensuring adequate resources and capacities at lower tiers and also provide the framework for mutual communication and collective intelligence about the interdependencies and indirect interactions between decisions and policies on these lower tiers. With appropriate forms of subsidiarity and an overall commitment to norms of fairness and justice and an open public sphere, representative government bodies would provide a framework to elaborate a national-popular will that transcends particular interests. In this sense parliamentary institutions would remain the principal site for elaborating national-popular hegemony around democratic projects.

An alternative is associational democracy,[5] with its proposals for a multiscalar, mixed constitution based on twin territorial and functional legislative chambers and a complex, competitive, and overlapping series of democratically organized associations that produce and/or deliver goods and services within a clearly defined meta-governance framework. His model of associationalism rests on voluntary associations that compete for members (and, in some cases, partial public funding) in providing economic, welfare, and political services. These associations would be accountable to key stakeholders—including suppliers, consumers, and "neighbours" as well as their own workers and managers—and be subject to definite (but not overdetailed) legal regulation and wide-ranging audit. Although there would obviously be wide scope for transnational as well as highly local associations, these would all operate within a context of democratically accountable (national) states that would each act as an "association of associations" for a given national territory—being charged in particular with the tasks of constitutional design, the "governance of governance," and the guarantee of basic freedoms, a minimum income, and basic social benefits. Finally, the national state (as well as all other associations) would operate in the context of free and open communication—a feature that Hirst regards as the most important guarantee of democratic accountability and certainly more important than infrequent plebiscitary elections.

Even if we ignore the inevitable selectivities in the elaboration of national-popular and/or associationalist projects, which always marginalize or exclude some interests, such "mixed constitutions" become harder to maintain when the bases of effective territorial representation are also under threat. One solution is to focus less on the mechanisms through which political rulers in specific national states are elected, appointed, and held accountable and more on the mechanisms that would enable a plurality of "demoi" to play an active role in decisionmaking and the holding of decision-makers to account, whether elected or appointed. To prevent this plurality degenerating into a series of blockades and stalemates, however, mechanisms are also needed to constitute an active "people" that comprises more than (1) the sum of individual electors casting their legitimating votes in infrequent elections (whether for parliamentary assemblies or voluntary associations) and/or (2) a disorganized plurality of competing interests and local economic and political organs (without means of open communication, negotiation, and negative coordination).

7. Romantic Public Irony

There are many recommendations for institutional design for good governance and, as experience shows, they are not only heavily contested but also prone to failure when adopted. This poses a key question about how to proceed in the face of failure. Four basic reactions to the failure are fatalistic or stoical resignation, denial, and cynical opportunism. The fatalist concludes that nothing can be achieved and therefore makes no effort. The stoic recognizes that failure is likely but goes through the motions in ritualistic fashion. Others deny that failure has occurred, continually moving the "goal posts" and engaging in spin. Others again seek to ensure that they "cash in" before the failure becomes evident, leaving others to pick up the losses. A fifth approach, recommended here, is romantic public irony. An ironist must simplify a complex, contradictory, and changing reality to be able to act—knowing that such necessary simplifications also distort reality and, worse, can generate failure. A romantic public ironist also acts on the assumption that success may be possible—thereby "thinking one thing and doing another." Moreover, given that she cannot guarantee success, the romantic public ironist can at least choose her mode of failure. But she should choose wisely, adopting a mode of governance that will minimize the likelihood of failure (see Box 1). A wise choice rejects the anarchy of the market or the topdown command of more or less unaccountable rulers in favour of self-organization, mobilizing the collective intelligence of stake-holders and other relevant partners in a form of participatory democracy. Thus, in contrast to cynics, ironists seek to involve others in policy-making, not for manipulative purposes but to promote conditions for negotiated consent and self-reflexive learning. Self-reflexive and participatory forms of governance are crucial means of defining the objectives as well as objects of governance and help to secure these objectives by reinforcing motivation and mobilizing capacities for selfreflection, self-regulation, and self-correction. This does not exclude resort to the anarchy of exchange or the hierarchy of formal organization as part of an appropriate repertoire of modes of coordination that are available to respond to signs of failure. But it does stipulate that public romantic irony is the most appropriate mechanism for working out the best modes of governance in particular situations and deciding when collibration is required. Other modes of coordination are subordinated to the logic of participatory governance in the interests of balancing efficiency, effectiveness, and democratic accountability.

The adoption of romantic public irony as an approach is a counsel of perfection. It represents a form of Pascalian wager—a bet on the possibility of finding collective and democratic solutions to apparently insoluble problems. The chances of success are enhanced if three conditions are met:

Box 1. Romantic Public Irony

- Expect failure, act as if you intend to succeed.
- If you are bound to fail in meta-governance, choose your mode of failure.
- Choose to fail wisely, that is, together, through participation and dialogue to choose different modes of governance for given purposes.
- This will reduce the chances of failure!

1) A flexible repertoire (requisite variety) of responses is maintained in order to be able to alter strategies and select those that work. Complexity excludes simple governance solutions and effective governance often requires a combination of mechanisms oriented to different scales, different temporal horizons, and so forth, oriented to the object to be governed. Strategies and tactics can be combined to reduce the likelihood of failure and to modify their balance as appropriate in the face of governance failure and turbulence in the policy environment.

2) There is continuing reflection on what would be an acceptable outcome in the case of incomplete success, on the implications of inadequacies in the market, government, and governance, and on the extent to which current actions are producing desired outcomes. This involves the monitoring of mechanisms to check for problems, resort to collibrating mechanisms to modulate the coordination mix, and the reflexive, negotiated reevaluation of objectives. And it requires learning about how to learn reflexively. There is a general danger of infinite regress here, of course; but this can be limited provided that reflexivity is combined with the other two principles.

3) The participants in meta-governance recognize the likelihood of failure but proceed as if success were possible. The supreme irony in this context is that the need for irony holds not only for individual attempts at governance using individual governance mechanisms but also for the practice of meta-governance.

These three principles are valid not only for the powerful but also for the powerless. Indeed, Karl Deutsch suggested that power can be defined as "the ability to afford not to learn from mistakes."[6] It follows that the powerless need to be more circumspect, reflexive, and capable of learning—for seizing even temporary advantages certainly depends on reflexivity and learning. This is powerfully conveyed by the Laura Balbo's homely metaphor of the "patchwork" continually performed by women in mixing different resources and strategies in their attempts to suture fragile social networks together.[7] There are innumerable examples of the importance of requisite variety and reflexivity in the everyday survival strategies and tactics of resistance among the poor, deprived, underprivileged, and oppressed in peasant communities, informal urban settlements, marginalized sectors, networks of the weak, and so on.[8] (see Chatterjee 2004; Hobsbawm 1959; and Scott 1985). And, if the powerless are not to retreat into fatalistic escape, stoic acceptance, or cynical exploitation of their fellows, a healthy dose of romantic irony is especially vital. Choosing to fail democratically and collectively is their least bad option—it increases the chances of developing requisite variety, encourages mutual learning and reflexivity, and provides the basis for shared understandings of their material and social situation that will reduce the risks of failure.

8. From Political Economy via political Ecology to Moral Economy

It is tempting to analyze the prospects for the development of an appropriate mix of representative, associational, and direct democracy without regard to the broader context in which this must occur. But, disregarding the continuing propensity to conduct internal and external wars for (sometimes allegedly) extraeconomic reasons, there remain a set of economic constraints rooted in the competitive, profit-oriented, market-mediated logic of the world market and the damaging, growth-oriented, resource-intensive logic of "industrialism" operating from local to planetary scales. The logic of capital accumulation, whether the dominant forces of production are purportedly "industrial" or "postindustrial," entails a competitive treadmill-oriented to ever-increasing production of wealth in the form of a massive accumulation of commodities. This treadmill operates not only among firms but also clusters, regions, and national states and is one of the principal limits to the denationalization of statehood and the harmonious internationalization of policy regimes. In addition, the logic of industrialism is not suspended by the alleged (but still partial) transition to post-industrialism and, indeed, could never be fully suspended. For a wholly postindustrial society is impossible. Immaterial production continues to depend on material production and is usually integrated into broader circuits of production, distribution, and consumption. Indeed, the shift to postindustrialism in advanced capitalist economies depends in part on the transfer of industrial production and its associated pollution elsewhere, modifying the ecological footprint of national economies and encouraging, in some cases, pollute-thy-neighbour policies that are unsustainable for one earth. When an integrated world market and global ecosystem characterized by uneven development and growing ecological vulnerabilities are combined with many competing economic and political entities endowed with unequal strategic capacities and power, the prospects are virtually nil within the existing economic and political order for effective coordination to resolve market and state failures, environmental problems, economic inequalities, and unequal access to opportunities for human flourishing. For the modes of economic and political calculation associated with profit-oriented, market-mediated accumulation and exclusive juridico-political sovereignties militate against the sacrifice and reciprocity required to overcome the problems generated by economic competition and political rivalries on a global scale. Cooperation within these logics is feasible where a positive-sum game can be played against other competitors and rivals, where the costs of cooperation can also be deferred into the future and/or displaced onto others. But it is not possible within these logics in a global negative-sum game against nature.

The sort of cooperation that I have in mind demands a radical break with these logics and joint moves towards (1) economic solidarity and reciprocity oriented to the stewardship of nature and the flourishing of future generations on a global scale; and towards (2) political subsidiarity and reciprocity oriented "to improving the conditions of the least advantaged" rather than entrenching existing inequalities and dependencies. While the second movement is reminiscent of John Rawls's liberal theory of justice,[9] its articulation with economic solidarity, political subsidiarity, and reciprocity gives it a very different meaning and different implications. In this sense, it is closer to another famous dictum—"from each according to his ability, to each according to his needs"[10]—but relates it to an even broader set of changes. In short, it is not enough to move from the critique of political economy to radical political ecology; a move is also required from political economy to a moral economy that puts at its centre a concern with human flourishing within a global community and with promoting reciprocal interdependence within a global ecology. And this can be achieved only through substantively asymmetrical rather than formally equal sacrifice.

9. Wisdom-Based Society

Having reviewed the complexities of political economy and political ecology and their implications for the future of national states, national identities, and civil society, it is tempting to fall back into fatalism, stoicism, denial, or opportunism. There are many examples of all four approaches in relation to climate change as well as to the prospects for perpetual peace. Another approach, as noted above, is romantic public irony. This presupposes a commitment to reciprocity and solidarity—to *homo reciprocus* and the organization of reciprocity around universal values. Given the growing threats from climate change, that represent a bigger threat to humankind (and, in case this appears to be too "species-ist," to a stable ecological order on a world scale) than nuclear proliferation or terrorism, the search for solutions needs more than additional information or better knowledge. Accepting the limits to a capitalist knowledge economy that dominates the world market, and thereby, the development of world society, we should seek to embed both nature and human creativity in a remoralized society. Thus, I conclude that we should be moving towards a wisdom-based society that draws on the collective good sense as well as accumulated knowledge of humankind. This would require that society be reorganized so that individuals may flourish, not at the expense of others, but as social beings in harmony with nature. This is reflected in the wise words that are so often attributed—wrongly—to Chief Seattle of the Cree Indians but nonetheless indicate the limits of the unfettered pursuit of wealth in the form of commodities:

> Only after the last tree has been cut down
> Only after the last river has been poisoned
> Only after the last fish has been caught
> Only then you will find out that money cannot be eaten

Notes

1 Benno Teschke, *The Myth of 1648: Class, Geopolitics and the Making of Modern International Relations* (London: Verso, 2003).

2 Noam Chomsky, *Failed States: the Abuse of Power and the Assault on Democracy* (Harmondsworth: Penguin, 2007); cf. William Blum, *Rogue State: A Guide to the World's Only Superpower* (London: Zed, 2001).

3 Cf. Chalmers J. Johnson, *Blowback: the Costs and Consequences of American Empire* (London: Little, Brown, 2000); Chalmers J. Johnson, *The Sorrows of Empire. Militarism, Secrecy, and the End of the Republic* (New York: Metropolitan, 2004); Chalmers J. Johnson, *Nemesis: the Last Days of the American Republic* (New York: Metropolitan, 2007).

4 Cf. Greg Albo, "The Limits of Eco-localism: Scale, Strategy, Socialism," *Socialist Register* (2007): 350-360.

5 Paul Q. Hirst, *Associational Democracy* (Cambridge: Polity, 1994).

6 Karl W. Deutsch, *The Nerves of Government. Models of Political Communication and Control* (New York: Free Press, 1963), 21.

7 Laura Balbo, "Crazy Quilts: Rethinking the Welfare State Debate from a Woman's Point of View," in A.S. Sassoon (ed.) *Women and the State* (London: Hutchinson, 1988), 45-71.

8 See Partha Chatterjee, *The Politics of the Governed: Reflections on Popular Politics in Most of the World* (Delhi: Permanent Black, 2004); Eric J. Hobsbawm, *Primitive Rebels* (Manchester: Manchester University Press, 1959); James C. Scott, *Weapons of the*

Weak: Everyday Forms of Peasant Resistance (New Haven: Yale University Press, 1985).

9 John Rawls, *A Theory of Justice* (Oxford: Oxford University Press, 1973).

10 Karl Marx, "Critique of the Gotha Programme," in *The First International and After* (Harmondsworth: Penguin, [1875] 1974), 339-359.

IV

Community in Restoration

Enlarging Civic Mentalities: The Roles of Moral Philosophy, Narrative Story-Telling and Social Theory

Rob Stones

In this paper I will address the issue of how we are to think about the character and role of civic virtues in the globalized twenty-first century. The very idea of civic virtue suggests, I would argue, a concern not only with the individual self, but also with the wider communities one belongs to, whether these be local, regional, national or global, or communities that crosscut these. At its most fundamental level, a virtuous concern with these communities and the people within them suggests that one wishes them well in a way that transcends one's own well-being and self-interest. Such concern can, of course, manifest itself in a number of forms, from the relatively passive through forms of low level but significant moral support to various forms of active civil or political assistance. Also, and more centrally to the present paper, the ability to translate a diffuse and vague concern for others into something more focused and meaningful is no simple task. I want to argue that the humanities and social sciences can play a major role in elucidating what such a translation requires, and thus in a strategy of education whose goal is to improve the quality of civic concern for others.

I want to argue that the capacity to engage adequately with the lives of others requires serious thought. This is serious thinking of the quality emphasised by Hannah Arendt when, in relation to the trial of Eichmann in Jerusalem, she spoke of the banality of the evil that had produced the holocaust. It was not wickedness or depravity, or some kind of metaphysical manifestation of evil, that most strikingly characterised Eichmann but, rather, what she called "thoughtlessness." Arendt's primary interest here, as has been noted by the creative and acute political philosopher Seyla Benhabib, was in the interrelationships between thinking—and its opposite, thoughtlessness—on the one hand, and moral judgement on the other.[1] Arendt wrote:

> Might the problem of good and evil, our faculty for telling right from wrong, be connected with our faculty of thought? . . . Could the activity of thinking as such, the habit of examining whatever happens to come to pass or attract attention, regardless of results and specific contents, could this activity be among the conditions that make men abstain from evil-doing or even actually "condition" them against it?"[2]

Serious thinking of this kind is at its best when it is not amorphous or vague, and in this paper I will outline a series of key categories and forms of conceptualisation, or, to put it differently, some structured ways of seeing, intrinsic to thinking seriously about others. What precisely is required from any individual or group by way of serious thinking will depend on where they are situated in the nexus of social roles, relations and moral predicaments. It will depend whether we are talking about political, economic, or other "elites," in positions of great power, or about individuals or groups with much more limited power, albeit still sufficient perhaps to be of import. It will depend also on which social domains we are focusing on. Serious thinking will vary in specifics depending on whether we are reflecting about practices in the fields of politics, the legal and judicial, journalism, the military, welfare, health, education, migration, trade, and so on. Deliberation and judgement in each of these will harbour particular demands, conflicts and challenges. We shall see that this requires a combination of general guidelines and a structured sense of how these can be related to more specific circumstances.

Following Benhabib's suggestive appropriation of a term taken from Kant and developed by Arendt, I will frame my guiding principles for the adequate exercise of civic virtues with the idea of "enlarged mentalities," which I will return to below. This frame and the guiding principles within it are fundamental as serious civic thinking demands disciplined commitment to training the mind to the point at which it has the capacities required for focused and meaningful engagement with others. The possession of these capacities is a precondition for the exercise of civic virtues, but the prior subjection of self to instruction in these capacities should also be seen as itself an intrinsic civic virtue. The failure of cultures and individuals to cultivate these capacities, and so therefore to surrender to thoughtlessness, should, in my view, come to be seen as morally unacceptable, as a breach of moral responsibility.

The guiding principles, or forms of conceptualisation, are drawn from an interdisciplinary combination of social theory, moral and political philosophy, and narrative story-telling. The guiding principles can thus be seen as the product of focusing these inputs onto the project of expanding the civic mentality. The domain of ethics and political philosophy is the first of these sources. Benhabib's work in this area, particularly that on communicative ethics and a deliberative model of democracy, provides some of the most important principles in this domain. As we shall see, this provides an initial ethical framework which sets standards for the civic imagination. These standards require from citizens a minimally adequate level of knowledge and understanding with respect to the situation and standpoint of relevant others. Secondly, the realm of narrative story-telling can often be decisive in stimulating the curiosity and emotional involvement of citizens to a point at which they care about, and can relate to, the lives of these others sufficiently to motivate them to engage further.

Narrative provides the bait for the hook which captures the citizen's interest and commitment to want to continue through the various steps and stages of civic engagement. Thus, narrative story-telling—and, in their own ways, a variety of other cultural forms—provides an important field of guiding sensibilities and ways of seeing that contribute something valuable and indispensable to the expansion of mentalities, or what, interchangeably, we can call "the civic imagination." Story-telling can broaden the ability of citizens to imagine, and relate to, the varied and complex lives of others, provoking empathy for aspects of these lives that are strange and previously unknown, but also for the things in those otherwise different human lives that are unerringly familiar. As it "pulls" people in to engage with the lives of others, story-telling can also convey details and insights about the experiences and being of others which are outside the scope and talent of moral philosophy and social theory. In turn, however, it needs the latter approaches because for all its strengths and ability to evoke sympathy, psychological and social complexity, and the palpable sense of "being there" with an emotional and phenomenological intensity hard to match in other genres: it cannot by itself provide the normative focus and criteria of judgement for which we look to moral and political philosophy; nor can it match social theory in its analytical and systematic treatment of varied situations, near and distant influences, power resources, counter-factuals, strategic possibilities, or the interaction between emotions, values, and practices.

The area of social theory, the third field, is invaluable in providing concepts that can systematically ground and anchor the lives of others within their social and historical context. C. Wright Mills's conception of the sociological imagination, coined in the late 1950s, is a fruitful starting point here as it emphasises the ways in which biographies are illuminated by being situated at the intersection of wider social structures and large forces of history. The converse, he notes, is also true, as we understand much more about the larger social and historical forces once we are able to relate them to the biographies of the people who animate them and are profoundly affected by them. There have been many useful and telling conceptual refinements in social theory since Mills' formulations that we can import to inform the guiding principles of enlarged civic mentalities. The tradition of structuration theory is central here in its ability to provide clarity and precision of focus to the analysis of the most immediate intersections and links between social and historical forces, on the one hand, and individual experience, on the other. This is a tradition to which I have an ecumenical approach and thus conceive more broadly than many,[3] and within which I include writings from such theorists as Pierre Bourdieu,[4] Anthony Giddens,[5] Nicos Mouzelis,[6] Andrew Sayer,[7] Ira J. Cohen,[8] William Sewell Junior,[9] Jeffrey Alexander,[10] Margaret Archer,[11] and Mustafa Emirbayer and Ann Mische,[12] amongst others. Key to structuration I regard the ontological principles that social life is made and remade by more or less skilled, knowledgeable and culturally immersed actors, and that there is a close but indeterminate relationship between the socially relational external world these actors inhabit and act within (what Alexander calls their external environments) and their own internal, phenomenological worlds, which are the most proximate influence on how they act. If we want to know, for example, why someone is so embittered, so without hope, or so committed to a cause, then we need to be able to link their states of mind to the social and historical conditions in which they have emerged. It is the task for social theorists to answer questions about the lives of others by learning as much as possible about anything that is relevant from within this nexus of being. The sociological imagination and the broad tradition of structuration, taken together, allow us to think about the configuration of social forces of many types, proximities and strengths that impinge upon, influence, and provide the context for, the lives of others we engage with emotionally and morally.

The emergent combination of all these constituents can serve to focus otherwise *ad hoc*, diffuse, accrued and case-specific knowledge of the lives of others. Space means that in this chapter I will only be able to indicate briefly, and in passing, what is involved in each guiding principle or form of conceptualisation. Nevertheless, in sketching principles with each of the three broad constituent threads in mind I am already implicitly indexing a relatively expansive range of literatures that are usually kept separate. This is partly because I want to bring out further the interdependency of these three themes from the humanities and social sciences, but also because I am confident that the variety of approaches have much in common with each other and that there is much to gain from indicating the points of mutual support they can provide. My intention is self-consciously one of synthesis, believing that all these writers are pushing in similar directions and that a richer picture of civic mentalities and civic virtues can emerge from a careful combination of their insights.

Perhaps one way of understanding what I want to achieve is by imagining a short one- or two-minute report on an evening TV news programme – possibly with a view of a saffron robed monk at the head of a march in the streets of Rangoon, or the swollen and bloodied face of a Cameroonian woman beaten by British guards as she was deported from the United Kingdom, or the sights of starving and traumatised children in Zimbabwe and Darfur, or gunfire in the streets of Ramallah or Bethlehem, or, moving away from the news, it may be something physically nearer such as the sight of someone sleeping on the streets as you pass by in one of the world's cities, or the knowledge that the father or mother of someone you vaguely know, somewhere else in your town, has lost their job, their house, their health, or their mind. We get a thin version of the world from the TV news, and the quality of the background knowledge or set of understandings we ourselves bring to what is given to us thinly there, and to what we notice or hear about in equally thin forms more locally, has to be very good if we are to make more of it than a series of fragmented, evanescent and barely meaningful sounds and images. No doubt it is true that more could be done with the presentation of news, and important and passionate debates about this are thankfully frequent and continuing. But there is a much larger horizon of meaning to be confronted here. For even the best possible presentation of news conceivable can only do so much. There are many other challenging sources of knowledge, information, and potential understanding to draw from—and this is behind the emphasis I have placed on the broad range of the arts, humanities and social sciences. In the process, it needs to be remembered constantly that neither all these other sources nor the two-minute TV news bulletin enter the minds of citizens in the same direct manner in which a serum from a syringe enters the bloodstream. Rather, the mentalities of the citizens who see, hear and read information matter greatly. It is, consequently, vital to create engaged and thoughtful civic mentalities, just as it is also essential that citizens have the conceptual capacities with which to direct and channel that engagement and thought, and to draw on these in making moral and practical judgements.

Our civic imagination, and hence the capacities that inform it, also has to be seen more holistically. We have to ask more of ourselves in this as in other ways. By drawing on and combining the varied storytellings, narrative forms and gestalt-type impacts of films, novels, art, documentaries and drama, as well as the typically thin fare of news, we can broaden out and deepen our sensibilities, just as the resources of social theory and moral and political philosophy can stretch us in other ways. We need to be able to think deeply and creatively within and across traditional spheres and boundaries, and to have the phenomenological capacities to reintegrate what we learn. To resist the sense of fragmentation and amorphous "noise" that too much unstructured information can create we need to make sure that our civic imagination is guided by renewed, considered and reintegrated conceptual forms, ways of seeing, that can help to produce sense rather than, to use Frederic Jameson's evocative and acutely accurate phrase, "cultural schizophrenia."[13]

Benhabib's relatively minimalist formulation of communicative ethics provides the underlying moral framework for the guiding principles I want to advocate. The phrase "enlarged mentalities" is employed in a specific way to indicate people's ability to grasp the standpoints of others and to take these into account in proposals, deliberations and arguments about what to do next.[14] This suggests a requirement to temper one's own views about what should be done with a conception of "what would count as a good reason for all others involved."[15] The strong ethical assumptions that form the basis for this are a *principle of universal moral respect* for all affected by a decision, and a *principle of egalitarian reciprocity* that all these people should consequently have the right for their perspectives and views to be adequately represented in the real or virtual conversation that leads up to it.[16] This means that the chronically excluded, the marginalised, and the silenced, all need to be listened to, and that everything within reason should be done to keep the conversation going. Benhabib notes that any citizen with a view about what should be done in a particular sphere of life should ideally be able to justify her preferences by articulating good reasons in public to everyone affected. The significance of the enlarged mentality arises from the importance given to the ongoing conversation this entails. For in order to successfully woo and convince others of her position the citizen articulating her own preferences and reasons must have the capacity to take the standpoints of all the relevant others. This capacity—to exercise a "reversibility of perspectives"—means being able "to identify the different viewpoints from which a situation can be interpreted and construed."[17] The citizen must have this capacity, which necessarily involves both narrative and interpretive skills, in order to be "able to state why what appears good, plausible, just, and expedient to her can also be considered so from the standpoint of all involved."[18]

In constructing this set of normative benchmarks Benhabib creates a synthesis of the Kantian inspired universalist model of moral conversation with the more Aristotelian and Hegelian emphases on, respectively, *phronesis* (practical wisdom in context) and *Sittlichkeit* (the centrality of a shared contextual ethos of background values and understandings). That is: i) contextual understanding of the situation and standpoints of others is provided by a structured set of background understandings, built up over time, and having their initial roots and resources in individuals' own communities of socialization and development (*Sittlichkeit*); whilst ii) a formal commitment of respect for the situations and standpoints of others (*Kantian universalism*); provides the basis and the repertoires for iii) the practical wisdom employed in situ, a practical wisdom that is attentive to social change and to challenges to, and elaborations of, contextual understandings by new voices, perspectives or messages emerging from the ongoing moral conversation. The continuing openness to the standpoint of others entails a "sensitivity to particulars which . . . is central for good and perspicacious judgement."[19] (*Aristotelian phronesis*)

It is important to register that this normative framework accepts that the participants may well have basic deontological commitments that they are not prepared to compromise or negotiate on. Benhabib herself, from her situated perspective, suggests that infringements of Kant's "negative duties"—not to harm, not to cheat, or otherwise violate the dignity of the moral person—remain morally impermissible. Likewise, prominent liberals from John Rawls to Will Kymlicka would regard their freedom and ability to "revise and alter their final ends"[20] as nonnegotiable. This is because we may come to question the value of our current ends and our essential interest in living a good life thus "requires an ability to revise our ends and to pursue those revised ends."[21] In a contribution to a volume on the *East Asian Challenge for Human Rights* (1999) the influential Canadian political philosopher Charles Taylor, influenced profoundly by Hegelian contextualism, has pointed to different but analogous commitments within cultures profoundly marked by Buddhist, Confucian, and Islamic religious traditions. Thus, for example, he points to a nonnegotiable commitment to nonviolence as a foundational pillar of an alternative reform Buddhism in Thailand, one he associates with the late monk Pra Phuttathat (Buddhadasa) and the social reformer Sulak Sivaraksa. In the process he notes the importance of interpreting the standpoints and background understandings of such others from a thoroughly immersed and holistic hermeneutic perspective. Thus, although the reform Buddhists of whom he speaks defend human rights, this stance, in contrast to western liberal conceptions of human rights:

> . . . isn't grounded on a doctrine of the dignity of human beings as something commanding respect. The injunction to respect comes rather as a consequence of the fundamental value of nonviolence, which also generates a whole host of other consequences (including the requirement for an ecologically responsible development and the need to set limits to growth). Human rights don't stand out, as they often do in the West, as a claim on their own, independent from the rest of our moral commitments, even sometimes in potential conflict with them.[22]

A consequence of different moral worldviews and principles within the communicative dialogue means that there is more to deliberative ethics than listening to and understanding the standpoints of others (as demanding as this can be), and then subsequently attempting to convince these others that one's own arguments should be accepted as "good, plausible and just, and expedient" from their (now understood) standpoints as much as from one's own. There is also the moment—which will be frequently encountered—when the other (alter) fails to be convinced and instead invokes her own argument about why you, as the initial agent-in-focus (ego), should be convinced by her moral argument, which should be accepted as "good, plausible and just, and expedient." At this point there is a stalemate. The most, and the best, each party can do at this point at the moralphilosophical level is to be as clear as possible about the moral precepts and principles they have employed to guide their argument, and to show how it has, and is, guiding their reasoning. Thus, for example, Ronald Dworkin, in his books *Sovereign Virtue* (2000) and *Is Democracy Possible Here?* (2006) sets out an impressively lucid statement of liberal principles, which he then uses as a basis from which to argue systematically for positions on issues ranging from terrorism and human rights, the defence of a tolerant secular state against a tolerant religious state, and the legitimacy of taxation based on an ex ante rather than an ex post principle of equality. In *Is Democracy Possible Here?* Dworkin states explicitly that his arguments involve the presumption that almost all Americans do in fact subscribe to (or could be persuaded that they did after serious dialogue and reflection) two fundamental liberal principles that he outlines in his opening chapter, principles that can both be seen as dimensions of dignity. The first of these principles is the intrinsic value of a human life and how it is lived, with the accompanying implication that it is not objectively less important how anyone else's life is lived.[23] The second principle echoes the "nonnegotiable" principles linked to Kymlicja and Rawls, above, and is that of personal responsibility "for realizing the success of his own life, a responsibility that includes exercising his judgement about what kind of life would be successful for him. He must not accept that anyone else has the right to dictate those personal values to him or impose them on his without his endorsement."[24] Truly in the spirit of deliberative communities, Dworkin consequently invites those who disagree with him—many in the conservative, Republican, ranks, he believes, subscribers to America's "red culture" as opposed to the "blue culture" of the Democrats—to state, explicitly, what alternative counter-principles they hold, and exactly what follows from these. If such a debate began it would then at least be clear for all to see what the disagreements were about. The points of conflict would be clear and so would the precise purposes of deliberation, argument and deepening mutual understanding.

Dworkin's is a strategy devised to rigorously expose the precise points of disagreement between participants in moral dialogue, but in its optimistic guise it is also a strategy aimed towards the idea of a convergence of viewpoints. This is not a convergence of viewpoints in which there would be no disagreement of conflict but a more limited one that would allow a meaningful debate about disagreements on how best to interpret fundamental values that all can either share or at least respect, rather than just the kind of angry and embattled restatement of entrenched positions that he believes to currently characterise US politics. The latter state, he believes, is dangerously close to a form of war between the trenches of two hostile armies. He is asking Americans to revisit their own deeper political and moral traditions and to bring these into direct confrontation with the surface views they hold on the major issues of the day. Perhaps counterintuitively, Charles Taylor, looking further afield, argues for something similar. Insisting on the significance of *Sittlichkeit* he argues that greater global convergence of moral positions will not come about, as some people suggest, through the rejection of traditions, but from what he calls "creative reimmersions" by different groups each *in their own* spiritual and cultural heritages, themselves of course not unaffected by international and global influences. Subsequent communication and dialogue *between* heritages need to take place on the basis of clearly articulated and rethought precepts. In turn, we can say, such precepts have to be brought into profound engagement with the perspectives, background understandings, and arguments of others espoused by the framework of communicative ethics. One can also imagine that such creative engagements *with quite other* positions and traditions could also have their own effects, in turn, on the creative reimmersions *within* cultures.[25] There will inevitably be conflicts and sticking points. However, for Benhabib the important thing is to keep the conversations going for as long as possible, thus requiring that all positions, however inviolable, need to be defended and argued for publicly and taking other people's standpoints into account. Her belief is that "only the very extreme cases of sexism, racism and religious bigotry consider any kind of argument futile or unnecessary."[26]

We have the first sketch here of the principles and conceptualisations that can guide the enlargement of civic mentalities, but it is also necessary to combine and integrate this initial framework with conceptual forms drawn from social theory. For Benhabib's emphasis on moral and political philosophy almost inevitably reproduces the relative weakness of most such approaches, which are too often uprooted from any close concern with the social, cultural, historical, political and economic specificity of particular cases. This, incidentally, is the reverse of approaches from the perspective of social theory and sociology, on the other hand, which have a tendency to adopt the rhetoric of the moral high ground without any effort to engage in the kind of sustained moral argument associated with moral and political philosophy.[27]

I will say more about social theory shortly. However, at the core of any widespread, popular strategy for the expansion of civic virtues, and certainly as a precondition for the kind of informed, respectful and egalitarian engagement with others demanded by Benhabib, is narrative story-telling and kindred cultural forms. By these I mean to indicate cultural forms that can provoke and vitalise the impulse to empathise with the pleasures, aspirations, values, anxieties, fears and sufferings of other human beings, near and far. Zygmunt Bauman invokes Levinas in arguing that one should rediscover a deeper moral impulse in order to open out to the Other in a selfless way that transcends, because it precedes, any thought of instrumentality or questions about "what is to be done."[28] This is a powerful moral injunction, and something like this "opening out to" is probably necessary in order to begin the journey of developing a truly moral concern for others. However, it isn't enough to meet the quite demanding requirements of a reversibility of perspectives required by the conception of enlarged mentalities. For the majority of mortals, those of us whose moral fibre falls short of the stuff of sainthood, need more to induce us towards a sustained and concerned engagement with others whose lives seem distant from ours, or with whom we are otherwise disengaged. Certainly one of the most powerful means of engaging an audience over a sustained period of time in the thoughts, actions and concerns of previously unknown or uncared for others is through narrative story-telling. By this I mean to include showing as well as telling. Of course, now, in our multimedia age, we are more often than not drawn into stories through both, through narratives which unfold and entice in simultaneous and juxtaposed sound and spectacle. The essence of the narrative form is the art of inveigling the audience to care what happens next, to want to turn the page, to see the next scene, to return to a thread of narrative, to see tomorrow's newspaper. Relevant to enlarged mentalities is that one of the most effective ways of inducing an audience to care what happens next is to make sure they care about the characters involved. The more one knows about a character, if their story is well told, then, all things being equal, the more one will care what happens to them. The responsibility of the story teller to engage us is consequently enormous. Richard Rorty, in similar vein, has famously argued that it is the novelist's and the ethnographer's "detailed descriptions of varieties of pain and humiliation . . . [that are] the modern intellectual's principal contribution to moral progress."[29] Rorty places great emphasis on detailed empirical descriptions of the lives of others, of accounts which are as concrete and historically specific as possible. In the spirit, if not the letter, of enlarged mentalities he argues such narratives can help us to notice our similarities with:

> . . . people whom we still instinctively think of as "they" rather than "us." We should try to notice our similarities with them . . . to see more and more traditional differences (of tribe, religion, race, customs, and the like) as unimportant when compared with similarities with respect to pain and humiliation.[30]

His argument is that the more richly imagined and contextualised other human beings, then the harder it is for us to disregard their human qualities, and so the more their existential states, particularly their suffering and humiliation, will matter to us. In his contribution to the Oxford Amnesty lectures of 1993, he cites a report from the Bosnia war zone in the early 1990s filed by the US journalist David Rieff, a report telling of murders and rapes committed by Serbians on Bosnian Muslims. Rorty's purpose is to demonstrate as best he can that these Serbs "do not think of themselves as violating human rights. For they are not doing these things to fellow human beings, but to *Muslims*."[31] Zygmunt Bauman has written something very similar about the dehumanising effects of bureaucratic distance and functional specialisation on the whitecollar perpetrators of the holocaust.[32] The moral to be taken from all of this is about the importance of not dehumanising, and the converse importance of feeding the humanising imagination with narrative based, richly detailed, and historically concrete stories. These need to be stories that can speak to us in our own pressured, fragmented, and often cold and blasé states of mind—as Simmel noted of the mental life of modernity's urban inhabitants around one hundred years ago[33]—by means of narrative tension and evocative similarity, familiarity or analogy, and then, whilst we are hooked, enlarging our mentalities, expanding our sense of solidarity.

Ken Plummer, a distinguished scholar of the micro processes of social interaction, has demonstrated, perhaps more than anybody else in the field of social theory, the social significance of story-telling and the close and sometimes unexpected relationship it can forge with questions of moral understanding and deliberation.[34] In *Intimate Citizenship: Private Decisions and Public Dialogues*, he notes the power of "dialogic projects" in the US, including the National Issues Forum, the Public Conversations Project, and the Public Dialogue Consortium, to enhance mutual respect through the exchange of standpoints and stories. On the intensely emotional issue of abortion, The Common Ground Network for Life and Choice, a wide-ranging network bringing together pro-choice and pro-life activists managed to ease tensions and foster common ground between opposing sides through the exchange of biographical information, life stories and narratives about how:

> . . . they came to their respective views. Discussions follow on matters on which both sides can agree, and this leads to working out more ways to improve communication, find common ground, and develop some kind of common politics. Finally, groups work together on achieving these goals. In dialogue-oriented groups that focus specifically on abortion, what often moves centre stage are the issue of adoption and the attempt to reduce sexual activity among teenagers. As one participant commented: "It was shockingly easy to identify issues we agree on, like the need for aid to pregnant women who are addicted to drugs, the need for better prenatal care, and the need to reduce unwanted pregnancy."[35]

The capacity of literature, film and other forms of narrative storytelling to evoke a deep sense of "being-there," emotional entanglements, and an almost involuntary moral involvement and urge to reciprocity, gives it the power to cast doubts on the sense of dividing moral and political philosophy from the depth analysis of social configurations. Stories, especially concrete and richly imagined ones that beguile the listener to utterly suspend her disbelief, lead one to identify intimately both with the intense predicaments and the routine conditions of human existence. The urgent practical responses that the empathetic and emotional immersion in these conditions often provokes would naturally seem to involve both moral judgement and social analysis. It is, therefore, important to build on the emotional force of stories to overcome the unhelpful division between morality and sociology. Benhabib's framework can play a pivotal role here. For on the one hand, its commitment to an interpretative-hermeneutic approach to the standpoints of others has a clear elective affinity with the world of narrative storytelling, while its explicitly normative justification and procedural principles provide a clear and systematic focus for the investigation of specifics within others' situations and standpoints. The latter emphasis, translating the interpretative-hermeneutic immersion in the stories of others into a systematic concern with specific aspects of their phenomenological world-views, expression of interests, and the forms and content of their argumentation over particular issues, has a similar affinity with the most refined and systematic social theoretical approaches to the standpoints and situations of the others within the moral conversation. All of these approaches need to be integrated in order to expand civic mentalities to the point at which they can follow through on the principles of universal moral respect and egalitarian reciprocity. Stories engage our civic and existential sensibilities; the normative framework—and the elucidation of the conflicting principles it can provoke—tells us what we need to know for the ongoing moral conversation to be adequate, and in this sense it helps to channel and focus the quest; and the conceptual and methodological armoury of the social sciences are required to get a more systematic grasp of the various actors' in situ understandings, beliefs and motivations, and also the ways in which these are related to the configurations of social forces that surround and inhabit those actors, only some of whose contours and influences even they themselves will fully comprehend.

It is thus the combination of the three approaches that can genuinely enlarge citizens' mentalities. Social theory can add further elements—technical, more specific and not yet elaborated—to an understanding of what needs to happen in order to optimise the process of civic engagement. To begin with, it is necessary to emphasise that there is an inevitable homology between the guiding conceptual forms required for the expansion of civic mentalities in theorists and intellectuals, on the one hand, and those required by citizens in general, from elite to everyday actors. Perhaps this is self-evident, but I feel it is worth spelling out nevertheless. That is, both theorists and citizens need to learn how to employ what I will call *civic ethno-methods*—a sequence of conceptual understandings and methodological procedures taken from the social sciences. *Civic ethno-methods* can be thought of as the cumulative relevant conceptual and practical know-how distilled from the repeated and sequential use of the civic mentality in response to the predicaments of different people in different times, places and situations. They indicate a harnessing of the sociological tradition of ethnomethodology founded by Harold Garfinkel to the domain of civic virtues. Garfinkel's work grew out of the phenomenological tradition and was particularly influenced by the German social theorist, Alfred Schutz, who argued that human beings' perceptions and apprehensions of the world depended upon:

i) typified notions of the characteristics of objects, including other people;
ii) and of how typical actions and sequences of actions were carried out ("recipe knowledge").

Garfinkel noted that in performing social practices human agents routinely and skilfully brought these typifications into interaction with the empirical sense data of immediate encounters, akin to what Benhabib referred to above as "sensitivity to particulars." These are the moments or social change, and of new voices and new details of lives being lived that practical wisdom is attentive to. I want to argue that we can think of the various forms of conceptualisation or guiding principles that need to structure and inform enlarged mentalities as typified notions in exactly the same way. These guiding forms will be typified conceptualisations of (or, more technically, working ontological conceptions of) both objects, including individual and collective agents and typical patterns and forms of organisation and social processes; typifications that are central to the understanding of moral and social life.

Notwithstanding what I have said about the need to ask a lot of ourselves it would clearly be too much to ask of citizens that they retain an interest and a recollection of the details of each and every civic issue and problem they encounter. However, what it is possible to ask, and for a responsible culture to teach, is the acquisition of a series of conceptual typifications of objects and processes. In other words, enlarged mentalities should involve, in the first instance, an expansion of moral and social conceptual capacities. The precise ways in which these typified capacities are applied in specific situations will depend upon skill, judgement and circumstance. Of course, some details of some situations and circumstances will be retained within the background understandings of memory, and these will coexist with sparser, more typified understandings. Adopting a term borrowed from Karl Mannheim, Garfinkel referred to the methodical processes that lie behind these and other kinds of skilled practical competencies as the "documentary method of interpretation" whereby a) more enduring background knowledge, including typifications of objects and a range of practices; and b) the empirical sense data of a specific situation, are brought into dialogue with each other.[36] A graphic and familiar example of this taken form the ethnomethodology literature involves the categories of interpretation used by coroners in attempting to interpret the empirical evidence to decide whether or not a reported death is a suicide. In one case an old woman was found gassed in the kitchen of her English cottage. Typifications of suicides were routinely invoked—loneliness, poverty, rugs and towels stuffed under the doors and window casements—and matched against the evidence.[37]

With respect to the exercise of civic virtues the background *knowledge* of the lives and standpoints of others that any citizen acquires over time will inevitably be structured by a series of typified conceptualisations. Within an enlarged civic mentality these typifications will be informed by conceptualisations taken from moral and social theory. In an analogous "documentary method of civic interpretation" these typifications, built up over time and relatively enduring, need to be brought into a dynamic relationship with the detailed empirical realities of new, particular cases (building up what I refer to below as "conjuncturally-specific knowledge") in order to make decisions, judgements and evaluations in the civic sphere. The challenge for a project of enlarging civic mentalities would be to work towards richer and more adequate stocks of typified conceptualisations of civic formations and their constitutive elements whilst also cultivating the sensibilities and capacities required to combine this background knowledge with the empirical sense data of specific situations. The ethical rigour in this approach lies, to a great extent, in the genuine commitment to build up typifications through which to seek out and respect the standpoints of others as opposed to any algorithmic blueprint or more detailed set of universalist maxims that apply always and everywhere no matter what the views and situations of those involved. This means that the developed and expanded civic imagination needs always to be brought into contact with the specifics of a situation, and with the plurality of standpoints within this, before any practical judgements are made about what should be done. Citizens will have to be prepared to do some work here in a manner parallel to the so-called etcetera clause in ethnomethodology. Garfinkel's lay actors always have a lot of additional work to do in order to competently pull off even the most mundane of everyday social interactions. Invoking the etcetera clause here refers to their having to draw on their index of past experiences, including their conceptual frameworks, to provide the extra information required to interpret the typically elliptical sentences and social actions they are presented with by others in the course of interaction. Citizens, likewise, need to undertake the extra work and graft in employing both relevant conceptualisations and other relevant background information to interpret the situations, events, actions and problems they are presented with. As with the moral outrage encountered by Garfinkel's students when they transgressed the expectations of others that they would do this extra work, I would argue that we should cultivate a sense of moral outrage and reprobation as the appropriate response to lazy and indolent judgements in the civic sphere. Deciding how to judge this will be no easy matter, but the expanded conception of enlarged mentalities should provide a more adequate starting point for debate over this.

It is useful here to consolidate the notion of civic ethnomethods through integration with Pierre Bourdieu's notion of habitus,[38] which can itself be seen as an extension of the phenomenological tradition within social theory we have already introduced. Habitus indicates the set of conceptual and practical understandings and dispositions, including typifications, that are learned, and then stored up, over time, and which can then be transposed to new situations. Analogies between similar but different situations and the transposability of appropriate forms of knowledge and understanding from one situation to another are key to the strengths that habitus affords. As Bourdieu puts it, stocks of knowledge, understandings, "matrices of perceptions (and) appreciations," and embodied practical know-how can be drawn on to address diverse situations "thanks to analogical transfers of schemes permitting the solution of similarly shaped problems."[39] It is worth noting that, notwithstanding the strength and usefulness of his notion of habitus, Bourdieu is not as systematic or insightful as Garfinkel, or other major figures in the broader micro-sociological tradition such as Goffman, about the in situ, contingent, processes of judgement. This is important in that these other writers are ultimately better equipped to inform analyses of those moments signalled by what we have called the "documentary method of civic interpretation," whereby judgement and performance, and trial and error, bring background understandings into complex manoeuvres of engagement with empirical sense data (including the empirical sense data acquired through attentive listening in processes of ethical deliberation) through fine grained phenomenological practices of synthesis and positioning, checking for normative cues and warning signs, or engaging in quick thinking improvisation or "repair work."[40]

Benhabib's synthesis of the Kantian inspired universalist model of moral conversation with the more Aristotelian and Hegelian emphases on *phronesis* and *Sittlichkeit* is made possible, I would argue, by a view of human understanding that rests upon a particular manifestation of the documentary method of interpretation. That is, a structured background understanding of the situations and standpoints of others, which is built up over time (*Sittlichkeit*), is structurally equivalent in Benhabib's argument to Garfinkel's background understandings or to Bourdieu's habitus. This habitus within the deliberative citizen is, when placed within the structuration tradition, immediately thought about as marked by social coordinates of various kinds and is itself explicitly differentiated and pluralized in a way that roughly mirrors the differentiated and pluralized social context in which it has been formed. It is from this embedded and complex vantage point, together with the moral commitment to an enlarged civic mentality, that the citizen commits to represent to her or himself "the multiplicity of viewpoints, the variety of perspectives, the layers of meaning which constitute a situation."[41]

As we have already noted, the continuing openness to the standpoint of others which is central to Benhabib's communicative ethics entails a "sensitivity to particulars which . . . is central for good and perspicacious judgement."[42] However, this sensitivity requires more conceptual guidance than just that provided by background understandings of *Sittlichkeit* and the resort to a rather vague and amorphous deployment of *phronesis* or practical wisdom. Social theory can provide further conceptual refinements to guide us to a better grasp of the standpoints and situations of others located at the intersection of particular social and historical forces. Some refinements will be more relevant to some dialogues and disputes than others, but each of them has significant implications for the nature, status and nuance of the viewpoints, mentalities and/or situations of dialogic participants. Space means I can only provide the roughest sketch of just a few of these, but even so the case is so compelling that this should be enough to convince even the most reluctant sceptic that the concepts of social theory have an indispensable role to play in guiding any civic mentality worth its salt. So, there are additional distinctions to be drawn within habitus between the relatively enduring and embodied skills, dispositions and orientations adapted and drawn on in a range of immediate practical settings, and the broader cultural dispositions and discourses that inform such actions, dispositions derived from the various "ways in which the social world is constructed for the actor by previous interpretations and collective languages."[43] There is a process of, primarily prereflective, interpretation and transmission whereby the general, historically specific, cultural discourses and constructions inform and colour those background understandings and typifications, illuminated by ethnomethodology, that themselves inform practical actions in situ.[44]

A profound understanding of the other in a moral dialogue requires, on the one hand, a grasp of relevant aspects of these general cultural discourses involving local, regional, and national collective memories, identifications, and commitments of plural kinds, and on the other hand, a grasp of the dynamics by which these discourses are employed, through analogical transfers in addressing, for example, the exigencies of a particular moral or ethical dispute. This frame can be deepened further through attention to Andrew Sayer's compelling recent volume *The Moral Significance of Class* (2005) in which he shows how values and emotions should be included much more vigorously within our conceptualisation of habitus. He shows just how powerful emotions and mixed feelings such as "envy, pride, resentment, anger and—in extreme situations as a consequence—consternation" can be, arguing that they " . . . are not to be counterposed to reason but are evaluative judgements about circumstances beyond people's control which are likely to affect their well-being and their commitments."[45] Sayer argues persuasively, and through sustained systematic argumentation, that emotional values, cares, concerns and commitments need to be connected to gender, class and cultural logics (and, following Taylor, we could add those of religion), but that these complexes then need to be reconnected to concrete circumstances. Unless we can grasp what circumstances these cares are about, and how exactly they affect the actor's well-being, we will not genuinely be able to understand why and how specific commitments, loyalties, inequalities and grievances—whether these are of class, gender, or religion—matter to the people they affect.[46]

Other refinements within social theory critical to the understanding of the pressures and influences moulding and buffeting the standpoint of others include distinctions between the more enduring and transposable background understandings and conceptual typifications of habitus, on the one hand, and, on the other hand, the dimension of "conjuncturally specific knowledge" within the viewpoints of particular others in relation to their immediate situations, including their strategic apprehension of all aspects of that context.[47] To this can be added Nicos Mouzelis's notion of the "positional"—which is itself derived from the notion of role examined at length by many sociologists, perhaps most perspicaciously by Robert Merton[48]—which is the site that provides the institutional location for the specific demands, pressures, duties, loyalties and such like experienced by actors, and which are never far away in deliberations and arguments about what to do next. Reflections upon the roles or positions of others will always involve a combination of reflection on relevant aspects of their habitus and also their conjuncturally specific knowledge. Mouzelis, informed now by the tradition of symbolic interactionism makes a further distinction, one that is self-evidently useful when thinking about openness and process within communicative ethics. This is between the positional and those "situational-interactional" moments within which actors perform, improvise and respond as sequences unfold in all their varying degrees of seeming inevitability and contingency.

There are several other conceptual typifications of the meso and macro spheres that can be drawn upon. Each of these can help one to think about how particular actors, or events, usually encountered superficially in a snapshot, as in the proverbial TV news, can be situated with respect to causal influences, pressures, facilitating conditions and constraints on their lives. At the mesolevel, between the individual actor and the large forces of history and epochal social structures, all actors are caught up in a web of relationships which can be influencing, moulding, facilitating or constraining depending on circumstances. Individual action always takes place in the midst of ongoing social relations, practices and structures. This mesolevel of the institutionalised relationships from within which individuals confront the strategic terrain of possibilities and constraints has been developed in various ways by a number of theorists and writers. Each of them emphasises the specialisation of roles and tasks, mutual interdependences, and relational structuring. This work includes the conceptual elaboration by symbolic interactionists of interactive webs of people "doing things" and Norbert Elias's general idea of figurations of mutual interdependencies,[49] and Ira J. Cohens's notion of positionpractice relations which include, amongst other things, the theorisation of vertical and horizontal sets of power relationships and interdependencies.[50]

There is a complex relationship between the micro, the meso and the kind of macro level indicated by Mills's sociostructural and historical forces. The civic imagination needs to take this on board as it engages with the experiences, emotions and sufferings of definable individuals. Thus—to finish with the kind of graphic example that could profitably be produced for each of the concepts outlined above—in a documentary film from the early 1990s, *The Good Woman of Bangkok*, we are presented with the story of Aoi, a woman from a rural village in Udon in the northeast of Thailand (*Isan*) who works in the sex trade in the Patpong area of Bangkok, an area filled with go-go bars, night clubs and massage parlours catering for Western tourists. The macro environment for this story is absent from the film, although we do receive intimations that not everything was as Arcadian in the region of Isan from which she had migrated, intimations that subvert the idealised stories told to themselves by typical clients. The close engagement with Aoi, through observational-interactional scenes, together with the insistent intimations that social deprivation, economic poverty and subtle forms of gender oppression were "push" factors behind Aoi's "choice" of work and destination, draw us in to her situation and its dilemmas. If, invoking the etcetera clause of the civic imagination, we do the extra work of providing a macro context for Aoi's biography we quickly learn, amongst other things, that millions of women migrated from Isan to Bangkok in the 1980s and early 1990s as Thailand's economic boom took hold, most of them finding their way into various service jobs in the tourist industry, many of them into the sex trade.[51] These macro movements of people were not unrelated to movements in the international financial and trade markets, to balance of payments issues—within which invisible earnings from tourism were immense, and to the policies and demands of the IMF, the World Bank and private international creditors. Enlarged civic mentalities need to grapple with the intersections of these forces if they are to truly understand not only the standpoints but also the situations of the others in the communicative dialogue. The ontological, typified concepts that apply at each of the micro, meso and macro levels will inevitably need to be complemented by more crosscutting substantive concepts and ways of seeing that are specific to the particular case and question at hand. In Aoi's case the substantive guiding categories will be, amongst others, those related to gender and to migration, with the latter then including within it: conceptions of initial migration; processes of settlement; uneven and combined adaptation to the environment of destination; and complex issues of memory and belonging; each fine-tuned by empirical application, debate and counter-debate, and all potentially informed by the more general and abstract kinds of ontological refinements outlined above.

I started by saying that the realisation of civic virtues in the globalized twenty-first century will require enlarged civic mentalities and serious thinking. I set out my intention to justify this statement by drawing from moral philosophy, narrative story-telling and social theory in order to present a set of guiding categories and forms of conceptualisation required for citizens to genuinely engage with the lives of others. In the course of the exposition an important paradox emerged which I will now make explicit. This is that the guiding principles that emerge from the three strands I have focused upon are typifications which carry with them the danger of reification, what Theodor Adorno called identity-thinking,[52] the risk that they will turn into dehumanising stereotypes, simply mapped onto a myriad of circumstances with no respect for the differences and specificities between them. This is because in order to act as guiding principles they have to possess the quality of being more or less generalisable across situations—this is the basis which allows their transposability. At the same time, their very rationale is to alert citizens to the variety, difference, complexity and *specificity* of particular life situations within particular social and historical circumstances, and to allow all of this to be systematically understood. And, finally, the greatest of the rewards from resisting the dangers of reification, it is within the specificity that one often finds something akin to the universal—elements of sameness, familiarity and "shockingly easy" empathy at the very heart of less consoling, more disquieting, elements of the strange and unfamiliar. Thus the typifications, which at their worst and most reified can give way to dehumanising stereotypes, are needed to provide civilizing structure and principles to civic mentalities, but they must continually be questioned and held in creative tension with a parallel openness and attention, humanising and demanding, towards specificity. I will expand and elaborate this project in subsequent publications, but for the moment I hope I have succeeded in convincing at least some readers not only that the project is a worthwhile one, but also to adopt it, in part or whole, and to play their own part in taking it further.

Acknowledgements: I would like to thank my discussant, Jae-Ryong Song, for insightful comments which allowed me to clarify a number of points in the original paper. I'd also like to thank Bob Jessop, Woosung Huh, and Joo Hyoung Ji, for responses to the paper that forced me to think about the content of the paper from new and productive angles.

Notes

1 Seyla Benhabib, "Judgement and the Moral Foundations of Politics in Hannah Arendt's Thought," in Seyla Benhabib (ed.) *Situating the Self: Gender, Community and Postmodernism in Contemporary Ethics* (Cambridge: Polity Press, 1992).

2 Hannah Arendt, *The Life of the Mind*, vol. 1 *of Thinking* (New York and London: Harcourt, Brace and Jovanovich, 1977); quoted in Benhabib, op. cit., 122.

3 Rob Stones, *Structuration Theory* (London: Palgrave Macmillan, 2005); Rob Stones, "Action and Agency," in John Scott (ed.) *Sociology: The Key Concepts* (London: Routledge, 2006); Rob Stones, "Theories of Social Action," in Bryan Turner (ed.) *The Blackwell Companion to Social Theory*, 3rd ed. (Oxford: Blackwell, 2008).

4 Pierre Bourdieu, *Outline of a Theory of Practice* (Richard Nice, trans.) (Cambridge: Cambridge University Press, 1977).

5 Anthony Giddens, *New Rules of Sociological Method: A Positive Critique of Interpretative Sociologies* (London: Macmillan, 1976; Cambridge: Polity Press, 1993); Anthony Giddens, *Central Problems in Social Theory: Action, Structure and Contradiction in Social Analysis* (London: Macmillan, 1979); Anthony Giddens, *The Constitution of Society: Outline of the Theory of Structuration* (Cambridge: Polity Press, 1984).

6 Nicos Mouzelis, *Back to Sociological Theory: The Construction of Social Orders* (London: Macmillan, 1991); Nicos Mouzelis, *Sociological Theory: What Went Wrong? Diagnoses and Remedies* (London: Routledge, 1995).

7 Andrew Sayer, *The Moral Significance of Class* (Cambridge: Cambridge University Press, 2005).

8 Ira J. Cohen, *Structuration Theory: Anthony Giddens and the Constitution of Social Life* (London: Macmillan, 1989).

9 William Sewell, "A Theory of Structure: Duality, Agency and Transformations," *American Journal of Sociology* 98 (1992): 1-29.

10 Jeffrey Alexander, *Action and Its Environments* (New York: Columbia University Press, 1988); Jeffrey Alexander, Bernhard Giesen, and Jason L. Mast, eds., *Social Performance: Symbolic Action, Cultural Pragmatics, and Ritual* (Cambridge: Cambridge University Press, 2006).

11 Margaret Archer, *Realist Social Theory: The Morphogenetic Approach* (Cambridge: Cambridge University Press, 1995).

12 Mustafa Emirbayer and Ann Mische, "What is Agency?" *American Journal of Sociology* 103 (1998): 962-1023.

13 Fredric Jameson, "Postmodernism, or the Cultural Logic of Late Capitalism," *New Left Review* 146 (1984): 53-92.

14 Cf. Hannah Arendt, "The Crisis in Culture," in *Between Past and Future: Six Exercises in Political Thought* (New York: Meridian, 1961); Seyla Benhabib, op. cit., 53-55; Seyla Benhabib, "Toward a Deliberative Model of Democratic Legitimacy," in Seyla Benhabib (ed.) *Democracy and Difference: Contesting the Boundaries of the Political* (Princeton, NJ: Princeton University Press, 1996), 72; Seyla Benhabib, *The Claims of Culture: Equality and Diversity in the Global Era* (Princeton, NJ: Princeton University Press, 2002), 115.

15 Seyla Benhabib, *op. cit.* (1992), 71-72.

16 *Ibid.*, 29.

17 *Ibid.*, 54.

18 Seyla Benhabib, *op. cit.* (1996), 72.

19 Seyla Benhabib, *op. cit.* (1992), 53-54.

20 John Rawls, *A Theory of Justice* (Cambridge, MA: Harvard University Press, 1971), 641.

21 Will Kymlicka, *Liberalism, Community and Culture* (Oxford: Oxford University Press, 1989), 34.

22 Charles Taylor, "Conditions of an Unforced Consensus on Human Rights," in Joanne R. Bauer and Daniel A. Bell (eds.) *The East Asian Challenge for Human Rights* (Cambridge: Cambridge University Press, 1999).

23 Ronald Dworkin, *Is Democracy Possible Here?: Principles for a New Political Debate* (Princeton, NJ: Princeton University Press, 2006), 9-17.

24 *Ibid.*, 10, and see 17-21.

25 See Charles Taylor, *op. cit.*, 140; cf. Mark Cladis, *A Communitarian Defence of Liberalism: Émile Durkheim and Contemporary Social Theory* (Stanford, CA: Stanford University Press, 1992), 227-239, on internal moral critiques; Rob Stones, "Rights, Social Theory and Political Philosophy: A Framework for Case Study Research," in Lydia Morris (ed.) *Rights: Sociological Perspectives* (London: Routledge, 2006), 140-142.

26 Seyla Benhabib, *op. cit.* (1992), 33.

27 See Rob Stones, *op. cit.*

28 Zygmunt Bauman, *Life in Fragments: Towards a Postmodern Morality* (Oxford: Blackwell, 1995), 64-65.

29 Richard Rorty, *Contingency, Irony and Solidarity* (Cambridge: Cambridge University Press, 1989), 192.

30 *Ibid.*,196 and 192

31 Richard Rorty, "Human Rights, Rationality, and Sentimentality," in Stephen Shute and Susan Hurley (eds.) *On Human Rights: The Oxford Amnesty Lectures 1993* (New York: Basic Books, 1993), 111-134.

32 Zygmunt Bauman, *Modernity and the Holocaust* (Cambridge: Polity Press, 1989).

33 Georg Simmel, "The Metropolis and Mental Life," in David Patrick Frisby and Mike Featherstone (eds.) *Simmel on Culture* (London: Sage, [1903] 1997).

34 Ken Plummer, *Telling Sexual Stories: Power, Change and Social Worlds* (London: Routledge, 1995); Ken Plummer, *Intimate Citizenship: Private Decisions and Public Dialogues* (Seattle and London: University of Washington Press, 2003); Ken Plummer, "Rights Work: Constructing Lesbian, Gay and Sexual Rights in Modern Times," in Lydia Morris (ed.) *Rights: Sociological Perspectives* (London: Routledge, 2006).

35 Ken Plummer, *op. cit.* (2003), 93.

36 Harold Garfinkel, *Studies in Ethnomethodology* (Englewood Cliffs, NJ: Prentice Hall, 1967).

37 See J. Heritage, "Harold Garfinkel," in Rob Stones (ed.) *Key Sociological Thinkers*, 2nd ed. (London: Palgrave Macmillan, 1999; New York: New York University Press, 2008); Atkinson J. Maxwell, *Discovering Suicide: Studies in the Social Organization of Sudden Death* (London: Macmillan, 1978).

38 Pierre Bourdieu, *Outline of a Theory of Practice* (Richard Nice, trans.) (Cambridge, Cambridge University Press, 1977), 78-87 and 159-171.

39 *Ibid.*, 83.

40 Cf. Martina Löw, "The Constitution of Space," *European Journal of Social Theory* 11 (February 2008): 25-49; Erving Goffman, *Behaviour in Public Places: Notes on the Social Organisation of Gatherings* (Glencoe: Free Press, 1963); Erving Goffman, *Interaction Ritual: Essay on Face-to-Face Behavior* (Garden City, NY: Anchor Books, 1967).

41 Seyla Benhabib, *op. cit.* (1992), 53.

42 *Ibid.*, 53-54.

43 Isaac Reed and Jeffrey Alexander, "Culture," in Bryan S. Turner (ed.) *The Cambridge Dictionary of Sociology* (Cambridge: Cambridge University Press, 2006), 114.

44 Cf. Jeffrey Alexander, *Action and Its Environments* (New York: Columbia University Press, 1988); William Sewell, "A Theory of Structure: Duality, Agency and Transformations," *American Journal of Sociology* 98 (1992): 1-29.

45 Andrew Sayer, *op. cit.*, 133.

46 *Ibid.*, 51.

47 Rob Stones, "Strategic Context Analysis: A New Research Strategy for Structuration Theory," *Sociology* 25.3 (1991); Rob Stones, *Sociological Reasoning* (London: Palgrave Macmillan, 1996), 98-99 and 105-158; Rob Stones, *op. cit.* (2005).

48 Robert Merton, "The Role-Set: Problems in Sociological Theory." *The British Journal of Sociology* 8 (1957): 106-120; Robert Merton, *Social Theory and Social Structure* (New York and London: The Free Press, 1968).

49 Norvert Elias, *What is Sociology?* (London: Hutchinson, 1978).

50 Ira J. Cohen, *op. cit,* 207-213. Also see Nicos Mouzelis, *op. cit.* (1991); Nicos Mouzelis, *op. cit.* (1995).

51 Pasuk Pongpaichit and Chris Baker, *Thailand's Boom!* (Chiang Mai: Silkworm Books, 1996); Ryan Bishop and Lillian Robinson, *Night Market: Sexual Cultures and the Thai Economic Miracle* (London: Routledge, 1998).

52 Theodor W. Adorno, Negative Dialectics (E. B. Ashton, trans.) (New York: Seabury Press, 1973).

From *Homo sapiens* to *Homo symbious*

Jae Chun Choe

Recently, I have been asked rather frequently to provide a biologist's view of our society. I was reluctant at first because I was not sure if I should dare to invade the territory—conventionally occupied by sociologists. However, having considered the issue further, I have in the end decided to accept the invitation.

I am a sociobiologist. Sociobiology was defined by its founder Edward O. Wilson (1975) as "a systematic study of social be-havior of animals including humans." Thus it seems reasonable for a sociobiologist to review social trends in *Homo sapiens*, a representative species of highly social animals. The theoretical background of sociobiology is the Darwinian theory of evolution.[1] Scholars, such as evolutionary biologists, who specialize in looking back in history to understand chains of cause and effect can certainly look forward into the future, because the future unfolds in a shape largely determined by inertia from the past and present.

1. Sociocultural Trends in the Early 21st Century

I can summarize my thoughts about future trends in human societies by defining our time as the age of the following six different, but certainly not mutually exclusive, changes:

The Age of Climate Change
The Age of Ageing
The Age of Women
The Age of Mixing
The Age of Creativity and Innovation
The Age of Science and Technology

Hardly anyone can argue against the idea that we are living in the age of unprecedented climate change. Until a few years ago there existed a diversity of opinions among climatologists as to whether the climate variation we are experiencing is real and caused by human activities.[2] However, I believe that there is now nearly unanimous agreement among experts that the world climate is indeed changing and that we, the human species, are the main causal agent.[3] The Norwegian Nobel committee has recently awarded the former U.S. Vice President Al Gore and the Intergovernmental Panel on Climate Change (IPCC) the 2007 Nobel Peace Prize "for their efforts to build up and disseminate greater knowledge about man-made climate change, and to lay the foundation for the measures that are needed to counteract such change." In addition to this rather monumental testimony, the issue of climate change has also been the main theme of the Davos World Economic Forum for the past three years in a row. Climate change or global warming in particular will have wide-ranging and fundamental effects on the natural world and human societies. I will return to this topic later in my discussion.

Nearly all developed countries are currently facing the problem of societal ageing. To biologists this poses a set of unusual and interesting research questions. What is the evolutionary significance of population ageing in the human species? Why have humans evolved to live well past their prime reproductive age, while in the rest of the natural world organisms die off as soon as their reproductive life stage is over? In addition to raising evolutionarily interesting questions, ageing has tremendous socioeconomic implications. In my recent book, *Living Two Lives from a Single Seed* (2005), I called for sweeping social changes such as the abolishment of the mandatory retirement system. Changes as a result of societal ageing are inevitable in nearly all aspects of our lives, including the national pension system. The need for innovative change is perhaps greater in Korea than any other country in the world, because Korea has the fastest rate of population ageing, mainly due to the world's lowest birth rate.

As more women come out to the professional world, the complexion and rules of society have changed rapidly. Such change is as apparent in Korea as in the West. Although the roots of sexual inequality run deep in this country, I dare to declare that the age of women has begun in Korea in all practical senses. I am not saying that Korea is a country of sexual equality, but the movement for psychological and institutional changes in the right direction is well underway. There will be a fair amount of trial and error but in the end, Korea will benefit greatly from the active participation of women in all social sectors.

The Korean myth of pure bloodlines has been a subject of recent international attention. Almost ten years ago, I suffered from intense personal attacks by the country's spiritual leaders when I published an article in which I argued that we, the Koreans, have our origins in mixed blood lines. Many intellectual and political leaders in the country expressed strong objections to my assertion and voiced their concerns that this idea could damage the national morale. Nonetheless, the recent human genome analyses of Korean people conducted by several genetics laboratories revealed the fact that indeed we have rather diverse genetic origins. To those that would argue that these revelations about our history could damage our national pride, I wish to argue that genetic mixing will only make us stronger and more beautiful. Indeed, the world is going through a period of fullscale mixing: not only genetic mixing between different peoples, but also exchanges of ideas, culture, and technology.

In a special feature article published on 16 March 2006, the news magazine *Time* calls the present time "the greatest age of creativity and innovation the world has ever known." It goes on to say that "the authorship of innovation is shifting from the Few to the Many." Science and technology allow creative ideas to become innovative machines. The 21st century promises to be another amazing era of science and technology.

2. A Tale of Two Caves

Having reviewed major sociocultural trends in contemporary human societies, let me now focus on a single issue, that is, the issue of climate change and related environmental problems. I chose to talk about this issue not only because it is a topic related to the theme of this symposium but also because it is likely to have the greatest impact on our lives.

Thinking of the main theme of this symposium from a Darwinian perspective, let me offer you a scenario I concocted to illustrate the ecological status of our species within the earth's ecosystem. I call it "A Tale of Two Caves" to parody a Charles Dickens' novel "A Tale of Two Cities." Let's all travel back to the Stone Age.

There were two families living in separate caves. One family had a head of household who was rather relaxed and tolerant. As a result, its family members were not concerned about preserving the nearby natural environment. They hunted and gathered as many animals, nuts and fruits as possible, often far more than they could consume at once. They were not concerned about keeping their cave clean, either. They threw away food leftovers and other waste within the cave and its vicinity.

On the contrary, the head of the other family was very picky and intolerant as far as cleanliness was concerned. Not only were the family members not allowed to litter within the cave, but also they were frequently called away from other activities for general house cleaning, to the point at which they did not have enough time for hunting and gathering. They also suffered a higher rate of mortality, particularly at night when they were forced to leave the safety of the cave in total darkness whenever nature called.

Let me now ask you a question based on this simulation. Which family do you think would have been more prosperous and left more offspring? My answer is the first family. Edward O. Wilson[4] argued that we have a genetic predisposition to love and protect nature. He termed such human nature "biophilia." However, I disagree with Wilson. I do not think that we are genetically programmed to protect the natural environment. In fact, I believe quite the opposite. We are a species who are expert in the exploitation of natural environments, as our astonishing population growth rates illustrate. It makes logical sense that the first family had more to eat and could produce more babies while the second family wasted their precious time protecting their environment, which was good for the environment and for the human population as a whole, but very costly to the family members themselves. Leaving more offspring and making them to survive to produce the next generation is the key to the success in an evolutionary game. When the first family found their cave too filthy and their immediate environment depleted of resources, they would then move to another cave in another area. Our problem now is that there are no more empty caves left for us to move to if we wish to evacuate from our own contaminated cave.

While I am in an imaginative mood, let me introduce another scenario. I am going to make an important announcement right now: "I am running for the presidency." (Let me make it absolutely clear that this is a scenario I introduce only to illustrate my point. I am NOT running for the presidency and don't want the media to get excited about this fictitious press conference.)

Our former president, Mr. Moo-hyun Rho, pledged during his campaign that he would move the capital to a new city, and he tried to keep his promise against all odds. Although I am not at all in favor of the transfer of the capital, I do agree with him about the fact that Seoul is too crowded to function properly as the capital. So, I have decided to improve upon his plan. Here is my campaign promise: I will transfer the whole country to a new place. If Seoul can no longer function as the capital of Korea, then in my opinion, the Korean peninsula is also too crowded to properly harbor a nation. Once I become president, I will hold a cabinet meeting and ask my cabinet members to help me decide to which country we should move our nation and its people. Let's say that we decided to move down under to Australia. What will the Australian government say when they receive the official letter notifying them of the plan to transfer our entire nation to their territory? There are no more caves uninhabited by humans on this planet, and the natural tendency to protect biodiversity and natural habitats is not in our genes. There is only one earth and we must learn to survive together on this planet.

We tend to think of Mother Nature as being all tooth and nail, based on Darwinian ideas of the "struggle for existence" and "survival of the fittest." It is true that competition for limited resources sets the stage for natural selection, but Darwin never suggested that all-out competition is the only way of life. He also discussed mutualism or symbiosis at length.

Who are the most successful creatures on this planet by numbers? Insects, of course. Who, then, are the most successful creatures by weight? Plants, or more specifically, flowering plants. How have these creatures become the dominant life forms on earth? They worked together. Insects help to pollinate plants and flowering plants provide nectar in return. Mutualism or symbiosis can be more powerful than reckless competition.

At this critical juncture of human history I would like to suggest *Homo symbious* as a new image for our species in the 21st century. Far too many of us think that we are no longer part of Nature. However, we are actually an integral part of many ecosystems. Think about the current ecological roles of domesticated cereal plants such as rice, wheat, barley, corn, and so forth. They were no more than weeds in the field until we began cultivating them about 10,000 years ago. Now they are the greatest landowners on this planet. How have they become so successful? The answer lies obviously in their symbiosis with the human species. In terms of scale, we are clearly among the most effective symbiotic species on earth. If we are to survive much longer on this planet, we need to humble ourselves by abandoning the name *Homo sapiens*, which means "wise human beings" and reestablish ourselves as *Homo symbious*.

Broadly defined, symbiosis is a relationship of two or more different organisms living in close association. It does not always mean a mutually beneficial relationship. *Homo symbious* maintains close associations not only with other species but also among ourselves. The concept of *Homo symbious* is social as well as environmental. *Homo symbious* strives to work for coexistence with other species and global peace among all people. The concept of *Homo symbious* is similar to that of *Homo reciprocus*, if not a little broader.

Although the biological basis for the idea of *Homo symbious* comes from such disciplines as ecology and evolutionary biology, it is also firmly rooted in ancient philosophies of both the West and the East. Aristotle had called the human species "social animals," and *The Analects* (論語) of Confucius talks about the spirit of *hwa-i-bu-dong* (和而不同), which can be translated into "affable but not adulatory" or more plainly "harmonious but not identical." Confucius has said, "The superior man is affable, but not adulatory; the man is adulatory, but not affable." The spirit of *Homo symbious* will enable us to build a global community in harmony with other nations as well as with Nature.

3. Consilience as a Way for the Future

Natural ecosystems are among the most complex systems in this world, and at the moment, natural ecosystems are out of balance. As a countermeasure against this unprecedented environmental and social crisis, I propose that the academic world adopt the idea of "consilience" or the unification of knowledge (*sensu*).[5] Consilience is a concept introduced by the 19th-century British philosopher William Whewell (1794-1866) in his book, *The Philosophy of the Inductive Sciences* (1840). It was then shelved for one and a half centuries before being resurrected by E. O. Wilson. While translating Wilson's book, I put "consilience" in a vessel called *tongseop* (統攝). Consilience, or *tongseop*, means deriving a common system of explanation for facts and theories by bridging the gaps between different branches of learning.

The branches of learning that we know today did not, in fact, exist until the Middle Ages. Throughout much of the Renaissance, most scholars were still typically equipped with "specialized" knowledge in almost all areas of learning. This is why we still use the term "Renaissance man" to describe an erudite person with broad knowledge in many fields. Knowledge, or rather, methods for exploring knowledge, generally began to split in the 16th century. It cannot be denied that this reductionism has contributed to tremendous advances in knowledge. By the end of the 20th century, however, we discovered that the entirety remained elusive even when we put together all the parts that we had so zealously sought.

Consilience or the unity of knowledge means the interlocking of cause-and-effect explanations across different disciplines, as for example, between physics and chemistry, chemistry and biology, and more ambitiously, biology, social sciences, and the humanities. Nearly half a century ago, Sir C. P. Snow lamented that there was a deep chasm between science and the humanities. Truth moves in ways that do not respect the strict borders that we draw to divide the branches of learning, because the divisions of learning do not exist in Nature. Academic disciplines were created by man for the sake of convenience in chasing the traces of truth under different circumstances. However, truth crosses over the borders of academic disciplines, at times in straight lines and at other times drawing gentle curves, while most modern truth-seekers are confined within the artificial boundaries of their own disciplines to struggle with but a fraction of the whole truth. Now, the time has come for us to cross these interdisciplinary borders freely and bravely to follow the trajectory of the truth. It is time that we eliminated the cumbersome process of passport checking every time a researcher attempts to cross academic borders.

Wilson[6] declares that the greatest task of the human mind was, and still is, the union of natural sciences and the humanities. I hope that the 21st century will be the century when we finally achieve this union. A successful union of the humanities and natural sciences will eventually lead to the consilience of all disciplines of learning. Only then may we begin to lay the groundwork for the establishment of a harmonized global community.

Notes

1 Charles Darwin, *On the Origin of Species by Means of Natural Selection* (London: John Murray, 1859); Charles Darwin, *The Descent of Man and Selection in Relation to Sex* (London: John Murray, 1971).

2 Patrick J. Michaels, ed., *Shattered Consensus: The True State of Global Warming* (Rowman & Littlefield Publishers, 2005).

3 Al Gore, *An Inconvenient Truth: The Planetary Emergency of Global Warming and What We Can Do About It* (Rodale Books, 2006).

4 Edward O. Wilson, *Biophilia: The Human Bond with Other Species* (Cambridge, MA: Harvard University Press, 1984).

5 Edward O. Wilson, *Consilience: The Unity of Knowledge* (New York: Vintage Books, 1998).

6 *Ibid.*

Sublime Beauty and Productive Circulation: The Role of a Third Space

Teckyoung Kwon

Reconsidering the dynamics between eye and mind, Maurice Merleau-Ponty quotes Valery and says that the painter "takes his body with him."[1] Does this quotation have anything to do with the reversed hierarchy between eye and mind, as Merleau-Ponty put the word, "mind" after "eye" in the title of his essay? Traditionally, we have learned that soul is more precious than body, and mind is more important than eye. The reason that he suspects the traditional hierarchy of mind over eye lies in the phenomenological view of the world and human beings, that is, we are born into the world. The world was here before me and will be here after me. It looked at me and will look at me. As I am looking at a tree, the tree is looking at me too. The premise that we are born into the world and that "the world is made of the same stuff as the body" (163) leads us to rethink the science and revisit Hegel's dialectics. Defining the human being in its relations with the world, Hegel says that life is a slave and death is the master, which adduces the primacy of body over mind.[2] We should consider his phenomenology of spirit seriously again due to our condition of being trapped in this technological world, beset by huge problems, namely, atrocious human relations and damaged natural environment. Those two phenomena remind us that science alone does not resolve the violence and lessen global warming. Recent technology has arrived at almost its summit in the history of the Enlightenment project, but our happiness is falling apart.

Many thinkers have diagnosed the reason that human happiness has not increased in proportion to the development of technology, notably including such materialists and psychoanalysts as Marx, Nietzsche, and Freud. Those early skeptics against Enlightenment have prevailed over the world these days, inspiring us to create a new paradigm of knowledge after almost thirty years of political corrections in the name of cultural studies. It has brought us visible differences in the field of gender, race, and sexuality, as we all know. However, the intellectual atmosphere changed after 9/11, after the terrorism awakened us to the fact of how much hatred lies hidden, apart from those liberal movements of cultural studies. Once more phenomenology is brought up and aesthetics accompanies it for a new system of knowledge. In such a context, this paper, broadening its scope towards the restoration of a proper relationship between nature and man, will explore the following possibility: phenomenological aesthetics for the proper relationship between the earth and men, through the reestablishment of the subject and the other in our community. In fact, the problem of communication in society is not really a different matter from that of the circulation of nature, and aesthetics is the best means of communicability in society because of its "subjective universality," as Kant once said. Though Kant was the apostle of Enlightenment and some of his ideas are not relevant to posthumanities, as Adorno had already noted, he is still the springboard from which we repeatedly start for a critique of beauty.[3]

For an alternative idea to the present society, saturated by speed and unlimited competition in the digital world, my effort will focus on the three numbers against the two numbers of the digital system. On this matter, the aesthetic phenomenology, or phenomenological aesthetics, of Merleau-Ponty and Jacques Lacan, among others, will be helpful due to their concern for the intersubjectivity between mind and body, the world and the earth. This paper will try to draw attention to productive circulation for the normal communication between the world and human beings in our posthuman times. We assume that "a third space" will be the prompt for the establishment of the proper relationships between man and nature, not to mention man and society.

The research begins with the explanation of the words "a Third" or "mystery of passivity" in the phenomenology of Merleau-Ponty and directs us to the Lacanian third space after briefly visiting the aesthetics of Kant and Hegel. The discussion will be focused specifically on their conceptions of Beauty and the Sublime. The comparison of those thinkers will reveal what the traditional minds ignored and the followers merely revised.

1. The Significance of "a Third" or "a Space" in the Phenomenology of Merleau-Ponty

Criticizing science for its possessive and absolute view of the object, Merleau-Ponty returns to Descartes not to adopt his cogito, but to elucidate why Descartes did not want to mention the pictorial. Painters know how our body works when they represent nature, since they experiences the motion of phenomenon with their vision: "Vision is attached to movement." The eye is the window for the mind to see through because we only see by looking at things, and "my body simultaneously sees and is seen." (EM, 162) As the blind man can see with his cane, vision is also a part of matter. Thus, the undividedness of the sensing and the sensed repeatedly echoes in Merleau-Ponty's phenomenology of perception. Materializing our mind, he puts much emphasis on things: "things have an internal equivalent in me." (EM, 164) As far as we see the world with our eyes, which are not divided from the world itself, we cannot see the world with objective vision. This is the reason that painting or the visual image is closer to the real than science, and why painters like Cezanne tried to capture the moment of nature in the midst of the moving thing. The moment a painter tries to penetrate into things, he realizes that he has been penetrated by things. As a result, the things that he is looking at are nothing but images, images that fly from him like shadows or ghosts: "Light, lighting, shadows, reflections, color, all the objects of his quest are not altogether real objects; like ghosts, they have only visual existence." (EM, 166) According to Merleau-Ponty, we cannot see things without "a third eye," something visible and invisible:

> Shall we say, then, that we look out from the inside, that there is a third eye which sees the paintings and even the mental images, as we used to speak of a third ear which grasped messages from the outside through the noises they caused inside us? (EM, 165)

From those passages we can estimate the reason that Descartes avoided talking about pictures and aesthetics in his schema of *Cogito*. He was not able to count a third eye or a third ear, which becomes inevitably an obstacle to his transparent subject, even if he says that "the blind see with their hands." The impossibility of distinguishing between body and soul, and what sees and what is seen, obviously caused an embarrassment for him, so Descartes turned from the real quickly: "the abyssal Being that Descartes opened up and so quickly closed again." (EM, 177)

Contrasting science to painting, Merleau-Ponty posits the painter's mode of representation at a higher position than that of technology, with such words as "prehuman way of seeing things" or "technique of body." Furthermore, he adds another, more interesting sentence to those expressions: "painting is an art of space." (EM, 184) What is the "space" that he is talking about? Is that the same word with a third eye or a third ear? In fact, Merleau-Ponty's following remark pushes us to the corner of puzzling: "Painting makes us see the same way in which we actually see the thing itself, even though the thing is absent. In particular, it makes us see *a space* where there is none." (EM, 172) What is the space that is seen when it is not there in fact? According to him, a space is a "place of body" when we see a landscape on the flat picture of the Renaissance period. When we look at that picture, a flat thing, we see the depth that is "a third dimension derived from the other two." (EM, 172) Where does this depth come from, a third, or a space that we see on the two flat dimensions? Isn't this the excess of body that the soul believes is its own house? In other words, the experience of body is a surplus that the soul can't control, own, or manipulate. Because of the excess of the body's experiences, we see "a mystery of passivity" (EM, 175) in the center of things. This is the space, an abyss where God exists. Because of this abyss, we are prohibited from the space, being allowed only a space, a particle of the Thing. We are engrossed in the world, surrounded by the things instead of standing in front of them. Technology can never control things and the world, not to mention human bodies. God (The Empty Space) forbids us from manipulating those things.

Reading "Eye and Mind" leads us to the ultimate question of what God's abyss signifies or what kinds of functions a space or a third takes in posthuman society. Or rather, we may ask how we can get the vision of the "prehuman" way of looking at the material world, which is inseparable from our body. On this matter, Merleau-Ponty does not examine further but stops at the point of the suggestion that we are in an imperative need of changing our way of perceiving the world.[4] He ends up his essay with the following remark:

> If no work is ever absolutely completed and done with, still each creation changes, alters, enlightens, deepens, confirms, exalts, recreates, or creates in advance all the others. If creations are not a possession, it is not only that, like all things, they pass away; it is also that they have almost all their life still before them." (EM, 190)

Does this passage sound like the intimate repetition adduced by Nietzsche, and Freud? Yet, the differences should also be examined carefully. The phenomenology of Merleau-Ponty rests on the number 3, the remains that is a third space, unlike Nietzsche's dichotomy of Apollo and Dionysus, or Freud's dynamics of the Pleasure Principle and the Reality Principle. We now turn to the analysis of the beautiful and of the sublime, illustrated by Kant, to make that distinction clear. Does Kant acknowledge a third space produced by the mediation between the beautiful and the sublime?

2. Kant's Dichotomy of the Beautiful and the Sublime

In the schema of Kant's philosophy, the number 3 is his favorite as he developed his idea into 3 categories in which the third critique functions as the bridge between the other two, pure reason and practical reason. He even categorized pleasure or taste into 3 different levels: the agreeable, the beautiful, and the good. The agreeable is the basic feeling, or lower desire of animals as well as humans. Its taste is solely subjective, as cows have a taste for plants while people favor bread and butter. The next level of taste is that of the beautiful. Its taste is also subjective, yet it leads us to reflection without being mediated by a concept. Thus, its taste is based on disinterestedness, while the taste of the good, which is the third level, is based on interestedness being mediated by a concept. Independent of interest, the beautiful leads us to the higher state of mind from the lower state of animal-like senses. Of the three delights, Kant presents the beautiful as a medium to bridge the agreeable to the good. The good should be achieved on the basis of senses, not by a concept but by experiencing the beautiful form. Thus art is to harmonize the agreeable, which is solely the subjective, with the good, which is solely universality:

> The result is that the judgment of taste, with its attendant consciousness

> of detachment from all interest, must involve a claim to validity for all men, and must do so apart from universality attached to objects, i.e., there must be coupled with it a claim to subjective universality. (CJ, 9)

On his emphasis on the function of art as "subjective universality," Kant suggests "a finality of form" as a necessary step for cognitive power: "The sole foundation of the judgment of taste is the form of finality of an object (or mode of representing it)." (CJ, 13) A good form provides the audience with the harmony of senses and reason in order to reach the reflection. The well-organized design or composition is a product of a genius. In his discussion of the medium of aesthetics, Kant seems to repeat Aristotle's *Poetics*, and in his emphasis on the genius who provides aesthetic harmony, he reminds us of Plato's poet, Ion, even though he broadens the scope of pleasure and the function of art in much more detailed, expository writing. In doing this, he insinuates the importance of Reason shedding light on the senses for reflection. Though he focuses on the 3 categories of delight as he classified our faculties in his three critiques, he does not go further for a third space. If we look into the analysis of the sublime, we can find where his concern is: it is on the distinction as well as comparison of two human faculties, Understanding and Reason.

Kant defined the sublime as the feeling experienced when Reason confronts the unconquerable violence of Nature such as huge storms, earthquakes, or terrible floods. Such an experience is a terrible and fearsome phenomenon itself, yet we feel sublime as our soul is purified behind a window or in a shelter. Kant characterizes this sublime feeling as a formless, incorrect, negative, or even distorted pleasure, compared to the beautiful, which is a formal, correct, and positive pleasure. Yet, the sublime belongs to the higher faculty as Reason, rather than to the beautiful as Understanding:

> Sublimity, therefore, does not reside in any of the things of nature, but only in our own mind, in so far as we may become conscious of our supe-

riority over nature within, and thus also over nature without us (as exerting influence upon us). (CJ, 27)

For Kant, Reason is the real source of imagination, a creative power of culture against primitive forces. Consistently, elaborating the primacy of Reason over Understanding, Kant does not pay any attention to the bridge between the beautiful and the sublime, opening the road into a dualism of these two faculties.

Another reason that Kant did not attend much to linking the two faculties as one, the sublime beauty, as Lacan does later, is because of his belief in man's faculty as higher than that of nature or animals. Indeed, he repeats that art, a product of reason, is more precious than Nature itself, a product of God: "an ideal of beautiful flowers, of a beautiful suite of furniture, or of a beautiful view, is unthinkable . . . ." (CJ, 19) Kant was essentially a man of the Enlightenment who could not deny the power of cognition, which should be obtained not by a beauty that is free and at large but by an ideal beauty fixed by a concept of "objective finality." (CJ, 16) If he accepts natural beauty on the same level as formal beauty, he becomes a man who denies the products of human beings, Culture and Civilization. Instead, he elaborates a great deal on why we need a genius as an ideal creator inspired by the grace of God. Only a genius can represent natural beauty according to the will of God: "Fine art is an art, so far as it has at the same time the appearance of being nature." (CJ, 34) Consequently, Kant seems to be ambivalent toward nature. On the one hand, he urges the higher status of cognitive power over a natural state; on the other hand, he asks that cognitive power should resemble the spirit of nature, implying that man should imitate the natural pattern of the cycle, a useful source on which today's ecological aesthetics can rely. As long as the cognitive power is a gift of God, a work of fine art cannot be independent of God's creation, Nature. Thus, Kant remarks that: "Nature proved beautiful when it wore the appearance of art; and art can only be termed beautiful, where we are conscious of its being art, while yet it has the appearance of nature." (CJ, 34)

Even though Kant did not define exactly what relations could be possible between natural beauty and aesthetic beauty, we can estimate it as the power of representation confronted by natural violence, as observed in the analysis of the sublime. If this estimation is right, the sublime could be the power of imagination, or sublimation, creating the work of art in the pattern of nature. Moreover, we can even formulate a third space from this context, if we push Kant's vision of the sublime to Reason, a creative inspiration for a mode of representation by imitating the cycle of nature. And also on the basis of such a productive circulation, we can formulate the function of communication in our society that Kant touched upon, yet did not fully develop in his comment on the effect of fine art. The effect of fine art is one of "advancing the culture of the mental powers in the interests of social communication." (CJ, 34) Though Kant enjoys the number 3 in his intellectual schema, he never really tries to formulate it as a third space, as we observed in his dichotomy of the beautiful and the sublime, in his dualism of Understanding and Reason. We should wait until Hegel devises a concrete, simple model in which two differences are tied together into one dialectic.

3. Plato Mediated by Aristotle: A Scientific Model of Hegel

In the history of art theory, it was Hegel who first applied a scientific method to art by means of mediation. With respect to the traditional reflections of art, he criticizes them as abstract and urges a more refined and concrete methodology. Consistently observing the dialectics of lord and bondsman, known as "master and slave dialectics," presented in his early days, Hegel enlarges the concept of the self-conscious in the field of fine art. In this way, Kant's universal mode of representation is mediated by a concrete medium of social as well as historical perspective. In his *Phenomenology of Spirit*, nothing exists by itself without being dependent on the other: the conscious exists as self-consciousness after being recognized by the other. In his schema of knowledge, life exists only after being recognized by death, just as a work of art exists in the dialectical relations of content and form. Communication and intersubjectivity are the key issues in Hegel's paradigm: "If consciousness fashions the thing without that initial absolute fear, it is an empty self-centered attitude." (PS, 119)

In this respect, Hegel analyzes the tragedy of Antigone into a good example of his dialectics to reveal how the subject, or selfconsciousness is born after the death of consciousness. In her struggle with Creon, who represents the law, Antigone suffers a great deal in her claim for the burial, entailing disaster for the kingdom. Her strife and conflict with Creon are escalated until they are finished and reborn as self-consciousness. Both of them are destroyed to be reborn into a true self-consciousness by means of negation: Creon was a bondsman, while Antigone was lord, and Creon should be negated by Antigone. To be the public law in society, Creon needs to suffer negation by Antigone's private claim of love for her brother. A genuine social subject should be born after the pure subject has been mediated by the other, a kind of death. Thus, recognition by death is indispensable for the ideal state of Spirit. The same goes for Art. In the Hegelian dialectics of master and slave, nothing stands by itself without being mediated by the other, whether it be death, society, history, or another individual, as we see in his interpretation of the tragedy of Antigone. With one simple concrete device, Hegel solves not only the Kantian dichotomy of Understanding and Reason, but also that of Plato's Idea and Aristotle's Form.

In the dialectics of form and content, Hegel adopts Plato's Idea as spirit or content and mediates it with Aristotle's Form. He also uses Kant's sublime as the energy for Romantic art, which is the perfect synthesis of Idea and artistic Form. First of all, he posits form and content in the context of time and place. The form of art reflects the spirit of the specific time and place because time and place (i.e., the world) are lord, while form is a bondsman. Form should be mediated by the other, a specific time and place:

> Now every man is a child of his time in every activity, whether political, religious, or scientific, and just as he has the task of bringing out the essential content and therefore the necessary form of that time, so it is the vocation of art to find for the spirit of a people the artistic expression corresponding to it.[5]

Based on the premise that Art is the supreme medium to represent the Absolute Spirit, Hegel regards the form of art with respect to history and to Romantic art of the 19th century in German literature as the highest form of art. The primitive form of art in the East is defined as "the symbolic," where the unity of the human ideal and the external world was not appropriately achieved. They are incompatible with each other because external nature was dominant over the human spirit. The second form is "the classic," where the spirituality of the human mind grows to the unity of spirit and the external world as seen in the Greek gods. The final form is "the Romantic art," in which spirit transcends the external world and reaches the highest point, the Absolute Spirit. In this way, Hegel, who believed firmly in the progress of history, as Kant did, thought that art is superior to nature since history as well as the form of art continually develops towards Absolute Spirit. In Romantic Art, which deepened the spirit of humanity in its own inwardness, the world in general was at first posited as negative.

It was Hegel who first tied the theory of the subject with aesthetic theory on the basis of negation. Self-consciousness is also a form of art that does not exist without being negated by society as well as history. Hegel also solved the discrepancy between the Cartesian *cogito* and paintings, the issue brought up by Merleau-Ponty, and at the same time, the dualism of Kantian Understanding and Reason. For the first time in intellectual history, the theory of the subject became equal to the theory of art by means of the dialectic of master and slave. In spite of Marx's criticism of Hegel as one who sacrificed material base for Spirit, Hegel was the founder of the Marxist criticism in which the base of interpretation should rest upon a social and historical background. Indeed, Hegel's mediation theory is echoed later even in Adorno, who examines the function of art in terms of a paradigm shift; "However strong historically the tendency towards a recurrence of pleasure may be, pleasure remains infantile when it asserts itself directly and without mediation."[6] Hegel's contribution to productive circulation through negation is so great that any later theory related to negation or intersubjectivity could not possibly escape his influence. Yet, his limitation lies exactly in that contribution because the paradigm shift following the Romantic spirit turned in the opposite direction, especially after Nazism and in the era of post-humanities.

Probably only a scientist still believes that history is progressive. Another limitation to Hegel's dialectics is the fact that it cannot produce any alternatives to the digital system wildly oscillating between "on" and "off." The phenomenology of spirit in the Enlightenment era did not allow the impossibility of "a third," an excess of the Earth for a productive circulation. In a word, his negation did not leave any possibility to be enlarged into Nature. He just stopped at the point of Romantic Art, where negation as world (in this case, society and history) was born.

For a productive circulation for the Post-Enlightenment Era, we should jump to Lacan's aesthetics, renewed after Nietzsche, Marx, and Freud, who were thought to be immensely indebted to Hegel's negation and did not really surpass him in terms of a third space.

4. A Third Space Mediated by the Earth: Lacan's Sublime Beauty

Lacan investigates the tragedy of Antigone in the opposite way from

Hegel. As a springboard to escape from the immense influence of Hegel's negation, Lacan reads it differently. Hegel posits Antigone's private love as a negation against Creon's law, in the result of which, a more mature public law as well as a more mature individual would be born. First of all, Lacan focuses on the sublime beauty of Antigone rather than on Creon. What makes her beautiful and sublime to the audience? Indeed, she is so cold and even cruel in her persistent claim for burial, and her drive for death almost renders her an irresistible force of Nature. She reminds us of the will of formidable Nature to destroy everything, as Kant described in the analysis of the sublime. Then, what happens to her, one who becomes the image of such a beautiful woman of faith to such a degree that no one suspects her nature as a lord of terror? Penetrating her death drive, Lacan sheds a light on Sophocles' drama, step by step, until it shows how language makes her a sublime beauty and how Creon's prohibition ensures that beauty. Her image is solely created by the dialogue and by the chorus on the stage protecting her from the repression of law. The crueler the law, the more sublime her image becomes, and thus she finally turns out to be an object of desire. In short, her image is solely created by the prohibition of law and the signifier of the symbolic.

The essence of the sublime is nothing, a death drive, a destructive force as Kant analyzed in the sublime. The fact that her beautiful image was solely created by words releases Lacan from the influences of Kant and Hegel. Kant did not view the violent power as an innate human necessity, a death drive, as Lacan did. Lacan therefore said that Kant did not know *jouissance*, as did most thinkers about Kant in their aesthetics. In this new vision, obviously helped by Freud's instinct, Lacan links the split of the sublime and the beautiful as one domain of sublime beauty. Antigone's sublime beauty as the effect of the law signifies the crucial point that she is mediated by the symbolic, the kingdom of Creon, without which she remains nothing. As a symbol of the primitive power of destruction or death, she is nothing without law: "I can only know of the Thing by means of the Law . . . for without the

Law the Thing is dead."[7] Here, we see a complete reversal from Hegel's dialectics of Lord and Bondsman. In Hegel's formulation, Creon is the bondsman who should be reborn after the strife and death wrought by Antigone, the lord. In other words, to be reborn into the social subject, into self-consciousness, Creon needs to be exposed to the negation of Antigone. What about Lacan, who also posits Antigone as master and Creon as slave? Unlike Hegel, whose concern was to construct an image of man in the Enlightenment Era, an ideal image embodying the Absolute Spirit, Lacan attended more to the destructive power of Nature as well as its inwardness in human nature. So, he thought Antigone should be negated by the symbolic of Creon, as the death drive should be repressed by the Name of Father. *Jouissance* was nothing if it was not mediated by the symbolic:

> Tragedy is that which spreads itself out in front so that the image may be produced. When analyzing it, we follow an inverse procedure; we study how the image had to be constructed in order to produce the desired effect. (S7, 273)

In the Lacanian domain, Antigone is mediated by Creon in order to become a fantasy object of desire, which is also the process for Creon to become the fantasy subject in his kingdom. Accordingly, Lacan equalizes the subject of desire to aesthetics. If the schema of "Creon with Antigone" is for the theory of art, "Kant with Sade" will be the theory of subject, or vice versa. Both theories are based on the sublimation (or repression) of *jouissance* to become a sublime subject as well as a desirable object. In other words, the faculty of sublimation becomes no more a necessity for the subject than for beauty in the posthuman era because the destructive power prevails over the world, and it exists in the form of the other. As long as sublime beauty is achieved only not by elimination of its destructive power but by its sublimation, the good is obtained from evil in a disguise. We cannot get rid of evil because it is always already there as a part of good.

From this clue, we can renew our perspective for our age when technological culture proceeds far enough to the point that the fear of terror becomes a part of our daily life.

As we know, Lacan posits Antigone as an excess of Creon, by which a surplus results, and this works as a cause of circulation. This surplus is nothing but a third space, a mystery of passivity in Merleau-Ponty's terms. However, Lacan never puts the name Antigone before Creon, as we see in "Creon with Antigone" or "Kant with Sade." What happens to him?

We can seek the answer from the Lacanian dynamics of the repressed subject and the desirable object. In the formulation of desire, $<>a. Even if the power of destruction exceeds the law, the law should be the subject, not to be trapped in perversion, not to be the slave of the object. For sanity, the subject should keep distance from the sublime beauty, unless it becomes an object of jouissance and disappears, resulting in *aphanisis* of the subject.[8] So, the formulation turns out to be reversed as a<>$, a perversion. In perversion, the subject changes into the slave of the object, losing distance from the object and finally being exposed to sado-masochistic destruction. Being negated by law, the essence of an image of sublime beauty is an empty space, which is always ready to return to its essence. If it is pushed too far, whether it be an erotic object, a commodity object, or even the aim of life, the sublime beauty falls apart into Nothing, a thing-in-itself, the Earth. That is why Lacan says that you enjoy your symptom or traverse your fantasy, and insists that our happiness solely depends on how we treat a third space, "the Real." The sublimated beauty is a metaphor for new humanity, and psychoanalysis becomes no more a field of psychology than is ethics or aesthetics.

5. Conclusion: The Encounter with Sublime Beauty

Hegelian negation, mainly by society, does not include recognition by the realm of Nature. Also, Nature is not regarded as an excess to be mediated by the symbolic order. So, the subject is not aware of the truth that a tree has been seen by you when you see the tree. Before you see, it has been already there. Neither intersubjectivity between nature and man nor a surplus, a third space, a cause of productive circulation, exists in Hegel's phenomenology. Doesn't this resemble a digital system of 0 and 1, where there is no place for a third space, as seen in perversion? There is a memorable episode about a sardine can. One day, Lacan and a friend were walking along a beach and saw a sardine can floating on the water far from them. His friend said that the can was not looking at him while he saw it. But Lacan knew that the can also looks at them. (S11, 95) The episode implies that the gaze works even among things, and that mankind is a part of things. This regard of things, or body, is in fact the crucial concept that Lacan shared with Merleau-Ponty under the name of "gaze." Shouldn't we also share the same perception with them, as long as the thing-in-itself remains beyond our grasp? We cannot see the moment we are born, yet things see it. Nature, the excess, the Real is the impossible, because it is visible and at the same time invisible: only eye can see the depth in the flat painting. Eye is an excess of mind. Only in this new perception can we keep an intimate relationship with things and preserve ourselves surrounded by Nature. As one of the Oriental thinkers, Lao-tzu sang in ancient times, in *Tao-Te-Ching* :

> Thirty spokes fit together into the hub of a wheel, and so the usefulness of a carriage depends upon what is nonexistent (the hollow centre). Clay is molded to make a hollow vessel, but the vessel's usefulness lies in its emptiness. A dwelling is made by cutting out doors and windows. And so the usefulness of dwelling depends upon empty spaces. Thus, what exists is advantageous, and what does not exist has its use.[7]

How can we explain our contradictory behavior when we are never aware of being seen by a tree, in spite the fact that we definitely see depth, a third dimension, in the two-dimensional picture? As Merleau-Ponty noted, we are not standing in front of Nature but surrounded by Nature, and this new phenomenological perspective will protect us from "perverse" (destructive) circulation. Only a symbiotic relationship with Nature can save our community, too.

Notes

1 Maurice Merleau-Ponty, "Eye and Mind," *The Primacy of Perception* (Carleton Dallery, trans.) (Evanston: Northwestern University Press, 1964), 162. Hereafter cited as EM.

2 G. W. F. Hegel, *Phenomenology of Spirit* (A. V. Miller, trans.) (New York: Oxford University Press, [1807] 1977). Hereafter cited as PS.

3 Immanuel Kant, "The Critique of Judgment," in Richard Kearney & David Rasmussen (eds.) *Continental Aesthetics* (Malden, MA: Blackwell, 2001). Hereafter cited as CJ.

4 Maurice Merleau-Ponty, *Phenomenology of Perception*, 2nd ed. (New York: Routledge & Kegan Paul, [1962] 2002), 239. "We perceive the world with our body. The body is a natural self and, as it were, the subject of perception."

5 G. W. F. Hegel, "Lectures on Aesthetics," in Richard Kearey and David Rasmussen (eds.) *Continental Aesthetics: Romanticism to Postmodernism* (New York: Blackwell, 2001), 121.

6 Theodor Adorno, *Aesthetic Theory* (New York: Routledge & Kegan Paul, 1970 [German], 1984 [English]), 21. "In periods following an age of asceticism, pleasure becomes an emancipatory force."

7 Jacques Lacan, *The Ethics of Psychoanalysis* (New York: Norton, 1992), 83. Abbreviated as S7.

8 Jacques Lacan, *The Four Fundamental Concepts of Psychoanalysis* (New York: Norton, 1978), 216. Abbreviated as S11.

9 Howard D. Smith, "Tao-Te-Ching LXIV," in *The Wisdom of the Taoists* (New York: A New Directions Book, 1980), 52.

References

Reinventing Humanity
Walter Reese-Schäfer

Axelrod, R. 2000. *Die Evolution der Kooperation*. 5. Aufl. München: Oldenbourg.

Berman, P. 1996. *A Tale of Two Utopias. The Political Journey of the Generation of 1968*. New York and London: W.W. Norton & Co.

Etzioni, A. 1996. *The New Golden Rule: Community and Morality in a Democratic Society*. New York: Basic Books.

———. 1997. *Die Verantwortungsgesellschaft. Individualismus und Moral in der heutigen Demokratie*. Frankfurt, New York: Campus.

Gutschker, T. 2002. *Aristotelische Diskurse. Aristoteles in der politischen Philosophie des 20. Jahrhunderts*. Stuttgart, Weimar: Metzler.

Hegel, G. W. F. 1970. *Wissenschaft der Logik. Theorie-Werkausgabe*. Hg. Eva Moldenhauer und Karl Markus Michel. Bd. 5. Frankfurt am Main.: Suhrkamp.

Heine, H. 1977. *Sämtliche Schriften*. Bd. 4. Hg. v. Klaus Briegleb. München: Hanser.

Höffe, O. 1999. *Demokratie im Zeitalter der Globalisierung*. München: Beck.

Joas, H. 1997. *Die Entstehung der Werte*. Frankfurt am Main.: Suhrkamp.

Kant, I. [1784]1977. "Beantwortung der Frage: Was ist Aufklärung?" Bd. 11. In *Werke in zwölf Bänden*, S. 53-61. Hg. v. Wilhelm Weischedel. Frankfurt am Main.: Suhrkamp.

Kraushaar, W. 2000. "Die erste globale Revolution." In *1968 als Mythos, Chiffre und Zäsur*, S. 19-52. Hamburg: Hamburger Ed.

Reese-Schäfer, W. 1997. "Ein kritischer Exkurs zum Gemeinschaftsbegriff in den USA und Europa: Von Tönnies über Parsons zu Plessner und Sennett." In *Grenzgötter der Moral. Der neuere europäisch-amerikanische Diskurs zur politischen Ethik*, S. 418-435. Frankfurt am Main.: Suhrkamp.

———. 1998. "Kollektive Ekstasen, Wertvorstellungen und Menschenrechtsnormen. Rezensionszu Hans Joas, Die Entstehung der Werte." *Soziologische Revue* 21.3: 281-289.

———. 2001. *Amitai Etzioni zur Einführung*. Hamburg: Junius.

———. 2006. *Richard Rorty zur Einführung*. Hamburg: Junius.

———. 2007. *Politisches Denken heute. Zivilgesellschaft, Globalisierung und Menschenrechte*. München und Wien: Oldenbourg.

Sartre, J. P. 1967. *Kritik der dialektischen Vernunft*. Bd. 1. *Theorie der gesellschaftlichen Praxis*. Reinbek: Rowohlt.

Tönnies, F. 1887. *Gemeinschaft und Gesellschaft. Grundbegriffe der reinen Soziologie*. Neudr. der 8. Aufl. 1935, 2. unveränd. Aufl. 1988. Darmstadt: Wissenschaftliche Buchgesellschaft.

Walzer, M. 1982. *Gibt es den gerechten Krieg?* Stuttgart: Klett-Cotta.

———. 1996. *Lokale Kritik – globale Standards. Zwei Formen moralischer Auseinandersetzung*. Hamburg: Rotbuch.

On Humanity in Transition: The Past, Present, and Future
Hwa Yol Jung

Afary, Janet, and Kevin B. Anderson. 2005. *Foucault and the Iranian Revolution*. Chicago: University of Chicago Press.

Arendt, Hannah. 1958. *The Human Condition*. Chicago: University of Chicago Press.

_________. 1972. *Crises of the Republic*. New York: Harcourt Brace Jovanovich.

Bacon, Francis. 1955. *Selected Writings of Francis Bacon*. Edited by Hugh G. Dick. New York: Modern Library.

Bakhtin, Mikhail M. 1986. *Speech Genres and Other Late Essays*. Translated by Vern W. McGee and edited by Caryl Emerson and Michael Holquist. Austin: University of Texas Press.

Bauman, Zygmunt. 1987. *Legislators and Interpreters*. Cambridge, UK: Polity Press.

_________. 2000. *Liquid Modernity*. Cambridge, UK: Polity Press.

Benhabib, Seyla. 2004. *The Rights of Others*. New York: Cambridge University Press.

Berlin, Isaiah. 1986. *The Hedgehog and the Fox*. New York: Simon and Schuster.

Bloom, Allan. 1987. *The Closing of the American Mind*. New York: Simon and Schuster.

Calvino, Italo. 1988. *Six Memos for the Next Millennium*. Cambridge, MA: Harvard University Press.

Camus, Albert. 1956. *The Rebel*. Translated by Anthony Bower. New York: Alfred A. Knopf.

Carson, Rachel L. 1965. *The Sense of Wonder*. New York: Harper and Row.

Chisolm, Lawrence W. 1963. *Fenollosa: The Far East and American Culture*. New Haven, CT: Yale University Press.

Cox, Harvey. 1969. *The Feast of Fools*. Cambridge, MA: Harvard University Press.

Derrida, Jacques. 2001. *On Cosmopolitanism and Forgiveness*. Translated by Mark Dooley and Michael Hughes. New York: Routledge.

Dosse, François. 1997. *History of Structuralism*. Vol. 2. Translated by Deborah Glassman. Minneapolis: University of Minnesota Press.

_________. 1999. *Empire of Meaning*. Translated by Hassan Melehy. Minneapolis: University of Minnesota Press.

Eaglestone, Robert. 2004. "Postmodernism and Ethics Against the Metaphysics of Comprehension." In *The Cambridge Companion to Postmodernism*, edited by Steven Connor, 182-195. New York: Cambridge University Press.

Eliade, Mircea. 1954. *The Myth of the Eternal Return*. Translated by Willard R. Trask. New York: Pantheon Books.

Feuerbach, Ludwig. 1966. *Principles of the Philosophy of the Future*. Translated by Manfred H. Vogel. Indianapolis: Bobbs-Merrill.

Fukuyama, Francis. 1992. *The End of History and the Last Man*. New York: Free Press.

Gilligan, Carol. 1982. *In a Different Voice*. Cambridge, MA: Harvard University Press.

Gilroy, Paul. 1993. *The Black Atlantic*. Cambridge, MA: Harvard University Press.

Glendon, Mary Ann. 1995. *Rights Talk*. New York: Free Press.

Glissant, Édouard. 1989. *Caribbean Discourse: Selected Essays*. Translated by J. Michael Dash. Charlottesville: University Press of Virginia.

_________. 1997. *Poetics of Relation*. Translated by Betsy Wing. Ann Arbor: University of Michigan Press.

Glover, Jonathan. 1999. *Humanity*. New Haven, CT: Yale University Press.

Gould, Carol C. 2004. *Globalizing Democracy and Human Rights*. New York: Cambridge University Press.

Gray, J. Glenn. 1967. *The Warriors*. New York: Harper and Row.

Hardt, Michael, and Antonio Negri. 2004. *Multitude*. New York: Penguin Press.

Hassan, Salah, and Iftikhav Dadi, eds. 2001. *Unpacking Europe*. Rotterdam, Belgium: Museum Boijmans Van Beuningen and NAi Publishers.

Havel, Václav. 1987. *Living in Truth*. Edited by Jan Vladislav. London: Faber and Faber.

_________. 1991. *Disturbing the Peace*. Translated by Paul Wilson. New York: Vintage Books.

_________. 1997. *The Art of the Impossible*. Translated by Paul Wilson and others. New York: Alfred A. Knopf.

Hegel, G. W. F. 1892. *Hegel's Lectures on the History of Philosophy*. Vol. 1. Translated by E. S. Haldane. London: Kegan Paul, Trench, Trüber.

Herder, Johann Gottfried. 1969. *J. G. Herder on Social and Political Culture*. Translated and edited by F. M. Barnard. Cambridge, UK: Cambridge University Press.

Ignatieff, Michael, ed. 2005. *American Exceptionalism and Human Rights*. Princeton, NJ: Princeton University Press.

Jonas, Hans. 1984. *The Imperative of Responsibility*. Chicago: University of Chicago Press.

Jullien, François. 2002. "Did Philosophers Have to Become Fixated on Truth?" (translated by Janet Lloyd). *Critical Inquiry* 28: 803-824.

_________. 2003. "China as Philosophical Tool." *Diogenes* 50: 15-21.

Jung, Hwa Yol. 1987. "Heidegger's Way with Sinitic Thinking." In *Heidegger and Asian Thought*, edited by Graham Parkes, 217-244. Honolulu: University of Hawaii Press.

_________. 1995. "The *Tao* of Transversality as a Global Approach to Truth: A Metacommentary on Calvin O. Schrag." *Man and World* 28: 11-31.

_________. 1999a. "Difference and Responsibility." In *Phänomenologie der Natur* (Phenomenology of Nature), a special issue of *Phänomenologische Forschungen*, edited by Kah Kyung Cho and Young-Ho Lee, 129-166. Freiburg/München: Karl Alber.

_________. 1999b. "Postmodernity, Eurocentrism, and the Future of Political Philosophy." In *Border Crossings*, edited by Fred Dallmayr, 277-296. Lanham, MD: Lexington Books.

_________. 2000. "Taking Responsibility Seriously." In *Phenomenology of the Political*, edited by Kevin Thompson and Lester Embree, 147-165. Dordrecht, The Netherlands: Kluwer.

_________. 2001. "John Macmurray and the Postmodern Condition: From Egocentricism to Heterocentricism." *Idealistic Studies* 31: 105-123.

_________. 2002a. "Enlightenment and the Question of the Other: A Postmodern Audition." *Human Studies* 25: 297-306.

_________. 2002b. "Introduction" to *Comparative Political Culture in the Age of Globalization*, 1-22. Lanham, MD: Lexington Books.

_________. 2002c. "Responsibility as First Ethics: Macmurray and Levinas." In *John Macmurray: Critical Perspectives*, edited by David Fergusson and Nigel Dower, 173-188. New York: Peter Lang.

_________. 2002d. "Transversality and Geophilosophy in the Age of Globalization." In *Calvin O. Schrag and the Task of Philosophy After Postmodernity*, edited by Martin Beck Matustík and William L. McBride, 74-90. Evanston, IL: Northwestern University Press.

_________. 2006a. "Transversality and Comparative Political Theory: A Tribute to Fred Dallmayr's Work." In *Letting Be: Fred Dallmayr's Cosmopolitical Vision*, edited by Stephen F. Schneck, 230-250. Notre Dame, IN: University of Notre Dame Press.

_________. 2006b. "Transversality and Comparative Culture." *Ex/Change* 16: 11-17.

_________. 2007a. "Edouard Glissant's Aesthetics of Relation as Diversality and Creolization." In *Postcolonialism and Political Theory*, edited by Nalini Therese Persram, 193-225. Lanham, MD: Lexington Books.

_________. 2007b. "Merleau-Ponty's Transversal Geophilosophy and Sinic Aesthetics of Nature." In *Merleau-Ponty and Environmental Philosophy*, edited by Suzanne L. Cataldi and William S. Hamrick, 235-257. Albany: State University of New York Press.

Kolakowski, Leszek. 1968. *Toward a Marxist Humanism*. Translated by Jane Zielonko Peel. New York: Grove Press.

Leopold, Aldo. 1987. *A Sand County Almanac*, spec. commemorative ed. New York: Oxford University Press.

Levinas, Emmanuel. 1999. *Alterity and Transcendence*. Translated by Michael B. Smith. New York: Columbia University Press.

Locke, John. 1960. *Two Treatises of Government*. Cambridge, UK: Cambridge University Press.

Macpherson, C. B. 1962. *The Political Theory of Possessive Individualism*. Oxford, UK: Clarendon Press.
Mahbubani, Kishore. 1998. *Can Asians Think?* Singapore: Times Books International.
Merleau-Ponty, Maurice. 1964. "Everywhere and Nowhere." In *Signs*, translated by Richard C. McCleary, 121-158. Evanston, IL: Northwestern University Press.
_________. 1969. *Humanism and Terror*. Translated by John O'Neill. Boston: Beacon Press.
Merry, Robert W. 2005. *Sands of Empire*. New York: Simon and Schuster.
Norton, Anne. 2004. *Leo Strauss and the Politics of American Empire*. New Haven, CT: Yale University Press.
Ozouf, Mona. 1988. *Festivals and the French Revolution*. Translated by Alan Sheridan. Cambridge, MA: Harvard University Press.
Ramsey, Ramsey Eric, and David James Miller, eds. *Experiences Between Philosophy and Communication*. Albany, NY: State University of New York Press.
Robinson, Fiona. 1999. *Globalizing Care*. Boulder, CO: Westview Press.
Said, Edward E. 1978. *Orientalism*. New York: Random House.
Sartre, Jean-Paul. 1965. *Anti-Semite and Jew*. Translated by George J. Becker. New York: Schocken Books.
Schrag, Calvin O. 2004. *Convergence Amidst Difference*. Albany: State University of New York Press.
Scruton, Roger. 1990. "Masaryk, Patocka and the Care of the Soul." In *Philosopher on Dover Beach*, 74-88. New York: St. Martin's Press.
Serres, Michel. 1995. *The Natural Contract*. Translated by Elizabeth MacArthur and William Paulson. Ann Arbor: University of Michigan Press.
Spence, Jonathan D. 1988. *The Question of Hu*. New York: Alfred A. Knopf.
Toulmin, Stephen. 1990. *Cosmopolis*. New York: Free Press.
Valladão, Alfredo G. A. 1996. *The Twenty-First Century Will Be American*. Translated by John Howe. London: Verso.
West, Cornel. 1990. "The New Cultural Politics of Difference." In *Out There*, edited by Russell Ferguson, Martha Gever, Trinh T. Minh-ha, and Cornel West, 19-36. New York: The New Museum of Contemporary Art.
Whitehead, Alfred North. 1954. *Adventures of Ideas*. New York: Macmillan.
Woolf, Virginia. 1938. *Three Guineas*. New York: Harcourt Brace.
Young, Robert J. C. 2001. *Postcolonialism*. Oxford, UK: Blackwell.

Beyond Freedom and Equality
John M. Dunn

Barry, Brian. 1965. *Political Argument*. London: Routledge.
Cavanagh, Matt. 2002. *Against Equality of Opportunity*. Oxford: Clarendon Press.
Constant, Benjamin. 1988. *Political Writings*. Edited by Biancamaria Fontana. Cambridge: Cambridge University Press.
Downs, Anthony. 1957. *An Economic Theory of Democracy*. New York: Harper & Row.
Dunn, John. 1980. *Political Obligation in Its Historical Context*. Cambridge: Cambridge University Press.
_________. 1984. *The Politics of Socialism*. Cambridge: Cambridge University Press.
_________. 1990. *Interpreting Political Responsibility*. Cambridge: Polity.
_________, ed. 1990. *The Economic Limits to Modern Politics*. Cambridge: Cambridge University Press.
_________. 1993. *Western Political Theory in the Face of the Future*. 2nd ed. Cambridge: Cambridge University Press.
_________. 2000. *The Cunning of Unreason: Making Sense of Politics*. London: Harper Collins.
_________. 2002. "Japan's Road to Political Paralysis: a Democratic Hope Mislaid." Third

Maruyama Memorial Lecture, Occasional Papers 2. Center of Japanese Studies, University of California, Berkeley.
_________. 2005. *Setting the People Free: The Story of Democracy*. London: Atlantic Books.
Dworkin, Ronald. 2000. *Sovereign Virtue*. Cambridge, Mass.: Harvard University Press.
Harding, Neil. 1992. "The Marxist-Leninist Detour." In *Democracy: The Unfinished Journey*, edited by John M. Dunn, 155-187. Oxford: Oxford University Press.
Hayek, Friedrich von. 1976. *Law, Legislation and Liberty: The Mirage of Social Justice*. Vol. 2. London: Routledge & Kegan Paul.
Israel, Jonathan I. 2000. *Radical Enlightenment*. Oxford: Oxford University Press.
_________. 2006. *Enlightenment Contested*. Oxford: Oxford University Press.
Kaufman, Andrew, Alison M. Jaggar, Keith Dowding, Soran Reader, and Ingrid Robeyns. 2006. "Symposium on Capabilities." *Journal of Political Philosophy* 16: 289.
Olson, Mancur. 1965. *The Logic of Collective Action*. Cambridge, Mass.: Harvard University Press.
Nussbaum, Martha. 2003. "Capabilities as Fundamental Entitlements: Sen and Social Justice." *Feminist Economics* 9: 33-59.
_________. 2006. *Frontiers of Justice*. Cambridge, Mass.: Harvard University Press.
Rawls, John. 1972. *A Theory of Justice*. Oxford: Oxford University Press.
Schumpeter, Joseph. 1950. *Capitalism, Socialism and Democracy*. London: George Allen & Unwin.
Sen, Amartya. 1985. *Commodities and Capabilities*. Amsterdam: North-Holland.
_________. 1999. *Development as Freedom*. New York: Alfred Knopf.
Wilensky, Harold L. 2002. *Rich Democracies: Political Economy, Public Policy, and Performance*. Berkeley: University of California Press.
Williams, Bernard. 1962. "The Idea of Equality." In *Philosophy, Politics and Society*, edited by P. Laslett and W.G. Runciman. 2nd series. Oxford: Blackwell.
_________. 1985. *Ethics and the Limits of Philosophy*. London: Fontana.
_________. 2005. *In the Beginning Was the Deed*. Princeton: Princeton University Press.
_________. 2006. *The Sense of the Past*. Princeton: Princeton University Press.

Global Governance in the Post-Cold War Era
Takashi Inoguchi

Ferguson, Niall. 2002. *Colossus: The Rise and Fall of the American Empire*. New York: Basic Books.
Friedman, Thomas. 2006. *The World Is Flat: A Brief History of the Twenty-first Century*. New York: Simon Schuster.
Gallup International. 2006. *Voice of the People*. London: Gallup International.
Held, David. 2004. *Debating Globalization*. Cambridge: Polity Press.
Huntington, Samuel. 1993. *The Third Wave*. Oklahoma: University of Oklahoma Press.
Ikenberry, G. John, and Ann-Marie Slaughter. 2006. *Forging a World of Liberty under Law: U.S. National Security in the 21st Century*. Woodrow Wilson School of Public and International Affairs, Princeton University.
Inoguchi, Takashi. 1988/1989. "Four Japanese Scenarios for the Future." *International Affairs* 65.1 (Winter): 15-28.
Kagan, Robert. 2006. *Dangerous Nation: America's Place in the World from its Earliest Days to the Dawn of the Twentieth Century*. New York: Knopf.
Mandelbaum, Michael. 2006. *The Case for Goliath: How America Acts as the World's Government in the Twenty-First Century*. New York: Simon Schuster.
Mann, Michael. 2005. *Incoherent Empire*. London: Pluto Press.

Beyond National Identities and Global Civil Society
Bob Jessop

Albo, G. 2007. "The Limits of Eco-localism: Scale, Strategy, Socialism." *Socialist Register*: 350-360.
Balbo, L. 1988. "Crazy Quilts: Rethinking the Welfare State Debate from a Woman's Point of View." In *Women and the State,* edited by A.S. Sassoon, 45-71. London: Hutchinson.
Blum, W. 2001. Rogue State—*A Guide to the World's Only Superpower*. London: Zed.
Chatterjee, P. 2004. *The Politics of the Governed. Reflections on Popular Politics in Most of the World*. Delhi: Permanent Black.
Chomsky, N. 2007. *Failed States: The Abuse of Power and the Assault on Democracy*. Harmondsworth: Penguin.
Deutsch, K. W. 1963. *The Nerves of Government. Models of Political Communication and Control*. New York: Free Press.
Gramsci, A. 1971. *Selections from the Prison Notebooks*. London: Lawrence & Wishart.
Habermas, J. 1989. *The Structural Transformation of the Public Sphere*. Cambridge: MIT Press.
Hirst, P.Q. 1994. *Associational Democracy*. Cambridge: Polity.
Hobsbawm, E. J. 1959. *Primitive Rebels*. Manchester: Manchester University Press.
Jessop, B. 2002. *The Future of the Capitalist State*. Cambridge: Polity.
Johnson, C. J. 2000. *Blowback: the Costs and Consequences of American Empire*. London: Little, Brown.
__________. 2004. *The Sorrows of Empire. Militarism, Secrecy, and the End of the Republic*. New York: Metropolitan.
__________. 2007. *Nemesis: the Last Days of the American Republic*. New York: Metropolitan.
Marx, K. [1875] 1974. "Critique of the Gotha Programme." In *The First International and After*, 339-359. Harmondsworth: Penguin.
Rawls, J. 1973. *A Theory of Justice*. Oxford: Oxford University Press.
Scott, J. C. 1985. *Weapons of the Weak: Everyday Forms of Peasant Resistance*. New Haven: Yale University Press.
Teschke, B. 2003. *The Myth of 1648: Class, Geopolitics and the Making of Modern International Relations*. London: Verso.

Enlarging Civic Mentalities: The Roles of Moral Philosophy, Narrative Story-Telling and Social Theory
Rob Stones

Alexander, J. C. 1988. *Action and Its Environments*. New York: Columbia University Press.
Alexander, J. C, and Smith P. 2003. "The Strong Program in Cultural Sociology: Elements of a Structural Hermeneutics." In *The Meanings of Social Life: A Cultural Sociology*, by J. Alexander. Oxford: Oxford University Press.
Alexander, J. C., B. Giesen, and J. Mast, eds. 2006. *Social Performance: Symbolic Action, Cultural Pragmatics, and Ritual*. Cambridge: Cambridge University Press.
Archer, M. 1995. *Realist Social Theory: The Morphogenetic Approach*. Cambridge: Cambridge University Press.
Arendt, H. 1961. "The Crisis in Culture." In *Between Past and Future: Six Exercises in Political Thought*. New York: Meridian.
__________. 1977. *The Life of the Mind*. Vol. 1 of *Thinking*. New York and London: Harcourt, Brace and Jovanovich.
Atkinson, J. Maxwell. 1978. *Discovering Suicide: Studies in the Social Organization of Sudden Death*. London: Macmillan.

Bauman, Z. 1989. *Modernity and the Holocaust.* Cambridge: Polity Press.

__________. 1995. *Life in Fragments: Towards a Postmodern Morality*. Oxford: Blackwell.

Benhabib, S. 1992a. "In the Shadow of Aristotle and Hegel: Communicative Ethics and Current Controversies in Practical Philosophy." In *Situating the Self: Gender, Community and Postmodernism in Contemporary Ethics.* Cambridge: Polity Press.

__________. 1992b. "Judgement and the Moral Foundations of Politics in Hannah Arendt's Thought." In *Situating the Self: Gender, Community and Postmodernism in Contemporary Ethics.* Cambridge: Polity Press.

__________. 1996. "Toward a Deliberative Model of Democratic Legitimacy." In *Democracy and Difference: Contesting the Boundaries of the Political*, edited by S.Benhabib. Princeton, NJ: Princeton University Press.

__________. 2002. *The Claims of Culture: Equality and Diversity in the Global Era*. Princeton, NJ: Princeton University Press.

Bishop, R., and Robinson, L. 1998. *Night Market: Sexual Cultures and the Thai Economic: Miracle.* London: Routledge.

Bourdieu, P. 1977. *Outline of a Theory of Practice.* Translated by Richard Nice. Cambridge: Cambridge University Press.

Cladis, M. 1992. *A Communitarian Defence of Liberalism: Émile Durkheim and Contemporary Social Theory*. Stanford, CA: Stanford University Press.

Cohen, I. J. 1989. *Structuration Theory: Anthony Giddens and the Constitution of Social Life.* London: Macmillan.

Elias, N. 1978. *What is Sociology?* London: Hutchinson.

Emirbayer, M., and A. Mische. 1998. "What is Agency?" *American Journal of Sociology* 103: 962-1023.

Garfinkel, H. 1967. *Studies in Ethnomethodology*. Englewood Cliffs, NJ: Prentice Hall.

Giddens, A. 1976. *New Rules of Sociological Method: A Positive Critique of Interpretative Sociologies.* London: Macmillan; Cambridge: Polity Press, 1993.

__________. 1979. *Central Problems in Social Theory: Action, Structure and Contradiction in Social Analysis.* London, Macmillan.

__________. 1984. *The Constitution of Society: Outline of the Theory of Structuration.* Cambridge: Polity Press.

Goffman, E. 1963. *Behaviour in Public Places: Notes on the Social Organisation of Gatherings.* Glencoe: Free Press.

__________. 1967. *Interaction Ritual: Essay on Face-to-Face Behavior*. Garden City, NY: Anchor Books.

Heritage, J. 1984. *Garfinkel and Ethnomethodology*. Cambridge: Polity Press.

__________. 2008. "Harold Garfinkel." In *Key Sociological Thinkers* (second edition), edited by Rob Stones. London: Palgrave Macmillan, 1999; New York: New York University Press.

Jameson, F. 1984. "Postmodernism, or the Cultural Logic of Late Capitalism." *New Left Review* 146: 53-92.

Kim, S. K., and R. Stones. 2007. "Film, Postmodernism and the Sociological Imagination: Exploring the Power of Local Stories in Southern Korea and Northern England." In *Reconstructing Postmodernism: Critical Debates*, edited by J. Powell and T. Owen, 103-121. New York: Nova Science Publishers.

Kymlicka, W. 1989. *Liberalism, Community and Culture.* Oxford: Oxford University Press.

Löw, M. 2008. "The Constitution of Space." *European Journal of Social Theory* 11 (February): 25-49.

Merton, R. K. 1957. "The Role-Set: Problems in Sociological Theory." *The British Journal of Sociology* 8: 106-120.

__________. 1968. *Social Theory and Social Structure*. New York and London: The Free Press.

Mills, C. Wright. 1959. *The Sociological Imagination.* Oxford: Oxford University Press.

Mouzelis, N. 1991. *Back to Sociological Theory: The Construction of Social Orders.* London: Macmillan.

__________. 1995. *Sociological Theory: What Went Wrong? Diagnoses and Remedies.* London: Routledge.

Plummer, K. 1995. *Telling Sexual Stories: Power, Change and Social Worlds*. London: Routledge.

_________. 2003. *Intimate Citizenship: Private Decisions and Public Dialogues*. Seattle and London: University of Washington Press.

_________. 2006. "Rights Work: Constructing Lesbian, Gay and Sexual Rights in Modern Times." In *Rights: Sociological Perspectives*, edited by Lydia Morris. London: Routledge.

Pongpaichit, Pasuk, and C. Baker. 1996. *Thailand's Boom!* Chiang Mai: Silkworm Books.

Rawls, J. 1971. *A Theory of Justice*. Cambridge, MA: Harvard University Press.

_________. 1993. *Political Liberalism*. New York: Colombia University Press.

Reed, I., and J. Alexander. 2006. "Culture." In *The Cambridge Dictionary of Sociology*, edited by B. S. Turner, 111-117. Cambridge: Cambridge University Press.

Rorty, R. 1989. *Contingency, Irony and Solidarity*. Cambridge: Cambridge University Press.

_________. 1993. "Human Rights, Rationality, and Sentimentality." In *On Human Rights: The Oxford Amnesty Lectures 1993*, edited by S. Shute and S. Hurley, 111-134. New York: Basic Books.

_________. 1999. "Globalization, the Politics of Identity and Social Hope." In *Philosophy and Social Hope*, 228-239. London: Penguin.

Sayer, A. 2005. *The Moral Significance of Class*. Cambridge: Cambridge University Press.

Schutz, A. 1962. "Commonsense and Scientific Interpretations of Human Action." In *Collected Papers*, Vol. 1. The Hague: Martinus Nijhoff.

Sewell, W. 1992. "A Theory of Structure: Duality, Agency and Transformations." *American Journal of Sociology* 98: 1-29.

Simmel, G. [1903] 1997. "The Metropolis and Mental Life." In *Simmel on Culture*, edited by D. Frisby and M. Featherstone. Reprint, London: Sage.

Stones, R. 1991. "Strategic Context Analysis: A New Research Strategy for Structuration Theory." *Sociology* 25.3: 673-95.

_________. 1996. *Sociological Reasoning*. London: Palgrave Macmillan.

_________. 2002. "Social Theory, Documentary Film and Distant Others: Simplicity and Subversion in *The Good Woman of Bangkok*." *European Journal of Cultural Studies* 5.2: 217-237.

_________. 2005. *Structuration Theory*. London: Palgrave Macmillan.

_________. 2006a. "Action and Agency." In *Sociology: The Key Concepts*, edited by John Scott. London: Routledge.

_________. 2006b. "Rights, Social Theory and Political Philosophy: A Framework for Case Study Research." In *Rights: Sociological Perspectives*, edited by L. Morris, 133-151. London: Routledge.

_________. 2008. "Theories of Social Action." In *The Blackwell Companion to Social Theory*, edited by Bryan Turner. 3rd ed. Oxford: Blackwell.

Taylor. C. 1999. "Conditions of an Unforced Consensus on Human Rights." In *The East Asian Challenge for Human Rights*, edited by J. R. Bauer and D. Bell. Cambridge: Cambridge University Press.

From *Homo sapiens* to *Homo symbious*
Jae Chun Choe

Choe, J. C. 2005. *Living Two Lives from a Single Seed* (in Korean). Seoul: Samsung Economics Institute.

Darwin, C. 1859. *On the Origin of Species by Means of Natural Selection*. London: John Murray.

_________. 1871. *The Descent of Man and Selection in Relation to Sex*. London: John Murray.

Gore, A. 2006. *An Inconvenient Truth: The Planetary Emergency of Global Warming and What We Can Do About It*. Rodale Books.

Michaels, P. J., ed. 2005. *Shattered Consensus: The True State of Global Warming.* Rowman & Littlefield Publishers.

Whewell, W. [1840] 1967. *The Philosophy of the Inductive Sciences.* Reprint, International Specialized Book Service.

Wilson, E. O. 1975. *Sociobiology: The New Synthesis.* Cambridge, MA: Harvard University Press.

_________. 1984. *Biophilia: The Human Bond with Other Species.* Cambridge, MA: Harvard University Press.

_________. 1998. *Consilience: The Unity of Knowledge.* New York: Vintage Books.

Sublime Beauty and Productive Circulation: The Role of a Third Space

Teckyoung Kwon

Adorno, Theodor. 1984. *Aesthetic Theory.* Edited by Gretel Adorno and Rolf Tiedemann and translated by C. Lenhardt. London: Routledge & Kegan Paul.

Hegel, G. W. F. [1807] 1977. *Phenomenology of Spirit.* Translated by A.V. Miller. New York: Oxford University Press.

_________. 2001. "Lectures on Aesthetics." In *Continental Aesthetics: Romanticism to Postmodernism*, edited by Richard Kearney & David Rasmussen, 99-126. New York: Blackwell.

Kant, Immanuel. 2001. "The Critique of Judgment." In *Continental Aesthetics*, edited by Richard Kearney & David Rasmussen, 5-27. Malden, MA: Blackwell.

Lacan, Jacques. 1978. *The Four Fundamental Concepts of Psychoanalysis.* Edited by J. A. Miller and translated by Alan Sheridan. New York: Norton.

_________. 1992. *The Ethics of Psychoanalysis.* Edited by J. A. Miller and translated by Dennis Porter. New York: Norton.

Merleau-Ponty, Maurice. 1964. "Eye and Mind." *The Primacy of Perception,* 159-190. Translated by Carleton Dallery. Evanston: Northwestern University Press.

_________. [1962] 2002. *Phenomenology of Perception.* Translated by Colin Smith. London: Routledge & Kegan Paul.

Smith, Howard D. 1980. *The Wisdom of the Taoists.* New York: A New Directions Book.

Notes on the Contributors

Jérôme Bindé is Director of the Office of Foresight at UNESCO. He is the director of the UNESCO World Report, *Towards Knowledge Societies* (2005), and the editor of Making Peace with the Earth (2007) and the anthologies: *Keys to the 21st Century* (2004) and *The Future of Values* (2004).

Jae Chun Choe is Chair Professor at Ewha Womans University, Seoul, Korea. His books include *Imagination Odyssey* (with Seoul Digital Forum, 2009), *Animals and Men* (2007), *Dialogue: Natural Science Meets the Humanities* (with Jung-il Doh, 2005), *Men Will Wear Make-up in the Age of Women* (2003), *The Evolution of Mating Systems in Insects and Arachnids* (1997), and *The Evolution of Social Behavior in Insects and Arachnids* (1997).

Inwon Choue is President of Kyung Hee University and Honorary Rector of the Global Academy for Future Civilizations, Seoul, Korea. His books include *Transversity* (2010), *Roundtable on the Furture Universities* (2010), *Politics Beyond Trammels: Political Discourse for Transcendental Engagement* (2006), *Dialogues Off the 20th Century* (with Dongsoo Lee et al., 2006), *The Dusk of Modern Civilization: Clashes and Beyond* (with Sangjun Kim, Euiyoung Kim et al., 2004), and *State and Choice* (1996).

John M. Dunn is Emeritus Professor of Political Theory at King's College, Cambridge, UK. His books include *Setting the People Free: The Story of Democracy* (2005), *The Cunning of Unreason: Making Sense of Politics* (2000), *Western Political Theory in the Face of the Future*

(1993), *Modern Revolutions: An Introduction to the Analysis of a Political Phenomenon* (1989), and *The Politics of Socialism: An Essay in Political Theory* (1984).

John A. Hall is Professor of Sociology at McGill University, Montreal, Canada. His books include *Ernest Gellner: An Intellectual Biography* (2010), *Coercion and Consent* (1994), *Liberalism* (1987), *Powers and Liberties* (1985), *Diagnoses of Our Time* (1981), and *The Sociology of Literature* (1979).

G. John Ikenberry is Albert G. Milbank Professor of Politics and International Affairs at Princeton University, USA. His books include *Liberal Order and Imperial Ambition: American Power and International Order* (2006), *State Power and World Markets: The International Political Economy* (with Joseph M. Grieco, 2002), *After Victory: Institutions, Strategic Restraint, and the Rebuilding of Order after Major Wars* (2000), *The State* (with John A. Hall, 1989), and *Reasons of State: Oil Politics and the Capacities of American Government* (1988).

Takashi Inoguchi is Professor Emeritus, University of Tokyo and Professor of Political Science at Chuo University, Tokyo, Japan. His books include *Globalisation, Pubic Opinion and the State* (2008), *Citizens and the State* (2008), *Political Cultures in Asia and Europe* (2006), *Values and Life-styles in Urban Asia* (2005), *Japanese Politics: An Introduction* (2005), *Global Governance: Germany and Japan in the International System* (2004), *Japanese Foreign Policy Today* (2002), *Japan's Asian Policy: Revival and Response* (2002), and *American Democracy Promotion* (2000).

Bob Jessop is Distinguished Professor of Sociology at Lancaster University, UK. His books include *State Power* (2007), *The Future of the Capitalist State* (2002), *State Theory* (1990), *Thatcherism* (1988), and *Nicos Poulantzas: Marxist Theory and Political Strategy* (1985).

Hwa Yol Jung is Emeritus Professor of Political Science at Moravian

College, Pennsylvania, USA. His books include *The Way of Ecopiety: Essays in Transversal Geophilosophy* (2009), *Rethinking Political Theory: Essays in Phenomenology and the Study of Politics* (1993), *The Question of Rationality and the Basic Grammar of Intercultural Texts* (1989), *The Crisis of Political Understanding: A Phenomenological Perspective in the Conduct of Political Inquiry* (1978), and *Foundation of Jacques Maritain's Political Philosophy* (1960).

Yersu Kim is former Rector of the Global Academy for Future Civilizations of Kyung Hee University. He was Professor of Philosophy at Seoul National University. He also served as Director of the Division of Philosophy and Ethics at UNESCO, Paris from 1995 to 2000. He authored *A Common Framework for the Ethics of the 21st Century* (English, 1999), *Language and Culture* (Korean, 1997), and *Role of the University in National Development* (English, 1980).

Teckyoung Kwon is Professor of English at the English Department at Kyung Hee University, Seoul, Korea. Her books include *Lacan, Chuang-Tzu, Korean Flag* (2003), *In the Realm of the Senses: Reading Films through Lacan* (2001), *How to Read Novels?* (1995), *Post-structuralist's Literary Theory* (1990), and *What is Postmodernism?* (1990).

Nam-In Lee is Professor of Philosophy at Seoul National University, Korea. His books include *Husserl's Phenomenology and Contemporary Philosophy* (2006), *Phenomenology and Hermeneutics: Husserl's Transcendental Phenomenology and Heidegger's Hermeneutic Phenomenology* (2004), and *Edmund Husserl's Phänomenologie der Instinkte* (1993).

Walter Reese-Schäfer is Professor of Political Theory and History of Ideas at the Georg-August-University, Göttingen, Germany. His books include *Platon interkulturell gelesen* (2009), *Aristoteles Interkulturell Gelesen* (2007), *Politisches Denken heute: Globalisierung, Zivilgesellschaft und Menschenrechte* (2007), *Grenzgötter der Moral: Der neuere europäisch-amerikanische Diskurs zur politischen Ethik* (2007),

Jürgen Habermas (2001), and *Was ist Kommunitarismus?* (2001).

Rob Stones is Professor of Sociology at the University of Essex, UK. His books include *Nature, Social Relations and Human Needs* (2009), *Key Sociological Thinkers* (2008, 2nd edition), *Structuration Theory* (2005), and *Sociological Reasoning: Towards a Past-Modern Sociology* (1996).

Wolfgang Welsch is Professor of Theoretical Philosophy at Friedrich Schiller University, Jena, Germany. His books include *Unsere Postmoderne Moderne* (2002), *Grenzgänge der Ästhetik* (1996), *Ästhetisches Denken* (1990), *Postmoderne: Pluralität als ethischer und politischer Wert* (1988), and *Aisthesis: Grundzüge und Perspektiven der Aristotelischen Sinneslehre* (1987).

Longxi Zhang is Chair Professor of Comparative Literature and Translation at the City University of Hong Kong, Hong Kong SAR. His books include *Unexpected Affinities: Reading across Cultures* (2007), *Allegoresis: Reading Canonical Literature East and West* (2005), *Out of the Cultural Ghetto* (2004), *Mighty Opposites: From Dichotomies to Differences in the Comparative Study of China* (1998), and *The Tao and the Logos: Literary Hermeneutics, East and West* (1992).

Index

D

E

N

O

P

S

V

W

X

Z